The Forbidden Abyss

A non-fiction novel series
Part One: *Brent Spiner & Vladimir Putin*

Gabrielle Chana

GABRIELLE CHANA BOOKS
Church of Gail *Publishers*

Copyright © 2016 Gabrielle Chana

All Rights Reserved.
No part of this book may be used or reproduced in any manner whatsoever without permission in writing from the publisher.

ISBN: 1530774128
ISBN-13: 978-1530774128

*A biographical novel about Jesus Christ,
through those
who have met Him.*

ACKNOWLEDGMENTS

This story is published in parts because it is an urgent story that the world needs to know; therefore, the author doesn't want to wait until she has written out the entire story, which covers from 1990 to now, before she releases the story.

Jesus Christ is a behind-the-scenes character in this story until 2012. In the part of the story that covers 2012 and onwards, Jesus Christ will be a prominent character, which will be a later book.

This first book of this non-fiction novel series lays the foundation for Jesus Christ's arrival, revealing the heroic hearts behind Jesus Christ's twenty-first century disciples, who are Gail and her men.

Brent Spiner, Vladimir Putin and other "main characters" in this true story have opened their hearts to me with courage, for their courage I am most thankful. It is not easy to reveal our vulnerabilities with transparency, but that is the only way to show who Jesus is, because He works with us as at the deepest recesses of our hearts, often forcing us to acknowledge truths that are painful and difficult. I have strived to accurately convey the innermost recesses of those who have conversed with Jesus or have seen Him in His appearances to us at Church of Gail. I have strived to tell this story with truth and transparency, because Jesus Christ forces us to shatter our illusions. May truth prevail.

Some incidents have been condensed dramatically to tell this story. Some of the scenes in this novel may not be a word for word accurate transcription of the event, but capture accurately the kind of relationship the people in the scene had with each other.

CAST OF CHARACTERS

Some fictional names are used in this story to protect the innocent. Only major or world famous characters are listed below. Other than the fictional names, this is a true story about Jesus Christ, seen through the eyes and ears of those who have met Him.

Brent Spiner	Brent Spiner
Gail Chana	Gail Chord Schuler
Loree McBride	Loree McBride
Matthew McConaughey	Matthew McConaughey
Jesus Christ	Jesus Christ
Terrance Jenkins	Terrance Jenkins
Vladimir Putin	Vladimir Putin
Hugh Jackman	Hugh Jackman
Lyudmila Putina	Lyudmila Putin
Larisa Putina	Larisa Putin
Rule 13	Rule 13
Zack Knight	Zack Knight
George Bush	George W. Bush
Laura Bush	Laura Bush
Gerard Butler	Gerard Butler
Camila Alves	Camila Alves
Barack Obama	Barack Obama
Kim Jong-il	Kim Jong-il
Dmitry Medvedev	Dmitry Medvedev
Bill Clinton	Bill Clinton
Yasuhira Fujiwara	Fujiwara no Yasuhira
Rich Arnold	Richard Arnold

Table of Contents

BRENT'S FORBIDDEN GROUND 11
1990 to 1992 11

September 1992 19
The Stalker for a Lifetime 19

The Northridge Earthquake 34
1992 to 1995 34

Loree's Birthday Bash at Spago's 47
1996 to 1997 47

Catherine the Great and King David 56
1040 B.C. to 2013 A.D. 56

The Vatican Agent 69
1998 to 1999 69

Gail Divorces Her Husband 93
2000 to 2001 93

Brent Spiner Returns 103
2006 to 2011 103

VLADIMIR & CATHERINE THE GREAT 110
2000 – The Kursk Submarine Disaster 110

Vladimir's Wife Who Never Died 120
2001 to 2002 120

The Marriage List 137
2003 to 2011 137

QUEBEC TRIAL 153
Brent Spiner's Leap of Courage: 2011 153

Jesus Christ Prepares for His Entrance 165

"When Jesus speaks, if we obey, he thrusts us
through the forbidden abyss, revealing truths that challenge our
perceptions and reform our hearts. We rise to new levels of understanding. If what we understand nourishes our heart, then we desire
truth, so we go forward with Him to learn more truths, through the
forbidden abyss. May the world experience the Jesus
I have known as they read these pages."

Gabrielle Chana (Gail Chord Schuler)

"According to God, all of what is happening has
already been foreseen, and the Jesuits are falling right into his
plan. You are his favorite person on the planet to work with, which
is why he's gone to such great lengths to protect you and your
loved ones. All we need do is keep up what we're doing and evolve
and adapt to the continuing threat. When we lose battles, our failures are part of God's ultimate plan. In the end we will
come out on top. God says you are the best.
"Gail, you rock!" is what he bellowed to
everyone at the news studio before
making his leave."

Brent Spiner on January 29, 2012

BRENT'S FORBIDDEN GROUND
1990 to 1992

Brent Spiner lay on his bed and dreamed of Gail that October day in 1990. He looked out his window from his Toyota at the Paramount Studios parking lot, and the tall, toothpick palms with their leaves, just tufts at the top, seemed motionless. The Southern California dry heat bore down on his head. His Gail no doubt felt a cold, crisp breeze, when she ventured outdoors from her apartment in Lynnwood, Washington. If he walked beside her, he'd see snow capped peaks, not the dusky far-off California mountains, which he could barely make out because of the smog. These California mountains only served to remind him, that this Gail perhaps was only a glorious figment of his imagination. For over a year he called her, with the number she gave him in her letters.

Brent had fallen in love with his fan, a nobody housewife and mother, who bared to him a soul far from ordinary. God, he couldn't get this woman out of his mind. Of course, he never talked to her, just called her number and heard her say, "Hello?"

Because he said nothing when he phoned her, she hung up on him. He just wanted to hear her voice. Despite millions of letters from fans, her photo and words stood out. From 1989 to 1990 he fell in love with a fan from his fan mail. She described in her letters to him what she felt raged in his heart, and the dreams he longed for and what her thoughts were about life and how life could bring meaning and purpose through her heart caressing his. No, those weren't her exact words, but it was her heart. She somehow felt the innermost longings of his heart and with those words, fulfilled his deepest longings.

His long, thin fingers caressed the pillow he held, imagining the pillow as her breast. His slender, feeling mouth wisped across the pillow, as if taking in her softness and womanliness from afar, soaking in dreams of loving her, of kissing her body. He sensed fires behind her soft eyes, and longed to fuel them. To find his solace for the day, he began looking for her letters through the pile. She had no idea how much he longed to read her words.

Something about her face, something in her eyes, in that photo she sent him—such sweet softness, such womanliness and courage. When she finally heard from him (August 1990) and made a tape for him and he heard her sing, he was smitten—it was over for him, he'd dream of Gail for the rest of his life.

His heart rose on angel's wings. The words she had written him over the past year, now leaped into his heart, so that his heart danced with feelings he never dreamed possible. She was an angel from heaven. How she managed to keep her soul so pure and divine, he had no idea, but she saw divinity in him, when he portrayed Data in "Pen Pals", when he tried to save a little girl from a dying

The Forbidden Abyss

planet, and she refused to believe that for him it was just a performance.

She believed in him, saw greatness in his eyes, and now he longed to be that great man she believed in, to make her proud of him, as he was so proud of her. The vastness of her soul she hinted at in her writings, though he perceived her husband had no idea what lingered in the depths she dared to divulge to him.

He knew she thought he didn't read her mail, so that gave her courage to bare it all to him, and he drank in her spirit as the most divine and pure soul he had ever encountered. His dreams of her inundated his days, imagining her as his companion day after day, longing to hear her sublime words, submerging himself in them over and over, and drowning in them. In awe, he wondered how one so high and vast, would long for him as her audience—yes, him, the humble, jaded actor. She was authentic, real, pure and passionate. Scared to bare it all, except to him. He absorbed from her vastness, because she saw it in him, when his character Data on the screen, saved the little girl from the dying planet.

When his letter of reply finally reached her, she read his words in amazement, "Thank you for sharing your thoughts with me, they were read with appreciation." Oh my God, she thought, he loved to read *her thoughts!* Perhaps he loved *her soul!* She had dared to expose all her forbidden dreams to him, because she knew for sure he would never read them with interest, but at least someone on earth would know that liberal and tolerant soul she had, that she feared to bare to her strict church-going crowd. He probably thinks I'm a wishy washy namby pamby, she had thought. But didn't he say he appreciated hearing her *thoughts?* Oh my God, somebody loves me for who I *really am*.

Her entire childhood, her mother drummed into her how unworthy she was, so that she now believed it. Because of this, when she dated guys in her twenties, she forced herself into a strict Christian mold, only revealing those parts of her personality sure to be acceptable to her church-going crowd, the only group where she felt she could find an acceptance that meant something to her.

But this world famous actor and awesome person, said he appreciated hearing those forbidden thoughts. He loved the *real Gail!*

To ensure her response to him would be acceptable and moral, she replied with a cassette tape of her singing, baring her soul to him more over *how* she sang, with passion and depths, than *what* she sang. She sang Christian hymns and played piano with a fire and passion that reached into depths that had long slumbered in him.

Hearing her sing, was like hearing an angel from heaven reach down into the deepest recesses of his soul, transforming dusty skeletons into mountaintops and majesty. His heart and soul became a torrent of emotion. He now wanted her. All of her. He wanted to rape all of her, have all of her and thrill her in his bed.

Oh my God, what a courageous and uplifting soul this woman had. The fire and passion in her voice, in the tape she mailed him of her singing, stirred his heart down to its deepest core. He knew he loved her. But, what should he do? Famous actor had fallen in love with nobody fan, a married woman, who was the most extraordinary woman in the world.

His nerves rattled him. Would she return his feelings? What about her husband? But all he wanted was to know she was real, and then to take what he could of her. Her letters showed she cared, but no romance for him emanated from her letters. She told him flat out she was married and had a kid.

Brent's Forbidden Ground

Sixteen hours on the set of *Star Trek: The Next Generation* drained his energy, after all the awful make-up came off, he rushed to his bed to make love to her in his dreams. He did this for a year, often living in a trailer on the set, equipped with a refrigerator, table, bed, like a miniature motel room, right on the Paramount Studios lot.

On his back, staring at the ceiling of his Hollywood Hills ranch style home, he imagined her in his arms, his arm seemed to sigh, as if in a dream, then reached for the phone, dialed her number, longing to hear her voice.

"Hello?" Yes, she was real. The tone in the voice, matched the spirit of her letters and the voice in her singing.

Her voice resonated through his mind. The words in her letters roamed through his consciousness. Those words swam through his heart and brain and colored all his hours. He got her first letters in 1989, her words and photos colored his life then and again and again. She soared in his dreams, his heart reached for pinnacles. Now in October 1990, he heard her voice in his mind, that voice that answered the phone, while he said nothing. Knowing she was real, he clicked the phone down as gently as a kiss.

Each time he called her, she answered with the same wonderment in her tone. Ah, she perhaps hoped it was him, but he could tell her reason overcame her heart, and she reasoned it off as a wrong number. But he always ended the call with a gentle click, like a kiss.

That voice followed him into Paramount studios, to his home, inside his car, on the hillsides. This sublimity, this infusion of wholeness and passion and courage she brought to him, so infused him that it flowed into the music he finally created for her. *Ol' Yellow Eyes Is Back* flowed with his love for her. He caressed her with his voice, with the songs he chose to nurture her beauty and the tranquility and sweetness she brought to the crannies in his heart.

Knowing now the angel was real, he had to love her. When he heard her sing; when she answered his letter to her with a tape of her singing, all Christian hymns, but hymns from the depths of her soul, that vast soul, that he so worshipped; all he suspected about her was true. He was in love with an angel of fire and passion from heaven.

He created a music album for her in response. With his music, he caressed that deep and beautiful soul. He sang words to make love to her, while he imagined her skin on his. That she'd transformed his life seemed to escape her. She thought him the big star, who tolerated her letters with token friendship, and not the actor who longed to experience all her crevices. How his feelings for her surged, how they dammed themselves inside his heart, seeping out for expression.

They seeped, they leaked out onto his bed, through feeling fingers, through his dreams, into whispers of longings, groanings, she never heard. They exploded onto his consciousness, they surged to the surface, they longed for expression.

And then, in May of 1991 she moved near him, to Seattle, only a one hour jet flight from Los Angeles. Her new phone number glared at him, his fingers longed to caress her, his lips longed to kiss her, his skin yearned to touch her.

May, the month of spring, the month of new beginnings. So close to him, so close to his lips, to his body, to all he longed for her. Nothing about the music he

The Forbidden Abyss

created for her came in any of her letters to him. She did not plan to buy his music. His heart fell.

He dialed her number, his heart jumped to his throat. "Hi, this is Brent Spiner. I—dream about you every night." The words lay trapped inside his heart. They never came out. No, that's not what he felt; it reached higher, to the skies, to sanctuaries. His heart had climbed pinnacles.

But she still wrote, she still cared. No, to bare his heart to her, to risk banishment, would send his heart to dungeons. But how he yearned for her skin to caress his, to surge their passions together into sublimity and beauty. His Bible belt upbringing haunted him, she went to church, and now attended revival meetings.

But so near to him now, he could reach out and touch her. But she wouldn't experience his love for her, if his music never reached her ears. He jumped into bed and dreamed about her again, He kissed the pillow and surged his passion into her. He reached for the phone. Did his hands quiver? He dialed her number.

"Hello?" she answered.

Oh my God, he could touch her now, he could hold her against him. . . the thrill of her, the yearnings he had for her. His heart seeped out in yearnings and whispers. "I want to rape you."

She hung up on him. His heart fell.

He rushed to call her. Oh, I'm so sorry. I didn't mean to scare you. I only wanted to kiss you. . . She wouldn't answer the phone, thought him a rapist or a criminal. After three rings, he stopped. He loved her. No more. He left her alone for now. Gave her some space. Then jumped into bed and loved her in his dreams. In his panic, he could only blurt out, "I want to rape you." It was over. The woman of his dreams would banish him for life.

Weeks later, Gene Roddenberry's assistant, Richard Arnold, visited his office at Paramount studios. Why was he here? "Brent, you need to know about one of your letter writers. I got a disturbing letter from her. I think she feels threatened by us. She seems to hint that she's getting inappropriate phone calls. Our studio may be implicated. Throw out all her letters. We can always say that we never got them."

"Really, what did she say?"

"I don't know. She won't say. But I'm going to write her and totally cut off my letters to her. This could be bad for our studio."

"Do me a favor and let me see the letters she writes you. I want to see for myself what she's saying."

Oh my God, he read her letters and, because he loved her, it really upset her that Richard cut her off. It was his fault, just because his heart slipped to his tongue when he called her. He sensed the pain he brought her, now that Rich had cut her off. He couldn't bear to be the cause of that pain, not when he worshiped the ground she walked on. He dialed her number.

"Hello?" She seemed down. He longed to kiss her lips.

"Hi, how are you?" He whispered to her.

"Who's this?"

He hung up on her, with a gentle click, like a kiss. He was so in love with her. She soared in his dreams, in fantasies on his bed. He reached for the phone to call her, to make love to her. No, she didn't know it was him when he called her. He couldn't stop dreaming about her. He wanted to marry her. Did he say that? Yes, he wanted to marry her. Yeah, he knew she was already married, but she seemed lonely, like a spar in a vast sea, searching and searching for happiness.

She had confided to him of her depression and the medications she was on. Not happy, but so beautiful, who deserved happiness, who deserved . . .him. So she wrote him. He could bring beauty and fulfillment to her, he understood what she longed for, sensed it in her words, in the transparency she brought to the pages and pages he read, of her soul, which reached into his.

He understood her, because her longings she bared into her voice as she sang, as she confided to him her secret longings, between words on the page, that he surmised through the spirit that they both shared, the spirit that longed for freedom from encumberments, from prisons, and from controllers and dictators.

Yes, she longed to be free, to express her longings, to flow her passions. He sensed it, he knew her better than she knew herself. Not happy in her marriage, that marriage suffocated her. He could break her free into longings and abandonments, could love her with fire and sublimity. How she soared as she sung; how she'd soar in his arms. Brilliance, beauty, charm—she had it all. She sang through his mind and soul. She consumed his days and permeated his life.

Yeah, he was the big shot Hollywood celebrity. He should have no problems marrying a nobody fan, even though, to him, she was the greatest somebody on planet earth.

Not able to get Gail out of his heart, he dreamed about her every day, so he had poured his heart into an album of love songs for her called *Ol' Yellow Eyes Is Back*.

Once he learned that Gail's friend had mailed her his album, he feared the worst. He changed his voice for his performance as Data, but his real voice, the one he used on the phone to say to her, "I want to rape you," would be an exact match to his voice in *Ol' Yellow Eyes Is Back*. He braced for the worst from the woman who had once dreamed of missionary service.

When a friend of Gail's mailed her his album in June 1991, Gail Chana realized that Brent Spiner, the world famous celebrity had created an album of love songs just for her.

Goodnight sweetheart, though I'm not beside you.
Goodnight sweetheart, still my love will guide you.

You'll never know how many dreams I've dreamed about you,
And just how empty they all feel without you.

Her friend mailed her his music. She figured it out. His voice on the phone matched the voice in the music. She wrote him, "I figured out that

The Forbidden Abyss

you are my mystery caller, the one who said, 'I want to rape you.'"

Her long letter full of feeling and brimming over with adoration for him continued. I realize you made this album for me. I adore you, but I can only be your friend.

Oh my God, he couldn't believe what he read in this letter he just got from her. She adored him, but couldn't go to bed with him, because she was married. Disappointed that he couldn't hold her in his arms, his heart leaped, because she swam in his words and embraced him in her soul. She had not banished him! He had put her into heaven, because his music stirred every recess of her heart.

His fingers trembled as he held the phone, just to hear her voice. At forty-two, he felt like a teenager in heat. He leaped for the phone, and let it ring and ring and ring.

"Hello?" Oh, her voice.

That summer of 1991, on a day when her Coast Guard husband was out to sea, his hands trembled so much when he held the phone to talk to her, he almost dropped the phone. He longed for her, whispered his heart to her. "Can I come over?"

"No. . .I don't think so. . ." She sounded disappointed.

My God, this woman wanted him more than her life, and she turned him down. "Why *not?*" he whispered.

"It wouldn't be right." How disappointed she sounded.

He clicked the phone down gently, like a kiss. He sensed that her heart melted at the sound of his voice, yet something in her gave her the steel to turn him down. This Jesus she worshipped stood between them. He knew the husband wasn't the reason. He sensed her husband lacked the depths to understand and love this woman as he did.

Though he got fifty marriage proposals a month through his fan mail, he began to get the feeling that she'd be the hardest woman to marry in the world. No, the hardest woman to even say "hello" to. His love for her would ruin his career, his sex life (no meaningful sex with any other woman after he fell in love with Gail–but then, he only wanted sex with Gail any ways). She'd ruin his chances for happiness with any other woman but her, and would force him to have the showgirl from hell as his girlfriend (while he dreamed every day about making love to Gail).

Yes, Jesuits deprived Gail Chana of wealth and renown. Like her ancestor king David, her passion was God and she found Him at age fourteen. Yes, Brent Spiner's Gail, with the genes of Catherine the Great and king David, and the great-niece of aviator Howard Hughes, loved her Lord Jesus Christ above fame, glamour or riches.

That voice Gail now heard on the phone was an exact match to what she heard in *Ol' Yellow Eyes Is Back.* It was the world famous Brent Spiner and he was head over heels in love with her! Oh God, why couldn't I meet him when I was single? Now I have to sin to go to him! Oh God, why, why? She could only give Brent one answer. "It wouldn't be right."

Celebrity Brent Spiner realized that for Jesus she turned him down, when he yearned for her love and body in 1991. She could not betray her Jesus by dumping a poor, even if cold husband, for a millionaire star. After hearing *Ol' Yellow Eyes Is Back*, Gail believed Brent had depths and greatness. Though she turned him down as a lover, she kept him as the man of her dreams.

Try, as she did, to convince herself that Jesus would not mind if she went to Brent, in her Bible readings adulterers were stoned. She loved Brent, but loved Jesus more. Jesus rescued her from despair as a fourteen year old, when she felt herself so ugly and unworthy, she wanted to die. When she learned that Jesus paid for all her sins on the cross and had forgiven her for all her ugliness, she felt she'd crawl around the earth three times to adore her Jesus forever. Her mother had drummed into her what a bad sinner she was, so that she believed it from the depths of her soul. She prayed every day that she could go to heaven, but knew she deserved hell. She always felt angry towards her enemies and couldn't love them like a good person would.

Scared to even open her mouth in school, she would go through an entire day at school, and only speak when forced. Afraid to say anything, because she knew all she did was wrong and evil. Jesus changed that and put a happy smile and some love and forgiveness in her heart. For this, she would adore Him forever.

Though it devastated her to remain with her cruel husband, she knew it would devastate her more, if she lost Jesus' favor in her life, and if she no longer sensed His presence when she prayed; so she turned Brent down, feeling like Abraham must have felt when he offered his son Isaac on the altar to God.

Perhaps the only thing she learned to love more than Jesus was the King James Bible. She had read it through from cover to cover to ensure her life pleased God. However, Brent came a very close second place to her love for the King James Bible and Jesus; because, like Jesus did for her, she found in Brent someone who loved and accepted her for who she really was, not the way she felt she must be, which was some elusive high standard that no human being could attain to.

Her entire life she strived for perfection in herself, to make herself worthy, trying to overcome a script her mother had drummed into her over and over, "You, no good. You selfish, like your father."

Brent, a brilliant judge of character, knew he transformed her away from her role as a dutiful, submissive wife and mother, who wouldn't admit to herself any part of her that broached her religious ideals. He saw her religion as a piece of clothing she wore, but not all the real her.

Only for Jesus, did she turn Brent down. Brent knew it. He respected her for it, and kissed her adored footsteps. But despite her refusal of his physical advances, she risked the streets to write him, and risked a broken heart to deny him her body, when she wanted to make love to him more than anything in the world. What a courageous and heroic soul this woman has, he thought. How he adored her courage and passion to all she believed in.

She made it up to Brent with words. Words, the only means where she could love Brent without sin. So she bared her heart on the page and wrote sheets and sheets to the man who consumed her every waking minute. She mailed him movies of herself that she made from her camcorder, sneaking the tapes to him in the mail when her husband was out. She talked to her camcorder as if it was Brent and sent off to him videocassette tapes to nurture him with her presence in the only way she could give it.

The Forbidden Abyss

On the piano, she sang *Moon River*, *I Could Have Danced All Night*, and songs from her favorite musicals. Though she made many mistakes, her beautiful soul shined in her voice, caressing Brent with her inner majesty and sublimity, making his feelings for her run deeper.

She cried into her pillow at night, "Oh Jesus, I prayed every day before I married my husband that I would only marry in Your will, and now I meet the man of my dreams and I can't marry him, because I'm already married! Why did you allow me to marry my husband, who kisses me like I'm a wall, when I now must turn down this intelligent, deep and sensitive man who worships the ground I walk on, and who loves the *real me?*

This is *so hard*. Because he *is* world famous and my husband is so poor compared to him, if I went to him, I would really hurt You. I wish so bad right now, that I was *single*. I want him so bad, but Lord, You and I are so close. I can*not* lose the sweet intimacy I have in prayer with You. Oh Lord, your will makes no sense to me at all!

Even though Brent did not share her passion for Jesus, he thought he'd never find a woman like this ever. She turned down her dream man, a millionaire star with a heart like gold, to remain with a nobody husband who kissed her like the wall, and degraded her. All for her Jesus.

But though she denied Brent her body, her writings reached into his soul and glimpsed his greatness.

He'd soon learn that another organization had an obsession with Gail, and they found his love for king David and Catherine the Great, a woman who turned him down for sex, a major threat.

September 1992
The Stalker for a Lifetime

A grueling day on the Star Trek set, the actors finally made it to the "green room" where actors go to prepare before a shoot, with plenty of space for actors to move around, and mirrors all over the place so they can practice their lines and see themselves. It even had small fridges so they could keep snacks and drinks in there, with a bed off to the side.

Patrick Stewart, his co-star, offered Brent a beer in the green room, while they were in a break between shooting scenes for the *Star Trek: The Next Generation* episode "A Fistful of Datas". Jesuit Loree McBride had spiked the beer with brain control drugs. Therefore, Brent felt ill to his stomach after Patrick Stewart offered him the beer, so he went to lie down on the bed. At first he thought he'd fallen asleep, but the drugs Loree put in his beer were slowly taking effect. He felt like himself, and felt conscious, but was dreaming and didn't know it. In this vivid, lifelike "dream" he thought Gail wandered into his studio. Upon seeing her, his soul soared out of bed. He thought she visited the studio and someone let her in. She had found him in bed, as if he waited for her, and dreamed for her to join.

Gail had finally arrived, his dream come to life. There were no words, only emotions as he felt her slip into bed, her limbs and body swirling him into passions and dreams. But it was Loree riding on top of him, sucking his penis, impersonating Gail to his drugged out mind and fantasies. .

Hours later, he opened his eyes, awakening from the dream and recalling with horror all of the details of what really happened. It didn't seem real at first. Because the dream was so vivid, he thought that perhaps it was the worst nightmare he'd ever had. With so many mirrors surrounding him and Loree in that Paramount Studios green room, reality overcame dreams, the brain control wore off, and he saw himself on all the mirrors, being raped from all different angles. The images of him and Loree in different sexual poses, flashed through his mind, as if each mirror image seared itself into his brain forever. One image with Loree on top. Another image, showing her from the side. Another, showing her rear bouncing up and down his penis. Oh my God, it wasn't Gail! Get these images out of my mind! Then I'll know this is just a dream. But, no, it was *not* brunette Gail, it was a *blonde*. Gail's not a *blonde*. And then he woke up, and it was a blonde, a woman the total opposite of his dream woman—Gail. Most definitely not his brunette Gail.

"I must have fallen asleep with Gail, and had a nightmare," he thought. He turned over in bed to hold Gail—and his eyes fell on Loree McBride, naked in his bed.

The Forbidden Abyss

He screamed, and jumped out of bed, almost out of his skin. "Get out of my room!"

Loree looked up, her mouth slipping into an evil, venomous smile. She hopped out of bed, satisfied with herself. She didn't say a word, winked at Brent, and waved.

"Oh, my God. She plans to return!" Brent thought, his mind spinning in disbelief.

She clicked the door shut. Oh, my Gail. I've betrayed you with a bitch. This can't be real. Tell me this is a nightmare. Oh, my God, it *is* real.

Brent Spiner felt the pain and guilt that a woman feels when a man has raped her and penetrated her most private part, along with the guilt that it had to somehow be his fault. He broke down in shock, trying to deny this had really happened to him, but the evidence was everywhere. The facts laughed at him, the rumpled sheets, the naked bodies, the feeling in his penis and anus that he had been violated. He wanted to vomit over and over, and gag himself out of his despair.

But as he stared down at the toilet, and tried to vomit, he could only offer dry heaves, while his heart felt as if it has been stabbed with a million knives. Who would believe that he had sex with Loree thinking she was Gail? He could only gag and gasp in horror, wailing between sniffles, gasping for his breath and sanity.

Oh God, let me die right now. I've lost the woman I'd die for and betrayed her, even worse I have betrayed all I believe in, all I care about. Is it possible to fall from the heavens and descend into hell overnight? My heart is tormented, searing and gashing in the fires of hell. All I feel is darkness and horror, and laughter. Laughter, Loree's laughter mocks me, bouncing off walls. Oh, I can't get Loree's laughter out of my head!

"You have betrayed the woman of your dreams." Loree's laughter cackled from the walls. "Your fucking penis drowned me with semen. I stuck my pussy all over your mouth and your butt, and you loved every minute of it! No, I wasn't your Gail. You loved it! And you love me!" Yes, he loved it, like a trashy pig, a heap of trash! But he thought she was Gail. How did Loree convince him he had made love to Gail? He scraped his fingers down his face in terror.

"Oh, God." He grasped for straws. This had to be a dream. But, no, this was *no* dream. Oh, God. No, it can't be real. His heart simmered, stewing and cooking. He looked for his heart, and couldn't find it. Did he have a heart left? He would have died for Gail, and now he had betrayed her by making love to a bitch.

What had he done?

Brent wailed and wailed, tears streamed down his face in a flood, until his howls seemed to echo like emptiness in a dark cavern, that only answered with laughter, his wails echoing like laughter from an endless cavern, like the emptiness of his heart. Just empty echoes and a long tunnel of broken dreams, and the foul smell of excrement, as Loree's left overs stained brown on his sheets.

Never in his life had he ever been violent or vulgar—traits he despised. For this reason, her drug rape traumatized him, making him feel like a monster in his own body, a monster that he abhorred. Loree's new creation, the monster who

Brent's Forbidden Ground

became Brent as he made love to Loree, horrified him so much, that he longed to crash his face that he now saw in the mirror, as the most abominable and horrid face he'd ever seen. He felt he didn't deserve to live. He, the monster he'd become, must die, must suffer torments for the terrors he had inflicted on all that was beautiful, on all the made life worth living. He loathed his existence, hated what he'd become. He, a monster, deserved to die.

Loree seemed to feed on his loathing and terror, how he now abhorred the vile reptile he had become. Goal accomplished, she licked her chops, savored her victory, gloating that she had shattered all his goodness, all that Gail could love in him, and had transformed him into a battered shell, so that when the good man came back into existence and saw what an evil reptile he'd become, and what that reptile had done with the good man's body; the good man, recoiled in horror, gasping for breath, hardly breathing at the audacity of the reptile's deeds. The reptile's vileness so tormented him, he began eyeing the drawers, mulling over in his mind, how he could crush that reptile out of existence by slashing his wrist, to stop forever that vile body that committed such terrors. His heart sentenced that reptile, himself, to the fires of hell. Brent, the reptile, had become a smelly worm that slithered in sewage.

Loree's laughter seemed to enrage the heavens and stir all the demons in hell, who gloated over their victory, because they had overcome a love that towered to the heavens, defiling it with vulgarities, so that Brent's sheets smelled of sewage. The foul smell raked his sinuses, stuffy from crying for hour and hours. While Brent wailed from a bottomless pit over the loss of all that had made his life worth living, Loree's wink and smile as she exited her crime scene, ensured Brent that she had more plans to ensure her devastation of the good man who wanted to marry Gail, would be complete.

Oh God, Gail must not see me. So vile, so disgusting. Mutilated, deformed, a monster—that's what I am now.

The Jesuit higher ups at Paramount Studios assigned Loree McBride as Brent Spiner's publicist just months before she became his stalker in September 1992. As his publicist, she would now be allowed access to Brent while he worked at Paramount Studios and would forever change the landscape of Brent's life.

To this day, those three weeks of September 1992, while Brent filmed "A Fistful of Datas" for his role on *Star Trek: The Next Generation*, continue to devastate him. Loree McBride's drug rape of Brent, using brain control on him, so that when he made love to Loree, he thought Loree was Gail, left scars in his heart and soul so deep, that Brent, who had never contemplated suicide, would contemplate it almost every day, the only thing stopping him—the thrill and majesty of Gail's love.

Over the years, he would deny the rape, or at least most of it. It didn't happen, it was only one day, not *three weeks*. Nothing so grotesque and violent could he have allowed. He would never betray the woman that he'd crawl ten miles on his knees to see, his Gail, with such a horrid act. Not for three weeks. Not when he worshipped the ground Gail walked on! How he wanted to die those torrid three weeks in September 1992!

As he drove his car underneath the Paramount Pictures cream and gold arch-

The Forbidden Abyss

es and into the studio parking lot, he felt his pulse rate quicken. He even now disliked the Spanish tile roofs of the studio, because it reminded him that Gail was far away in Seattle, surrounded by evergreen mountains and cool, crisp air and she had never been here in the Southern California sun with him making love to him. He looked about and saw no sign of Loree. Once he parked his car, he phoned his friend and co-star Levar Burton from inside his car.

"Hey Brent, what's going on with you and Loree?"

Brent wailed on the phone for at least a minute. "Give me time to get myself together. Hey, what I'm about to tell you remains top secret, alright?"

"Sure," Levar paused, as if bracing for the worst. "Hey, I don't like Loree. Something's not right about her."

"Levar, it's horrible. . .I was in the green room. You know, where we go to prepare before a shoot. Patrick Stewart got me a beer, and I set it down for just a second, and that's when Loree spiked it with some mind control drugs. I wasn't feeling well after I drank the spiked drink, so I went to lay down. That's when I started having a vivid dream about making love to Gail."

"My God, Brent. There are mirrors all over the place in that room."

'Yeah, so we can see ourselves as we rehearse between shoots, but I saw myself being raped by Loree in those mirrors from all these different angles!" Brent wailed and couldn't stop.

"How did Loree get in bed with you?"

"Well, I was feeling ill, so I went to lay down. I started having a dream about Gail when Loree walked in. My vision was so hazy I thought it was Gail. It was the mind control drugs." Brent wailed so much, he couldn't talk.

"Alright, Brent, whenever you're ready. . .Hey, let's talk about this at my place, okay? After work, come on over to my house."

That evening, Levar held Brent in his arms and rocked Brent from behind, while Brent told Levar his story. "I started having a dream about Gail. . ." Brent sniffed and cried. "Levar, I can't tell you. This just can't be real!"

"Calm down. I'm holding you in my arms. I believe you, Brent. I believe everything you're saying, and I know you love Gail." Levar checked out Brent's rear, with swollen flesh, bleeding and oozing, and stitches everywhere. "Wow, how did Loree do *this* to you?"

"My vision was so hazy, I thought Gail and I were making love. It was the mind control drugs. That's when Loree climbed on me and started raping me."

"What did she do, Brent?"

"She got on top of me cowgirl, so she was doing me on top."

"Brent, you have such a long penis. How in the world—"

"Yeah, and the weird thing is she was able to sit all the way down on it. All 18.25 inches! It was pretty freaky."

"Was that the only sex you had with her?"

"No, we did it all three holes, vaginally, orally and anal. It was really horrible."

"How long did it last?"

"After about twenty minutes, I ejaculated, and she got off and then sucked my penis. Then she got back on top of me and this time she sat on it again, but she put it in her anus. It was all three."

"Did you think you were doing all three holes with Gail?"

"No, I just thought Gail and I were doing it vaginally. It was so weird, because I was thinking Gail and I were in the missionary position the whole time. Regular sex."

"If you thought it was regular sex, how do you know you did all three holes?"

"Because the memories came flooding back to me after the drugs started to wear off."

"That's awful, Brent."

"They came back pretty vividly."

"Exactly how long did your sex with Loree last?"

"I'm unsure since I was drugged out pretty bad, but it had to be at least a few hours. Then I woke up with her in bed with me. I kicked her out, wondering what happened. That's when I started to remember. . ." Brent wailed and his body heaved.

Levar tightened his grip on the forlorn soul who was grasping at straws, just to keep his sanity. "Don't you think you ought to tell Gail about this?"

Brent's face became ashen. "No! Don't tell her Levar. Promise me."

"Really?"

"It's too dangerous to tell her. Not as long as Loree still roams about Paramount Studios. Loree keeps threatening to kill Gail, if I tell her. After what she's done to me, she's capable of anything."

Loree came back at another time when Brent went to bed after eating dinner. She'd slipped the drugs into his food. The next thing he knew, he was dreaming about loving Gail again. It was such a calming solace that he had forgotten everything about the rape, focusing only on loving Gail, in his own quiet, personal space, and in heaven. He couldn't think about anything else.

In reality, Loree, with a dildo or fake penis harnessed around her waist, was thrusting into his anus. She grasped him, and using her strap on dildo, thrusted into his anus like a man, spanking him with her hand until his buttocks were red with hand prints. Next, with her fist, she bashed her fist in and out, and up and down, ripping his anus with violent, fast, rapid fire strokes, beating him inside with her fist; her arms became covered with blood and feces, that spattered everywhere, flinging about, and saturating the sheets with a lake of blood and bit and pieces of feces.

Her eyes became a fire, as she arched her back in ecstasy, experiencing an orgasm from her violent thrusts, and from the blood and feces spattering all over her body and arms and sheets. Her face and eyes gleamed, fuming with ecstasy, thrilled at her conquest, feeling her power and strength, possessed and ecstatic, over her control of the famous Star Trek star, helpless under her grip, as if all the devils inside her steamed with glory over the terror they inflicted in the hearts of Brent and Gail. How Loree's soul thrilled to the mountaintops over her conquest for the forces of evil.

The brain control drugs Loree injected into him, somewhat numbed the pain as she jammed her fist into his rear over and over, but once the drugs wore off, his rear felt like a thousand knives every time he moved.

Hours later, he awakened, as if coming out of anesthesia, his rectum feeling as if it had been stabbed with a thousand knives. The details flooded back to

The Forbidden Abyss

him, like a horror movie of memories that seemed endless. All the agonizing pain he felt when she smashed her fist into his rectum, came back to him with full force, as if he was experiencing her thrusting motions in the here and now, with each Loree moment a memory alive rambling about his consciousness, so real and vivid, he could not shove the experience away, unable to escape as it all played back in his mind. He withdrew into himself again, hating himself for being so dirty and vulgar and violated. Oh God, he had to stop her, but how? How in *the world did she get away with this*? Must he stop sleeping? Eating? Drinking? Oh God, what will she do next?

On another day, she had slipped him the drugs, and brought in the cat they used on the set to play 'Spot'. She took her strap on dildo and started slapping the cat in the face with it, beating the animal heartlessly, and laughing. Then when she knew the drugs were at full effect, she shouted, "Brent, have sex with the cat!"

When the memories flooded back the next morning after the deed, as he awakened and the brain control wore off, he remember forcing his penis inside Spot's tiny vagina. It was awful for her, and she was screeching. She was yowling and meowing, and Loree laughed and laughed.

Spot was so traumatized that they had to get a new cat to play the role. The color and breed of cat changed during the episodes, due to the sexual trauma the animal had received. She would no longer come near Brent, she'd run away, and anytime she saw something phallic, she meowed and had a panic attack, like she was shell shocked.

When Levar and Brent ate hot dogs for lunch they got at the studio cafe, Spot walked up to them; then, upon seeing Brent, panicked, and scampered away. Brent hung his head in shame that he had tortured an innocent animal with his penis, feeling fully to blame, because it was *his* penis, after all, that had committed the heinous act. He loved that cat. He tried to apologize to her, crying, "Spot. I didn't mean to hurt you. Please, please, forgive me. Oh please forgive me, Spot." Spot yowled and ran away.

Brent thought, is this what Gail will do if she finds out what I've done? Brent imagined the look of horror on Gail's face, if he dared to reveal to her what his body had done the past week, to Spot, to Loree. . .Gail would run away from me, just like Spot. I'd scare her away forever. And to think before I tormented Spot, the cat used to cuddle on my lap. Now one look at me and she races down the hallway. My relationship with Gail has been scarred forever. Brent fought back tears, bit his lower lip, which quivered. Gail will never want anything to do with me anymore.

Loree stabbed injections into him and spiked his drinks and his meals at the Paramount studios commissary. She put him into another dimension, so that he could not separate fantasy from reality. He ended up in the emergency room. She fisted him so hard, ripping his flesh apart, blood spewed out from his rear onto the floor.

With no pity for the torture she inflicted on him, she laughed at him, "Ha! I got you. You know you like this. You love this. If you dare tell Gail about this, I'll kill her, just like I might kill you. But I think I'd rather have all this glorious

Brent's Forbidden Ground

sex with you, to keep you alive, so we can make love!" Her laughter rocked the walls of his studio, like a vampire who had just sucked all the blood out of him and wanted more, after ravaging his neck and exposing his jugular vein.

He inundated himself with painkillers to perform his scenes as Data in "The Fistful of Datas", unable to keep his legs together as he walked in some scenes, walking with a limp, which the studio wrote into the scene as comedy. Loree seemed to read his mind and followed him everywhere in the studio when he was on breaks from filming.

Brent was staying late at the studio one night. Macaulay Culkin had come to visit that evening, because he was a huge fan of the show and wanted to meet Brent. Brent sat down with him and engaged him in some discussion about the show. After having a nice long chat, they both went to bed. It was nothing unusual.

But as it turned out later on, that's not what really happened.

During the middle of their conversation, what actually happened, was Brent got up to go use the restroom, and when he came back, Loree handed Macaulay a drink.

"What's in it?" Macaulay said, looking at her quizzically, trying not to be rude, by not accepting the drink.

"It's something called 'Jesus Juice'," she said.

Figuring it to be some kind of alcoholic drink, Macaulay drank it.

Brent barged into the room to stop it, screaming, "No! No! Don't drink the 'Jesus Juice' Macaulay Culkin. You're going to get raped! Y*ou're going to get raped!*"

Loree scowled at Brent, and launched towards Brent and attacked him, slamming a needle into his throat. He struggled and screamed. The viper's drugs sunk into his veins like toxic venom.

Once the drugs started, he was thrust into another nightmare. She had him get down on his knees and suck Macaulay Culkin's penis.

Loree laughed, snapping pictures with her camera.

When Brent awakened the next morning, the memories of the previous night flooded back into his consciousness, with a vividness that assured him this was very real. He thought, please tell me this is just a bad dream! Or perhaps I'm crazy and none of this is real. Please make it not true! Please let me just be crazy. Oh, my God. It's true! It really happened. I really did this. I want to die. He scrambled through his drawers, looking for something sharp, a knife, scissors, anything to cut his wrist.

While Brent stumbled about looking for a knife to slit his wrist, he thought about Gail and how his death would affect her. His face pale and grim, he clenched his teeth. "I can't do it. Gail needs me to stay alive. She'll die if I kill myself."

His hands trembled, he looked in the mirror, despising what he saw. He, the instrument of evil and torture. His face became ashen as the blood ran from his face. More memories surfaced, tormenting him. The revulsion overwhelmed him, he ran to the bathroom to vomit. Out came the bile, as he retched in horror over the toilet, and saw that part of his vomit had clear flecks, like bits of oil that swam on the surface. These flecks fizzled, turning silver and then black. "Oh,

The Forbidden Abyss

my God. What kind of drug is this bitch using on me?"

The pinnacle of the rape happened one afternoon after he had just got out on break. At that point, Brent was afraid to eat, worried about possible contaminants in his food, so he brought his own food from home, and hid his water bottles. He toted them all around the studio with him in bags so that no one else could touch them. But Loree had drugged the water coming from the water fountain, so when he ran out of water on set (he used to sweat a lot under all that make up so he would drink a lot of water, and it had been ten hours on set already), he consumed the drugs when he stopped at the fountain. The next thing he remembered, he walked back on set, and the day continued as normal.

The next day, once the brain control wore off, Brent had perfect recall of what *really* happened. Though, at this stage, he was so drugged out, that his psychiatrists later wondered if perhaps these events may have been false memories that Jesuit forced into him, just to torment him.

Loree took his hand in the hallway, and led him out of the back of the building, taking him out to her car where she proceeded to drive all the way from Los Angeles to the San Francisco zoo.

At the zoo, she had a camera with her, and a set of keys that allowed her access to the inside of all the animal pens. She took him from cage to cage and made him have sex with all the animals and took pictures, laughing the whole time.

Donkeys, wild dogs, turtles, monkeys, snakes, and an elephant. He felt their semen not just inside him, but all over him, foul, disgusting, sick. The elephant tore his insides so badly that they had to call the paramedics to stop the bleeding and stitch him back up.

Then she made him do it again. He begged her, "No, Loree, please! My anus is bleeding! For the love of all that is holy my anus is bleeding!"

It tore him up really bad. The elephant was so powerful it pushed its penis right through his rear, ripping flesh and smashing organs.

He cried the whole time, shuddering, as the elephant raped him again and again. His horror reached new heights that day.

She brought out eels, stuffing baby, very tiny moray eels into the head of his penis, and shoved the big ones up his butt.

Scientists later decided that the part about the elephant penis may have been a false memory, inserted into Brent's brain to torment him.

Regardless of what really happened, Brent's injuries put him in the hospital with stitches all over his rear, offering oozing, putrefying flesh to the beholder. His sex with Loree and her zoo animals pierced his body and soul like a million knives.

Now she had pictures of him, being raped, making his degraded image forever prisoner on those film reels. With photographic evidence, he would never be able to escape, and should he ever shed the memories of what happened, those photos would bring it all back.

Feeling like pure filth, he couldn't face up to what he did. He thought, if I explain all of this to Gail, I'll scare her away. She'll see how sick and contaminated I am, and will know I am an evil and awful person. Oh, this is all my fault.

Brent's Forbidden Ground

How could I allow this to happen? I'm so horrible, such a monster, I don't deserve to live.

No matter where he went, she leaped on him from hidden corners, jabbing brain control drugs into him. She even put brain control drugs into the water fountain he drank from. She trailed him like a bloodhound.

"Ah, so you went to the big shots and they took my side!" Loree's laughter cackled off the walls. "You better not tell that Gail about me, or I'll do worse to her than what I've done to you. I'll kill her."

It took a month and many stitches to heal. The anal sex she gave him with a dildo and her fist, so ravished his rectum, that his rectum became butchered steak. She captured it all on film. "Oh, how he loves violent sex." Loree flipped her hair, clapping her hands together, cackling with laughter. "Brent has a side to him that he only reveals to *me. I've got pictures to prove it.*"

She carefully neglected to point out the stark contrast between his violent sex with Loree and his tender, committed love songs for Gail, who admitted to Brent that she had trained for Christian missionary service.

Though he tried to suppress the horror, Loree shoved her "evidence", the pictures she took to the Paramount studio heads, down his throat, stabbing him to death with it. Gloating in her victory, her rape devastated a love that towered to the heavens.

Gail noticed his unusual silence that three weeks in September 1992. September 15th was her birthday and he didn't call her. "Is something wrong?' she wrote him. "Have I offended you?"

Silence.

"Why won't you call me? What's wrong? Oh, something's terribly wrong." He never ignored her when she cried, but he was ignoring her! Oh, it's because I turned him down and now I've lost him. Oh Lord, how I must suffer for honoring your Bible and your laws. She cried so much, she couldn't sleep, couldn't eat, and stopped attending church.

All her heart she had flowed into Brent and the flow had been blocked. It jammed into a wall that seemed a million miles thick. All she had lived for the past year, dammed up in torrents inside her, so that her heart exploded with pain and she cried all through the days and days that Brent gave her silence on her phones.

To make matters worse, she knew Brent read of her despair in her letters to him, and his silence towards her continued, even when he knew she was groveling in depression because of his silence!

"Oh, something terrible's happened. Something awful. Lord, I'm so depressed. My heart is bleeding all over the floor and I can't stop the bleeding. I'm going to die if You don't help me."

Though Gail denied Brent her body, she had given him all else, all her time, all her heart and all her soul. Normally in church Sunday morning and evening and Wednesday night, she skipped church for a week, barely having the strength to get out of bed. Depression overwhelmed her. Tears flowed like a waterfall. As she drove on the freeway, she cried so much, she could barely see the road. The

The Forbidden Abyss

love she wanted to flow to him was blocked. Her heart had hit a wall.

A lady at her church named Lesleigh, sensed her despair long distance through prayer, and laid flat on the ground to pray for Gail. At that moment when Lesleigh prayed, Jesus gave Gail peace about Brent, her depression over his silence lifted.

Gail had surrendered her feelings for Brent to Jesus and decided she could love him through prayer. Now the dam of love she had for him was no longer blocked. It would flow to him through prayer. She decided to pray for Brent for the rest of her life. That decision made her feel she was still loving him, and so her spirits lifted. After weeks of torment over his silence, she could sleep at night, because she could now love him through prayer. Yes, prayers could go beyond his silence and the blockade that stood between them; and Jesus somehow would flow her love to him through the heavens. She wrote Brent to tell him this.

Brent went to go talk to Levar about getting rid of Loree. Levar was the only one Brent confided in at the time.

"After that few hours with her, did you have any other sex with her?" Levar asked him, laying a hand on his arm.

"Yes, she kept breaking into my room. I started drinking from bottled water, but she would contaminate the water while I wasn't looking and give me the drugs again, and wound up doing even worse things to me."

"Oh my God, Brent." Because Brent wailed so much, Levar just cuddled and rocked him for several minutes.

"She started raping me with a strap on, then she moved up to fisting. She got more and more perverted. She put her hand in my butt, made a fist and thrusted in and out of my anus with her fist."

Levar took another look at Brent's rear. "My God, she really ripped into your flesh. That explains all the blood I saw in the green room. Couldn't you feel the pain?"

"It didn't hurt while she was doing it, because of the drugs. This was all happening on and off for a few weeks. I'm so horrified, Levar. I've betrayed Gail and done such horrible things. I'm in so much pain, physical and emotional. I just want to die!"

"Is there any way to get away from Loree?"

"It seems that Paramount Studios wants her in the studio!"

"Brent, can't you stay away from her mind control drugs?"

"It's not like I can't eat or drink. She contaminates everything with mind control drugs, even the water fountain!"

"Oh, my God."

"Levar, she seems to have friends everywhere. She has connections in the media—she told me, so it must be true. She's threatened my job—and Gail's life. I've been trying to figure out where she comes from and how to keep her from entering the studio. Can you help me? Because my bodyguards aren't doing their job, and they're letting her meddle with my drinks and food, and letting her get into the studio. She, apparently, has a lot of friends."

"I want you to sleep with me. You're going to sleep in my arms tonight and every night until we get this thing licked." Levar held Brent from behind, rocked him to sleep, and went to guard the door.

"Oh, Levar. Loree is so icky. I don't want her anywhere near me. I get the shudders every time I see or hear her. When I wake up with her in my bed, I feel like a spider has crawled into bed with me."

"Brent, you need to tell Gail about this. Gail's crying her eyes out over you and you're giving her silence! You need her really bad right now. I think she'd understand. She could hold you up, Brent."

Brent's face became ashen and his hands trembled. "If Loree catches me calling Gail, she'll kill Gail." Brent's lips twitched and tears streamed down his face. "Loree said she'd kill Gail if I tell her. As long as she's still wandering around the studio, I can't call Gail!"

"Here, call Gail right now, from my cell phone."

"No, Levar—" Brent eased back from Levar and looked down at the floor, nodding his head in disbelief, then staring ahead with a blank stare, a faraway look, as if a nightmare played over and over in his mind, and he saw monsters and ghosts, knives and blood, fists rapid fire into his anus, evil grins, laughter—images whirling about, screaming at him, jumping at him. "Levar!" Brent screamed. "I'm going mad! Levar! Is that you? Is this real? Am I here at your house, or am I at the studio? Levar! What's real and what isn't? Levar!" Brent broke down and wailed, releasing all the shame, all the resentment, all the hatred he felt for Loree. He raced for Levar's kitchen, looked for a knife, scraped his hands through Levar's kitchen drawer, hands trembled, fingers scurried, trying to find a knife of the right size. But he shook so much, when he reached for knives, he dropped them, his hands shook so violently.

Suddenly, Brent felt strong arms about him, which clutched both his arms and held them back. "No, Brent! You're not going to do this! Brent, this is real. I am Levar and I will protect you from Loree. Stop it, Brent! Stop it!"

"I can't tell Gail, Levar! Don't tell Gail! Loree will kill her. Loree will kill her."

"Alright. Alright, Brent, I promise. I won't tell Gail. Calm down. Calm down."

Brent wailed and wailed in Levar's arms. "Not as long as Loree still roams about the studio." Brent's voice, had become husky, from hours and hours of wailing. Levar was horrified how his best friend had been transformed from a well adjusted, happy and loving friend into a man who looked ready for the state mental hospital. "Loree stuffs her purse with knives. The guards caught her with knives. She said she was a chef, that's why she had to carry them, so they let her through." Brent scowled. "Loree's so crazy. I really think if I tell Gail, she'll stalk Gail next."

Levar noticed that his best friend turned ashen white. "Alright, Brent, I swear over my dead body, I won't tell Gail."

Brent stared at Levar in disbelief. "Over your dead body, you won't tell Gail?"

"Over my dead body." He cuddled Brent from behind. Levar wanted to get past this and focus on a solution. Though he felt Gail could help Brent now, he could see that to bring Gail into the picture could bring in complications that would destroy Brent. "Can't you beat these mind control drugs?"

"They're tricky. You feel as if you're still yourself, and feel fully conscious, but don't realize you're drugged. Even though I feel ill from them, when I'm on them, I don't think I'm delirious. It's sort of like having a dream, but you don't know that you are dreaming. So everything makes sense at the time."

"Can't you see the drugs or get rid of them in your system? Maybe make yourself throw up, whenever you feel ill, 'cause they make you feel ill. Have you tried that?"

"Even though they made me sick to my stomach, I didn't throw up the first time. But I started to realize that whenever I feel sick, it's Loree's brain control drugs, so I made myself throw up after that."

"What do the drugs look like? Did you see them in your vomit?"

"They are clear and colorless, almost like water. That's why it's easy to sneak them into food and drink."

"How'd you figure *this out*?"

"Well, when the drug mixes with air, it slowly turns silver and then black, cause that's what happens to my vomit, when I'm under Loree's brain control drugs.

Levar tried to comfort and protect Brent, but it was no use, and every time they tried to thwart her, she would just find another way to get him. Brent finally summoned up the courage to tell Paramount about being raped.

"Loree has already talked to us about this matter. You raped her, and we won't ban her from the studio. We expect you to behave honorably around her, or else. . ."

"She spiked my drink. She's tried to kill me."

The studio executive looked over Brent, with a scowl, as if he disdained the very presence of the star that made his show shine.

"I see. Loree owns the studio." Brent could not hold back the tears. "You think I enjoy sex that does *this!*" Brent revealed his rear, filled with stitches and raw and oozing flesh.

The executive winced at the sight. "My, you really like it rough, don't you? I won't hear of this anymore. How could such a beautiful woman do this to you?"

"Brain control drugs!"

"Get out of here." The executive scowled. 'You're a disgrace to this studio. Treat Loree with the respect she deserves. You just couldn't resist her body, could you? Her beauty just overwhelmed you with lust. If you don't give her the respect she deserves, we'll write Data out of the show. We'll explain to the public that we can't have a rapist working for Paramount Studios." The executive paused and looked out the window. "One more thing, not a word of this to anyone, you understand?" He stared Brent down, as if in a dare. "If we find you have leaked this to anyone, we'll paint you as a rapist to the media. Don't forget—we have photographic evidence."

How Brent loved Gail and how this tore at his heart. He recalled Loree's words, "You tell Gail about our sex and I'll kill her!" Brent realized if he lost his job as Data, that he'd be out on the streets and unable to protect Gail. "Yes, sir."

The executives then produced a contract that made him promise in writing that he would not tell anyone about the rape, or else they'd be entitled to smear him to the press as a rapist. If Brent refused to sign this contract, he'd lose his job.

His heart racked with pain, sinking so low, he wasn't sure he could ever feel happy again. Now, if Gail wanted to, he could never marry her, at least not any

Brent's Forbidden Ground

time soon.

Even worse, he felt he betrayed all that made him feel worthy as a man. He could barely restrain his tears, but if he ended up in jail, either as a rapist or because of his debts, how could he keep Gail as his pen friend, or even protect her, if he needed to, in the future? Also, his co-stars made his job at Paramount a great place to work, and he had really bonded with them. So, he decided to stay with Paramount for them, for his job as Data and so that he could stay off the streets, to stay afloat for Gail.

He had just finished paying off a huge debt and was finally no longer in danger from his creditors. If he lost his job, he knew he'd be on the streets, and possibly in debtor's prison. He wasn't nearly as rich as the press made him out to be.

The world did not know of the huge debt he had incurred before he landed his famous job as Data of *Star Trek: The Next Generation*. So Brent signed the Paramount contract, promising not to tell anyone about the rape, giving Paramount permission to smear him to the press if he did. Perhaps, he could weasel out of this contract later, he thought.

The contract also made him promise not to bring charges against Paramount for defamation; that is, if he violated this contract and thus forced them to go to the press and expose him as a rapist. In other words, he must not tell anyone about the September 1992 rape or about this contract he made with Paramount, or he'd lose his job and would have to pay back Paramount any earnings he made after he signed this contract with them.

Brent never violated his contract, until after it became invalid in 1999, because it had an illegal purpose (to protect a criminal—Loree). Once he invalidated the contract, Loree continued to intimidate Brent into silence about her crimes, by threatening to kill Gail if he dared to communicate with Gail.

Though he brought criminal charges against Loree in 1998, the Jesuits always got her out of jail on technicalities.

Therefore, Gail never knew the full details of his rape with Loree until 2012. Brent also needed the money from his Paramount job, and he actually loved the job, because he loved his co-stars and his role as Data. So, despite Loree, Brent strived to have a good relationship with Paramount, who, after 1999, actually seemed embarrassed about Loree. The Jesuits made sure Brent never had enough money to survive without his Paramount earnings, forcing him to remain dependent on Paramount for financial survival.

It wasn't the fault of his co-stars that the higher-ups at Paramount were Jesuits. The Jesuits made sure that, despite Brent's genius intelligence, he had a pitiful career after *Star Trek The Next Generation* finished its television run in 1994. He landed no other roles in Hollywood that made him as famous as Data.

Now, in September 1992, he learned the truth, that Paramount Studios sponsored Loree McBride, and encouraged her to rape him, allowing her in the studio, even when she had knives, claiming to believe her story that she was a cook.

So he came back to the studio later to tell Levar about his meeting with the executives, and he ran right back into Loree McBride. She now knew he had signed the contract, and felt herself invincible.

She was standing outside his studio room door, with her hands behind her back holding a syringe full of drugs, grinning at him.

He stepped backward in fright, and she lunged, plunging the syringe into his neck, then threw him into the room. He struggled fiercely, and so she hit him over the head with a frying pan, sending him stumbling into the bed.

Then she tied him down with ropes on the bed, spread eagle.

In horror, he watched her undress. The door creaked open again. It was Levar, and he held his finger to his lips to shush Brent, so Brent wouldn't give away that Levar was behind Loree, because she didn't see him.

The last thing he remembered was her slowly removing her top, and a split second later, Levar rushed into the room. But Brent had passed out.

When he awakened, still tied to the bed, Loree and Levar were gone. But blood was everywhere.

I got to get out of here, he thought.

He struggled and bit the ropes about his body, to free himself, and then got up. A pool of blood led from the bed, to the door, and all the way out into the hallway. He followed the blood all the way outside, to the far back of the studio, fearing the worst.

Levar stood there, facing the dumpster. Brent trotted up beside him, "What happened?" Then Brent looked into the dumpster and saw Loree McBride.

Levar had killed her.

"This is between you, me, and this gallon of gasoline," Levar said, lighting his match to light up a cigarette. He offered Brent a cigarette.

Shaking his head in astonishment, Brent refused.

Levar threw the match into the dumpster, causing the dumpster to erupt into flames. The sound of the flames licking Loree's body filled the air. Putting his arm around Brent's shoulder, Levar stood there with Brent, listening to the flames, seeing the sparks fly, and feeling the heat from the dumpster. They just stood there, watching the flames. To Brent, feeling the heat and seeing the sparks—the surreal became real. The sounds—the crackling and the sparks leaping from the dumpster against the night sky and the heat from the dumpster—reassured Brent that Loree could torment him or Gail no more.

As the night went on, they decided to camp out and to wait until the blaze finished, roasting marshmallows and singing a few songs while passing around some beer. Brent felt his spirits lift.

After that, Brent figured everything would be all right.

"Just focus on Gail, and try to put this behind you," Levar said.

So for a while, Brent did. Brent even joked, with a happy, carefree air, about having sex on an episode, on the Joan Rivers Show in November 1992. Yes, he thought, he had finally disposed of that devil, and she would never come back. Let's turn all my negative energy into positive energy, and just focus on Gail.

Traumatized by the September 1992 rape, he blocked it all out, as if it never happened, like he had a horrible nightmare and now he woke up and everything was okay.

But Loree returned in December 1992. When he saw her, he thought, "Oh my God, am I seeing a ghost?" He felt the terror return, his heart palpitated with fear.

Brent's Forbidden Ground

He didn't believe in clones in December 1992, so he thought, "My God, this woman can do anything! I can't even kill her!"

So when she made threats on Gail's life in December 1992, he didn't question her. He knew she could do it.

Two days after Gail finally found peace about Brent's silence; Brent called her, around September 25, 1992, but offered no explanations for his silence.

Gail sighed in relief. He was not saying "goodbye". To her, it was as if those three weeks of silence and emotional death that Brent gave her in September 1992 never happened. But to protect him from Satan, who she suspected messed with her Brent; she typed out for him the words from the book *War on the Saints*.

She now realized how much Brent had become a part of her. In a moment of weakness, in early October 1992, she wrote Brent that she would go to him, if he really wanted her. The whole time she waited for his response, she prayed flat on the floor and asked Jesus to mess it up, if He didn't want her with Brent. Brent had become her heart and soul, her arms and legs, and almost her entire reason for existence.

Brent never told Gail until July 2012 why he didn't call her for three weeks in September. Gail guessed that perhaps Paramount studios ordered him to stop writing her for some strange reason. She correctly sensed that Paramount studios opposed the love between her and Brent. "I don't get the impression that Star Trek likes women who write letters to their stars quoting the Bible all the time." But Brent was from Texas—Bible belt U.S.A. She sensed he shared many of her Judeo-Christian values.

But she had no idea that Paramount studios used a Jesuit drug rapist on him, who almost killed him, and threatened to kill her, that horrifying three weeks in September 1992.

Because Brent genuinely loved Gail, he sensed that Gail's decision to go to him, may have been brought on by his three weeks of silence against her in September 1992. Unless she persisted with this decision, he would not encourage her to violate her moral standards. After his experience with Loree, he developed an overwhelming respect for a woman who would turn him down for sex, when she wanted him more than anything in the world, and who only turned him down to honor her religion.

He did not act on Gail's proposal to take her in his bed and as his wife that October 1992. His wounds had not yet healed from the rape, and how could he explain this to Gail without violating his contract with Paramount? So he ignored her offer.

To maintain Gail's respect right now became his prime concern. During that three week nightmare of horrors in September 1992, Gail's love for him was the only thing that kept him from suicide, he didn't want to do anything to risk losing her love.

The Northridge Earthquake 1992 to 1995

Loree made Brent realize just how much he loved Gail, and how much he needed her respect. Without Gail's love, he was certain he would go mad. Only the beauty and meaning that Gail brought to him, kept him sane that torrid three weeks in September 1992. He was now willing to die for Gail.

For three weeks in September 1992, Loree used Brent's body to betray the most awesome love in the universe, forcing him to make love to the cat Spot, used on his show, so that the cat hissed at him in horror. His brain deluded and dazed, he raped the cat, almost killing it—he suppressed the rest, it just couldn't be real. He'd made love to a monster, Loree McBride, over and over for *three weeks*, thinking all the while he made love to Gail.

By the end of October 1992, Brent had physically healed from the rape. But after the rape, Brent quit calling Gail on her birthdays and holidays, unlike before September 1992 when he never missed a holiday with Gail. He had to exercise more caution because Loree came back into his life in December 1992, and threatened to burn down Gail's home, or blow her up in her car. In fact, Loree blew up one of her clones in a car in July 2001, right after Gail's divorce, to show Brent she could do it.

Immediately after the rape in September 1992, Brent realized Paramount supported Loree and opposed his love for Gail. Because when he threatened to report Loree for the rapes, Loree told him about her plan with Paramount to make Brent out to be a rapist instead. So Paramount supported Loree McBride, and took her side.

When Brent realized that Paramount supported Loree against his love for Gail, he loved his costars. He stayed for them; and stayed for his role as Data. He couldn't just walk away. Brent loved all his friends there, it wasn't their fault. But the Paramount higher ups were all Jesuits.

So, a little bit after he appeared on the Joan Rivers show, before Christmas 1992, Loree returned one day pretending she was already Brent's girlfriend. Which he thought was just part of her game with him, but little did he know how far that game was going to go. He guessed she decided to step it up after the last plot failed. She just met him outside the studio one evening, and he swore he saw a ghost! She had died! Levar killed her. She followed him to his car, then when he drove away, she followed him to his home, and continued to stalk him.

It got worse the closer he and Gail got to each other. Loree would back off a little when he and Gail weren't speaking as much.

One day, in 1993, his bosses at Paramount said it was time for him to make some public appearances with his new "girlfriend". He knew from September

Brent's Forbidden Ground

1992 that they were already in on it (because of when he told them about Loree's rape, initially), and from there on out, it was a nightmare come to life.

Loree started her publicity campaign as Brent Spiner's girlfriend around 1993. She began appearing with Brent at Star Trek conventions and making public appearances with him, and told everyone she was Brent's publicist, when she was really his stalker.

"You will not be my girlfriend," he told Loree.

"Okay, if you don't make me your girlfriend, I'll just kill that bitch Gail." She flipped her hair, defiant and triumphant.

Brent felt then (because he didn't believe in clones) that he had just watched this woman come back from the dead, and had experienced such a horrific rape by her prior, that he thought she could do exactly as she wanted, and decided to sacrifice himself to save Gail.

Though somewhat concerned about how Gail would react if she learned about Loree as his girlfriend, Brent wasn't ready to tell Gail about the rape; even though he knew Gail would be confused and devastated over his public appearances with Loree. But, by 1993, Jesuits had injected Loree into his life, and he couldn't get away to tell Gail. He feared that Loree had a wiretap on all his phone conversations for a while. He was not sure of this, but it made him exercise extreme caution in his phone calls to Gail, so Gail never received any type of phone call from him on holidays.

"You tell that bitch what I'm doing with you, and I'll kill her," Loree laughed. "Oh would it be fun to blow her up in her car! Or perhaps I'll bomb her apartment."

It seemed Loree bided her time, waiting to see if he would make a move towards Gail. Loree already knew that he called Gail at times, so he had to change when and where he called Gail in an attempt to throw Loree off guard and make her think that he had stopped trying to talk to Gail.

Loree began plastering photos of herself with Brent on the Internet and in the tabloids, gloating over her power over Brent, that he could not stop it. Most of these photos Jesuits doctored to make her appear nicer than she was. But some of the photos were real, especially the ones where Brent stared at her like she was a viper. Jesuits made sure to remove any photos of Brent looking miserable with Loree from public view. Jesuits had to fake all the photos that made him appear to enjoy her company. They started faking them when they realized how unhappy he looked in the real ones. Even the photo of a pregnant, stringy haired Loree with Brent, allegedly in 2002, when she carried his baby, was fake, with Brent etched into the photo to make him appear to have been by her side.

Early 1993, Loree had reappeared, and stalked Brent again. Horrified, Brent felt Loree had power like God, because he did not believe in clones back then.

Brent decided he had to break his contract with Paramount, and planned to someday tell off the Paramount executives and then would refuse to have Loree as his Paramount Studios official girlfriend.

The only problem was that he wasn't nearly as rich as the world thought he was. He had started his job as the famous Data of *Star Trek: The Next Genera-*

The Forbidden Abyss

tion in big debt, so that from 1987 to 1989 his earnings from Star Trek basically paid off his creditors. If not for the miracle of landing the role of Data, he could very possibly have been on the streets or in debtor's prison by 1990. In fact, all his earnings from his first year as the famous Data, just paid off all his creditors.

Just when he was beginning to put some money into savings, Loree McBride jammed herself into his life in September 1992. Even worse, to establish to the world that she was really Brent's girlfriend, she made it a point to steal Brent's credit cards at every opportunity, and then would head for the malls on spending sprees, spending thousands of dollars on clothes, make up and whatever she wanted. News of her spending sprees made it to the tabloids, which was part of her press campaign to make it appear Brent lavished his money on her.

Whenever this happened Brent was furious. "You have no right to my credit cards!"

Loree held up one of his cards and flashed it before him. "Hey, what kind of girlfriend would I be, if you didn't lavish your money on me. The whole world knows you adore me!"

"Shit." Brent cursed. He really hated this Loree, but knew if he confronted her about this, she'd raise so much hell, he'd rather suffer in his bank account.

Loree laughed. "This is the payment for all the glorious sex I give you! If I'm to be a proper girlfriend, then my lover must reward me financially for all the glorious sex I give him!" Loree's raucous laughter bounced off the walls of his home so loud inside his house, the roof almost caved in.

Brent tried locking his credit cards in a safe, but Loree got inside all his safes, even blowing them up a couple times, and, amazingly, the credit cards always managed to stay intact after the explosion.

He tried keeping his cards on himself at all times, but this didn't work because by forging his signatures to letters or email correspondences, she somehow managed to contact his credit card companies and have them issue her a card.

Finally he decided that he needed to pay off all his cards and then close down all the credit card accounts, except perhaps one or two that he would watch over like a hawk.

Paying off the cards would be no easy matter, because Loree always found a card and then went on spending sprees.

But his goal was to pay off all his cards and his creditors, and then monitor the one or two credit cards he kept open like a hawk. Next, he would put his money into investments.

Once he had enough money in investments, so that he no longer needed Paramount's money to survive, he would break his contract with Paramount to have Loree as his girlfriend, telling them that she is a murderer and therefore his contract with them was illegal and could not be enforced.

From December 1991 to December 1993, Gail studied writing under award winning writer Jim Murphy. Because God refused her Brent as a lover, she would love him with her writings.

God was grooming His writer. If Gail went to Brent in 1992, she probably would not have bothered to learn how to write. She only learned how to write to make it up to Brent that it was immoral for her to give him her body. She sensed something rare and high about their love and longed to express it somehow.

It would not be a sin to love him with her writings! Her husband would never suspect that she learned to write to make love to Brent through her writings. To make sure her writings would satisfy his need for intimacy with her, she determined to write only masterpieces for this awesome Brent who had depths and breadths that thrilled her. Her love scenes must soar to the heavens. Determined to write love scenes that would be as good as having his body in bed, she rewrote the love scenes in *Silver Skies* about a thousand times to ensure that reading her love scenes would satisfy his need for her body. It tormented her to turn Brent down, because she longed to nurture, caress and soar her lover to the highest heavens with her body, to nourish his manliness, his greatness and his soul. Yes, she could love Brent with her writings! Jesus would not oppose that. What an awesome way to honor her forbidden love. Therefore, her monument of love for Brent became her novel *Silver Skies*. Her writings, especially the love scenes, must be so awesome, that to Brent it would be as good as having her in bed.

Perhaps, she dreamed, Hollywood would even make a movie based on her writings that he could act in! Oh, how proud he would be of her, that her love for him inspired her to write a masterpiece to honor their love. Maybe because of her writings, he'd win Academy Award for Best Actor. The very thought thrilled her to her core. A love this vast deserved a masterpiece and she filled her days with mastery of the writing craft, for the man who had lifted her heart from despair to glory.

She enrolled in The Institute of Children's Literature (1991 to 1993) and pursued her study of the writing craft like a future Olympic hopeful would prepare for the gold medal. With every brain cell she had within her, she determined to write nothing less than a masterpiece. What an awesome way to love her Brent!

Brent soon learned Loree's bribes mattered more than justice for his helpless Gail. Loree played Dr. Jekyll to the public and Mr. Hyde with him. The powerful Loree seemed to own the police. As he slept, his penis in an involuntary erection, she burst through the bedroom window of his one-story Hollywood Hills home with a baseball bat, glass shattering everywhere. With Jesuit precision, her vagina landed right on his erect penis. She then plopped a gallon of lubricant next to him and screamed, "Time to make love, Brent!" Glass fragments pierced him, and he struggled and bled, while he wrangled with her on top of his penis.

In his nightmares, from 1992 on, Loree burst through Gail's windows, shattering glass everywhere, then jumped onto Gail's bed in her sleep and stabbed her to death. Her bizarre, obsessive behavior with him so differed from her public self, who, besides those who dealt with him day after day, would believe him if exposed her treachery? Loree, a publicist, aware of public stereotypes, played her role with perfection, playing the glamorous Hollywood woman who bedded Brent in public, so opposite her real self—the raging, obsessive mad woman who stalked Brent in private.

Though he came across as a joker in public, his jokes covered deep hurts. To keep his Gail alive, he played Loree's game, his public love life with the drug-

The Forbidden Abyss

rapist a performance. Helpless under Loree's rage, nothing escaped her. She found him everywhere he went. If he dared a step towards Gail, Loree jumped to harm his true love, breathing out death threats. She threatened to kill Gail if he exposed her to Gail.

From 1990 to 2011, Brent only lived to hover over and protect Gail. It nauseated him how Loree McBride transformed him away from the man who sang in *Ol' Yellow Eyes Is Back*, the album he created in 1990 for his Gail. Without Gail, he would have ended it all, his celebrity a curse, because he knew it threatened the Jesuits, so that they tormented him with Loree.

The all powerful Loree always managed to break into his house. The video cassette tapes that Gail made for him from 1991 to 1993 on her camcorder, where she sang to him and played on her piano, Loree confiscated. He caught her in the act, ripping out all the film from Gail's videocassettes and eating the film. She flung the tapes outside the window. He saw a pile of broken tapes on the ground outside his house. So Loree destroyed all the private movies Gail sent him in the 1990s, and Gail had not made extra copies of them—too dangerous with her jealous husband roaming about her apartment, who threatened to divorce her if she continued to write Brent.

How Jesuits deluded the world about Brent's fame, portraying him as the millionaire playboy star, a fit match for their playgirl Loree. Brent couldn't talk to Gail from 1993 until the time she finally understood why he had Loree. Loree threatened Gail's death if he took a step in her direction. Scars on his rectum and body reminded him that Loree meant business.

Yes, Loree transformed him from a man with a heart in the heavens for Gail (1990 to 1992), to a man who jumped at every corner (1993 and onwards), expecting a frenzied woman to hit him over the head with a fry pan or stab him with an injection of brain control drugs.

One day Loree giggled and laughed, "I can't believe that bitch sends you all her religious crap. Doesn't she know you don't believe in God?"

"She has a right to believe what she wants."

"At least I don't preach at you like she does."

"Well, I think people have a right to believe what they want, as long as it doesn't harm anyone." Brent glared at Loree. He didn't care to go into a discourse with her, but he most definitely would not allow her to believe that he preferred her company to Gail, who was an angel compared to Loree.

Loree fumed, and made fists, frustrated that her sparkling good looks didn't make a dent on Brent's adoration of Gail.

One day in July 1993, Jesuits gave Gail's son a sudden asthma attack, apparently from some pollen, which landed him in the Seattle's Children's Hospital. Loree knew about Gail's son in the hospital, because the Jesuits increased the pollen count to make her son sick. So when Brent went to call Gail to comfort and support her, Loree had cut all the phone lines in the house, making him unable to call her to support her while her son was hospitalized. Because he tried to call Gail, and Loree caught him, which she always did, she punished and threatened him again.

Brent's Forbidden Ground

Because he committed the forbidden sin in trying to call Gail, he expected retaliation. He found all her syringes and flushed them down the toilet. This infuriated her, because those syringes were the first thing she went for.

She then put a gun to Brent's back and led him down to his basement, where she tied him up. Using a plasma torch to his chastity belt, she was able to remove the belt. The belt protected his genitals from Loree, and could electrify her if she tried to rape him.

"Yeah, I've had it with your fucking chastity belt. Now it's your turn to get electrocuted!" She laughed, while she started electrocuting his testicles with some kind of cattle prod. Then she hooked him up to an electro-ejaculator, which was a machine that basically milked a man like a cow, only it was semen. It hurt pretty badly.

He had no food in the basement. She planned to let him starve to force him to eat her food laced with drugs to control his mind, so she left him in the basement for days.

But he just refused to eat. He had betrayed Gail enough with his body, even if against his will, and he'd rather die than do it again.

Loree knew he would try to escape right away if he heard her slam the door or heard the car leave, so she wouldn't leave, but prepared him food from the house and sprinkled in the drugs. She figured he'd be so starved, that he would eventually give in. But the September 1992 rape terror still raked his memories, and he'd rather starve than have her drugged food, and she realized she had a lost cause.

After a while, she let him go.

Gail had just returned from the hospital with her son. He rushed to the phone and called Gail to comfort her.

It infuriated Loree that despite her physical beauty, that nothing she did could remove Gail from Brent's heart. The next day at midnight, Loree phoned Gail and blasted her voice into the phone, low like a man's voice—the voice she used when she fumed with jealousy and frustration. She roared her voice at Gail, "Hey *bitch*! What the *fuck* are you doing to my boyfriend!"

Gail laughed it off as some Paramount studios wacko that she knew Brent would *never want*. She had no idea about Loree at this time, and thought that Brent's three weeks of silence against her in September 1992 was a Paramount studios issue only, that perhaps Paramount threatened to fire Brent because he phoned a married woman fan. Brent so adored her, she never dreamed that he had sex with another woman, and, of course, it never crossed her mind that a woman could rape a man. A virgin when she married her husband, Gail's mind and heart were too pure to imagine the truth.

Though she did know that the New Age Satanic Star Trek studio would frown upon Bible thumpers, like herself; so she reasoned the problem lay there. But despite her Bible belt background, she sensed Brent, from Texas (Bible belt country), respected her. And she never preached at Brent. He was the only person she totally bared her soul to at this time in her life. She relished her soul mate Brent, even if he worked for the Satanic Star Trek studio. By this time, Brent had put his co-stars Levar Burton and Gates McFadden on the phone to talk to her, though they did not identify themselves, Gail recognized their voices. She liked Brent and his co-stars, thinking they were cool and tolerant people,

The Forbidden Abyss

what Gail really was deep down underneath. These traits she secretly admired in Brent and his co-stars, despite the intolerant King James Bible only crowd she hung around with through her husband and church.

Though Brent despised Loree and she terrified him, Brent kept Loree as his "girlfriend", because he really thought she would kill Gail. Loree was capable of doing such horrific things.

When he reported Loree to the police, they took her side, "You must have done something terrible to make this beautiful woman so mad. What have you done?" Loree McBride "owned" all of the police. She had bribed them.

July 1993 Gail had started her novel *Silver Skies* for Brent, while her family was stationed in Seattle. She was studying at The Institute of Children's Literature, and had started her novel that summer of 1993.

He missed the days when he could go to his sparsely furnished Hollywood Hills house to relax and dream of Gail or perhaps phone her, just to hear her voice. Now when he stared at the immaculate bare wood floors and the living room with its pristine modern couch and armchair, it seemed that memories of Loree's presence there polluted the heaven it had been to lounge about lazily in his house, dreaming of Gail and even trying his hand at screenwriting, because Gail had decided to become a writer for him. Ah, that was the good old days from 1990 up until September 1992. And then Loree happened. Now, if he worked on a screenplay, Loree would pounce on him. "Did you talk to Gail today?"

"What makes you think that?"

"Well, you're an actor, not a writer, and you have this crazy idea that your Gail will become the next big Hollywood screenwriter! Ha! Nobody's ever heard of her! Just 'cause she's written you a Star Trek teleplay, that you know will go nowhere."

"I'm an actor. I read screenplays all the time. I'm sick of all the sorry scripts I read, and think perhaps I can write something I'd like to act in."

"Don't all of a sudden turn into a screenwriter, or I might decide to wiretap all your communications. You talk to Gail, I'll kill her."

"Shit." Brent left the room, to get away from the monster.

"Boy, if your Gail heard you talk! Ha!" Loree laughed. "That bitch would you throw you out." Loree jumped onto Brent's sofa and swung her dildo. "Then I'll have you all to myself."

"Excuse me, I have to run to the toilet."

Loree began removing her shirt and bared her breasts to Brent, and leaped towards him.

Brent sprinted to the bathroom. "I think I'm going to throw up." He slammed the bathroom door behind him, locking it, while he stared down at the toilet. He double checked his chastity belt, made sure it covered his penis, then put his finger on the button to make it electrocute if Loree touched him.

He eased open his bathroom door and looked both ways, didn't see Loree, then sprinted out towards the front door and out to his yard. Loree had left behind a pile of burning dildos in his front yard.

Loree was vicious when Gail started her novel for Brent in 1993. "Hey Brent

Brent's Forbidden Ground

sweetheart, I have something to show you." She grabbed Brent by the arm and led him to the pristine modern sofa in his living room, where a photo album lay open.

"What's this about, Loree?"

"I'm a Jesuit," she said.

"What's *that?*" he said.

"It's a very powerful organization. We worship the true Christ. Let me show you what Jesuits have done." She flipped through the pages of the photo album, and each page featured photos of tortured, mutilated people: concentration camp scenes from Hitler's Germany, naked men and women in skeleton bodies, bones protruding, eyes hollowed out, tormented faces staring up at hatchets about to land on their neck, and eyes filled with terror on every page, bodies cut into pieces like butchered steak, and mountains and mountains of corpses.

Brent stared in horror at the photographs, many of them concentration camp scenes, where his fellow Jews had been tortured and annihilated.

"This is what we do to our enemies and we don't like the book Gail is writing, nor do we want you to get near her or to tell her that I'm a Jesuit, and that this is what we will do to Gail, if you won't let me be your girlfriend and if you don't cooperate with me." She sat straight and tall, her eyes with a determined glaze, like the look of a cult religious leader who pronounced doom on all who would not follow her into a Jim Jones doomsday.

Brent figured a Jesuit was some weird religious cult. "What's the big deal about being a Jesuit?"

"'Cause I'm proud to be a Jesuit and wanted to show you what we can do to Gail. I belong to a very powerful organization."

After viewing the photographs, he stayed up all night crying, staring at the ceiling of his bedroom, as if staring into a forbidden abyss. He didn't know what a Jesuit was, but he had had personal experience with Loree, and knew what *she was*. He decided to save Gail, he'd sacrifice himself, risk his life, and tolerate the presence of a human being who made him want to vomit.

Loree's ability to break into his house at whim, to make copies of his house key, even though he had not given his keys to anybody who could copy them for her, her ability to use brain control drugs on him and most of all her ability to come alive again after Levar killed her, convinced Brent she could do as she damn well pleased. He had no doubt Loree would kill and torture Gail, just like he saw in these photographs; so he played her game, made public appearances with her, while he loathed every minute he had to see, feel or hear her the presence of this black widow spider.

She hounded Brent every day. He was constantly running for his life. She met him everywhere—in his yard, his car, his workplace. Everywhere. Sometimes she would just do something creepy like leaving a pile of burning dildos in his yard, or drawing penises all over the side of his house in lipstick. Other times, she would surprise him by hiding in his car or closets, and attacking him, slapping and scratching him like some kind of demon. She was like a cat with rabies. He couldn't even keep her out of his house. She always managed to break in somehow, as if she somehow got a copy of his house key. Despite her terror over his life, Brent never ever considered giving up Gail. Though he was sure a lesser man would have.

The Forbidden Abyss

Brent felt shame that in January 1994 Paramount Studios sent Gail that letter saying to never write him again. It all started with her son, when he was in the hospital in July 1993 for asthma and pneumonia, right when Loree had him locked up in the basement, and cut the lines to all his phones, so that he couldn't call her.

Gail was concerned that Brent gave her silence when her son was in the hospital in July 1993, and the hospital noticed her "stress" and referred her to their social worker. She confided to this social worker about Brent, only if he would keep secret what she told him about Brent. He lied. The social worker wrote a report about Gail claiming she was crazy for believing that she and Brent had a "relationship". Her husband got the social worker's statement in the mail in November 1993.

Then her stupid and vulgar husband, when he read the social worker's statement in November 1993, demanded Gail give him the Paramount studios address, which she did. She watched her husband compose an idiotic letter, where he threatened to give Brent bad press, if anyone from Paramount contacted Gail, while he threatened Gail with divorce if she ever wrote Brent again.

In December 1993, Brent appeared to the front door of Gail's first story apartment and whispered her name. He wanted to confirm to her how much she meant to him, in case Paramount did something because of her husband's letter. She peeked out her son's window, and Brent flashed the lights on and off inside a sparkling, white truck he'd rented to drive out to her apartment, so she could see him. He wore a disguise, a black wig with a black moustache. Then he backed out and zoomed out of the parking lot like lightning, in his sparkling, white truck.

The Jesuits used Gail's husband to ignite a situation with Paramount by having him write that nasty letter to the studio.

So, in January 1994, Gail received a Fed Ex letter from Paramount Studios, which ignited Jesus Christ.

When Gail's ex husband got the evil Fed Ex letter on Saturday evening January 15th, he handed it to Gail and she read it. It forbade her to ever have any communications with Paramount Studios and accused her and her family of harassment. It also claimed that Brent never contacted her beyond an autograph photo.

So disgusted by the lies in the letter, she mumbled to herself, "Brent never sent me an autograph photo. He sent me a letter". She noticed that Brent did not sign the Fed Ex letter, but felt disappointed in him, because the letter made it to her apartment and her husband signed for it at the door.

Her husband handed it over to her, and she read it, feeling that Paramount Studios betrayed her, and it confused her about Brent. It so upset her, that she only got three hours of sleep that night. She did notice that Brent did not sign it and suspected sabotage.

The next day, she went to church quite upset. After church, she prayed for three hours on her knees, stretched over her futon, from one to four in the afternoon, begging Jesus with tears to forgive her for disgracing His great name. "Oh Jesus, I'm so sorry." She wiped her eyes and cried some more, feeling humiliated and ashamed for all the passion and faith she had poured into Brent, from 1991 to then (January 1994), because she responded to his romance on the

Brent's Forbidden Ground

phone, when he called her on the phone and made tender and passionate love to her, caressing her with his velvet voice. "I should have had the character to never encourage Brent in any sort of romance, because I'm married. I have disgraced Your great name, because I claim to be Yours.

"Please forgive me. I'm so sorry. I thought Brent was a deep and awesome man, committed to me, because he sang, 'When I fall in love, it will be forever' and that you approved of our love, and that we had a love that soared to the heavens. What a stupid sucker I have been. I tried to do what was right and I thought loving Brent was right, because our love was so awesome. How he has disappointed me! And how I have disappointed You!

"But, it appears, the way I went about it was all wrong. I never should have returned his romantic feelings. I should have kept my correspondence with him purely platonic and I never should have lost my head over this guy. Oh Jesus, I'm so distressed for you! I have disgraced you by my foolish behavior with Brent. I sure have come a long ways since those days that I trained for missionary service as a young lady, haven't I?

"Imagine, I turned down a chance to be an Air Force officer to go to Bible College, but now I'm guilty of adultery, because I didn't turn down an evil Hollywood actor who made love to me on the phone as a married woman. All those horrible things I've heard about Hollywood from my church are true! How I've disgraced You! How I've let you down! Please forgive me. I'm so, so sorry.

"Oh, I should have known better. All the preachers warned me as a young lady about the Hollywood cesspool. Why did I ever doubt them? Why did I think Brent was different from mainstream Hollywood? Oh, I've made such a mess of my life. Please forgive me for disgracing you! I will be wiser about Brent. I won't disgrace you anymore about him. I'm so sorry, Jesus. Please forgive me. I'm so sorry."

Out to the apartment dumpster she trounced, tossing the evil Paramount letter into the dumpster: her way of ending forever her communications with Brent.

Twelve hours after Gail prayed for that three hours, crying tears of shame and begging Jesus to forgive her, Jesus sent to Paramount Studios the Northridge earthquake.

It hit Hollywood in the wee hours of the morning.

Gail was not watching the news the day after her three hours of prayer, and when she went outside for a bit, around four in the afternoon on Monday, January 17, 1994, her son came running to her. "Mommy, did you hear about the earthquake that just hit Southern California?"

Gail rushed into her apartment to watch the news. Her Jesus had answered her three hour prayer from yesterday!

The earthquake had hit Paramount Studios very early in the morning, before the sun came up, around twelve hours after she prayed for three hours in shame to Jesus. Her jaw dropped in disbelief!

How could she, such an adulterous and sinful woman, get an answer to prayer *like this?* Jesus sent the Northridge earthquake to Paramount Studios! This was Jesus' message to Paramount for what they did to her!

When Gail read the paper the next day, she learned that the only Hollywood people who died worked for Paramount Studios.

"Oh, my God, Jesus. So this is the answer to my three hour prayer! I don't

The Forbidden Abyss

deserve such an answer. I've dreamed of making love to a man who is not my husband."

It was Paramount Studios, not Brent, which sent her that Fed Ex letter. Brent would not give up his Gail, and when they ordered her not to write him anymore, he got a wiretap on her phone and listened to her at all times with a device he used to hear all she said to him on her wiretapped phone.

When she answered her phone around dinnertime on January 17th, she heard strange beeps and noises on her phone, Brent's way of letting her know that he had obtained a wiretap on her phone, and that she would no longer need to write him to communicate with him. While experiencing the earthquake himself, he wanted to let her know in his own way, that he was okay, and that he still cared for her, and wanted to hear from her. That's why he wiretapped her phone!

Because of Brent's wiretap on her phone, she only had to dial her own number and get a "blank" on her phone now to talk to Brent. She could now talk to the "blank", and Brent would hear every word she said on the "blank".

Jesus seemed to tell her through the sermons she heard in church Sunday night on January 16, 1994, to never write Paramount again, and she never did. She promised Jesus she would obey Him in this matter. She could now talk to Brent by dialing her own number and obtaining a "blank"! But the earthquake seemed to indicate that Jesus favored her somehow. It boggled her mind, that, she, such an adulterous sinner, could pray down an earthquake to Paramount Studios!

"How clever Brent is," she thought, because his wiretap of her phone enabled her to continue her communication with him, despite their enemies, and she wouldn't need to communicate with Brent through Paramount anymore. All she had to do was pick up her phone, dial her own number, get a "blank" and talk to Brent. But she knew that whoever her enemy was, they made Jesus very angry!

"Jesus did tell me to encourage Brent, when I went to the funeral of that little girl in November 1992. I remember that. Yes, that was Him who told me to keep loving Brent, to remain Brent's friend, even though I was married, that everything was falling into some sort of divine plan. When I came back from that funeral and hit the random mode on my CD player and that song 'Somewhere' from *West Side* Story was the first song that played.

"Yes, Jesus really did speak to me then, when He told me in His still, small voice, through the words of that song 'There's a place for us, somewhere a place for us. Peace and quiet and open air, wait for us, someday. There's a time for us, someday a time for us. Time together, with time to spare, time to look, time to care. . .' I don't get it, but by loving Brent, I have not sinned. Jesus seems to tell me that the sinner is Paramount Studios. They got the earthquake, not me."

Brent was glad she noticed that he didn't sign his name in the Fed Ex letter. The studio acted on his behalf, without his permission, in an attempt to keep Gail from him, to break up their love. In fact, if Loree hadn't locked him up in the basement when Gail's son was in the hospital, it's very possible the social worker's statement over Gail's "stress" never would have happened, and then Gail's husband never would have written that nasty letter that enraged Paramount Studios.

Brent already knew how deep they were willing to go when they allowed

Brent's Forbidden Ground

Loree McBride to enter the studio and repeatedly rape him in September 1992.

He wanted Gail to know that it was indeed him who made love to her with sweet longings over the phone in the early 1990s, caressing her with his voice as her written words caressed his soul.

When Brent awakened the next morning, Loree waited for him at his dining room table. "Good morning, Brent. I've made eggs, your favorite!"

Brent jumped at the sight of her. "I'll pass, thank you."

Loree then flung the contents of the skillet onto a plate in front of him—and, rather than chicken eggs, they were actually jumbo sized human eggs. Brent didn't know it then, but they were from the Jesuit cloning labs. "They're fertilized. Just like you like it. *Kiss me, Brent!*" She flung herself over the counter to assault him.

Brent leaped for his life and almost dropped everything as he ran for the front door and whisked out of his house. I have to lose this woman, he thought.

He sold his one-story Hollywood Hills ranch house in 1994 for only one reason: to get rid of Loree McBride. He told no one about it who could tell Loree, and took bits and pieces of furniture over to his new Beverly Hills home little by little, to make it appear he wasn't moving, that he was just selling some of his furniture.

Finally, one day, totally moved into his Beverly Hills home, he collapsed onto the sofa in his new home and hoped and prayed Loree would not locate him. He made sure that in his new home, the bedroom was on the second floor! Now she couldn't crash through his bedroom window to attack him in his bed, like she did at his one-story Hollywood Hills home. Part of him knew moving to a new home was a long shot, because when the new tenants would move to his old home, she'd get kicked out and go looking for him again. But it did earn him about two months of peace.

When he failed to show up for months at his Hollywood Hills home, and another family moved in, she located his new house, and showed up at his Beverly Hills home.

In 2003, he would move again to try and get away from her. This time to Malibu, a bigger place where he'd have more room to keep her away from him inside the house.

Loree flew with him on jets to Star Trek conventions and everywhere. Paramount insisted that Loree McBride, Brent's Paramount Studios girlfriend, must go with him everywhere. From 1993 to 2000, he wasn't allowed to be anywhere without her, or he'd be fired from his job as Data for *Star Trek: The Next Generation*.

When Brent appeared with Loree at Star Trek conventions, he would stare at her with nervousness, because though she acted normal in front of a crowd, he knew what he was in for behind closed doors. Because he looked so miserable with Loree in the real photographs of them together in public, Jesuits doctored all these photographs, changing facial expressions or inserting a different Brent into the picture, to make him appear happy with his drug rapist. They also toned down Loree's viciousness and softened her facial expressions.

Brent followed Gail when she moved to her hometown Houston, Texas in

The Forbidden Abyss

1995. Actually her husband was stationed in Galveston, and Gail moved to baseball player Nolan Ryan's hometown Alvin, Texas, deciding not to live on the island, in case of hurricanes. Or at least that's what she told her husband, who did not know that Houston, Texas was Brent's hometown. Brent's mother lived in Houston, so Brent flew out to Houston to visit Gail. He would sit in a long, black limousine with very dark windows, so that no one could see him inside the limousine, which was parked in the parking lot of Gail's apartment complex.

When Gail drove into her apartment's parking lot, she noticed the long, black limousine with dark, tinted windows. Several times when she pulled into her parking lot, it was there. She smiled to herself, thinking, I bet that's Brent in there. I can't believe how he adores me.

In December 2011, when Gail confessed to Brent that she suspected he was inside that limousine, which often sat in her apartment's parking lot, he laughed. "Well, damn, there goes my cover!"

She went on a sewing binge, buying some peach colored fabric and shared her sewing exploits with Brent on the wiretapped phone. She sewed some curtains to cover her sliding glass door with ruffles and tie backs.

One time when Gail went out, Brent sneaked over to her apartment from his limousine and surveyed the inside of her apartment, admiring the peach curtains that hung over her sliding glass door. My, this woman can sew. He let her know of his admiration of her sewing abilities when she finished the curtains by flooding her wiretapped phone with beepy sounds to applaud her accomplishment.

When he peeked into her apartment, he wanted so bad to know what her home looked like, especially where she slept. He wanted to wrap himself up in those curtains.

Sometimes, even with Loree in his house, Gail would play whole sermons on her wiretapped phone for Brent to listen to. She shared all of her life with Brent, including her religion. From her Alvin, Texas apartment in 1995, by dialing her own number, she could get a "blank" on her phone that would last for hours. She used that as her way to share her life with Brent for hours. Though Brent may not have been a Christian, he thought it was pretty cute that she played her favorite sermons for him. It was just a part of her.

Sometimes when Loree was with him, Brent listened to Gail's King James Bible preachers from his wiretap of her phone. Loree would run out of the room to go throw up. Brent was glad when this happened, glad that the preaching brought pain to her, because it helped him get rid of her.

He'd given up being disgusted by all of Loree's fake photos on the Internet. Some of them were accurate, like the one where she scowled with an angry face. But sometimes she looked much sweeter than she really was. Jesuits doctored the photos. None of the sweet photos of her were accurate. She was always nastiness.

Yeah, she was a real bitch, kind of like Rachel from Gail's novel *Silver Skies*, or even like Lore from Gail's teleplay *Lal*. Really crazy and mean.

Loree's Birthday Bash at Spago's 1996 to 1997

Early 1996, Gail mentioned Jack Chick's book *Smokescreens* to Brent on her wiretapped phone. She discussed how this book exposed the Jesuit Order of the Roman Catholic Church and their involvement in the Nazi holocaust. Brent decided to go ahead and look this book up to get more information about what was going on with Loree. He ordered this book from Jack Chick and saw the same concentration camp photos in them that Loree had showed him in 1993—the same photos that kept him up all night, crying, when he was terrified over what Loree might do to Gail.

Oh my God, he thought, this Loree was not kidding when she said she was a Jesuit! This is more than just a Paramount conspiracy. I better do exactly what this bitch wants, because it appears this Jesuit Order is a very powerful organization

It seemed the more disgusted he got about her, the more the Jesuits created photographs of him with Loree, making them appear to attend functions together.

Loree and her two dogs had managed to move into Brent's house in the spring of 1996. She somehow always got a copy of his keys and just moved herself and her dogs in. It was all a part of her plan, because if he didn't let her move in, she would kill Gail.

Once she moved in, Brent had to bolt his bedroom door every night. Now moved into his house, Loree attacked Brent often, especially whenever she caught Brent talking to Gail on the phone, because he sometimes impersonated another person to talk to Gail on the phone. Brent's impersonations were so brilliant that Gail did not know it was Brent speaking to her when she picked up the phone and thought it a "wrong number".

Though he let Loree live in his house, he refused to let her sleep in his bed. She slept in her own room.

Every morning, he'd wake up and check his body and sheets to make sure nothing happened during the night. It would be hard to get out of bed, because he'd be very sleepy from having slept lightly and awakening every few hours to make sure she wasn't in the room. He then checked his cameras which rolled during the night while he slept, to see if she managed to break into his bedroom somehow and do something to him. If there was no "evidence", he'd reset the cameras to film his bedroom again.

After donning his electrified chastity belt, he would ease open his bedroom door, dead bolt it behind him, so she couldn't sneak into his bedroom while he was gone.

The Forbidden Abyss

Then, not knowing what lay beyond his bedroom door, his heart palpitated as he descended the stairs

She had whacked him with the butt of a gun and with frying pans and baseball bats several times, so he began wearing bulletproof vests and football helmets every time he ventured outside of his bedroom. He always wore his chastity belt that covered his genitals. It would electrify Loree if she tried to rape him.

To ensure that she couldn't put him on her brain control drugs, he never ate any food from the house. He got a lot of fast food mostly, or went out to eat. Sometimes it wasn't very healthy, but at least it didn't have brain control drugs in it.

Now that she had officially moved in, she upped her game. One day she put a gun to Brent's back, shoving the barrel into his back so hard that she gave him a bruise, then led him down to his basement door and tied him up. Flinging open the basement door, she flung him down the steps, his body flying down the steps. She left him there at the bottom of the steps, and took off.

Brent had no idea where she was going. It was the day of her birthday, June 26, 1996. With him tied up, she went for his credit cards, then called all of their friends and relatives, and gave herself a big birthday bash on June 26, 1996.

Using her contacts in the media, Loree published a lie in the paper that Brent sponsored the party for her. That's the day Gail learned about Loree, when she read about the bash in the *Houston Chronicle*. "Brent Spiner hosted a huge birthday dinner for his girlfriend Loree McBride at Spago's in Los Angeles, and boy was it some celebration. 'The food was great,' Sylvia said about her son. She had just returned from a trip out to Los Angeles to visit her son, Brent, who plays Data in *Star Trek: The Next Generation*."

However, this was a strange birthday bash that Brent gave for his "girlfriend" Loree, because Brent, tied up with ropes in his basement, wasn't invited.

Brent struggled with the ropes the whole time she was gone, but to no avail. When she descended to the basement, his heart raced. He hoped she had not found some syringes, to inject brain control drugs into him, while she went out.

"I tell you what. I'm a nice girl and will let you go." She began to loosen the ropes from off of him. She smirked at him, knowing that Gail had just read the *Houston Chronicle* and was crying her eyes out right now. Brent never called Gail on her birthday or major holidays anymore. Loree stopped that after she raped Brent in September 1992, so Loree knew this would really sting.

With her hands on her hips, she smiled. "Your Gail *finally* knows about your 'girlfriend.' She read about me in the *Houston Chronicle*."

Loree laughed and dragged him to the room where she often slept, pounced onto her bed and jumped up and down on it, swinging a dildo. "It's party time!" She handed him the machine (a receiver) he used to listen to her talk from her wiretapped phone. It was like a little speaker, where he had volume control and could even listen to Gail with headphones or ear pieces.

His face fell when he heard Gail wailing as if her life was at an end on his receiver. "Oh, Brent, why do you have a girlfriend? How could you do this to me!" Then came a long wail, sniffles, until her voice sounded muffled and raspy. "I've risked the streets to communicate with you. You know my husband would divorce me because I continue to communicate with you against his

Brent's Forbidden Ground

wishes. And now I realize that I've risked the streets for you for *nothing!* Because of your girlfriend, if my husband kicks me out on the streets because I have disobeyed him to communicate with you, I'll be homeless!" Gail read to him over and over what she had read in the *Houston Chronicle*, that he had sponsored a big birthday bash for Loree McBride as his girlfriend.

"What birthday bash is she talking about?"

Loree shoved the paper into his face and pointed at the snippet that described the bash. "Right there. With any luck, this article might make her so miserable she might kill herself, then I'll have you all to myself."

So thrilled over her conquest, Loree swung the dildo all night, jumping up and down on her bed.

Brent never could bear to bring his Gail any pain. After listening to Gail cry for hours, he laid down an ultimatum with Loree. "I'm going to make a public statement that I did not sponsor this bash. This is outrageous. I would never do this to my Gail!" Brent fought back tears as he listened to Gail wailing on his receiver.

Loree laughed so loud, the walls almost shook. "Oh, I wouldn't do that if I was you. You paid for it with your credit cards."

"What!?"

"Oh yeah. It was so much fun. Everybody was there, except you, of course. Almost like a big wedding reception."

He called his credit card company, "Hey, can you tell me what charges were made to my account in the past week?"

So he rolled his eyes when he read for himself in the Houston Chronicle that he had apparently thrown her a "birthday bash". He was infuriated that she racked up about twenty thousand dollars in debt on his credit cards for a birthday bash that devastated the woman he would die for.

Gail read the Houston Chronicle every day when she lived in Texas (1994 to 1997), to learn anything and everything about her Brent, because his mother lived in Houston then. When Gail read a comment supposedly by his mother on June 26, 1996, alleging that Brent hosted a big birthday bash for his girlfriend at Spago's in Los Angeles, she cried for a month.

Loree nudged up to Brent. "I expect you to make some television appearances now, and talk about me in your television interviews. Make sure to mention my two dogs roaming about your house. I'm getting sick of everybody asking whether I am your girlfriend. People question the articles I've published that state we are a couple. I want *you* to tell the world we are a couple!"

Brent stared at her in disgust. "I really hate you. I think I've had enough of this crap. I'm not playing your game anymore!" He wished so bad he could call up Gail and explain everything to her, but still felt unsure that Gail would believe him, because he couldn't even convince Paramount about Loree.

But hearing Gail crying her eyes out through his wiretap of her phone, made him determined to rectify the situation.

With a flip of her hair, Loree said, "If you try to expose me, let me show you what I'll do to your Gail." She grabbed his arm and led him to the sofa, on the coffee table in front she opened up a huge photo album, the first page that opened up, showed a corpse, with head decapitated, arms and legs ripped off and

The Forbidden Abyss

near the body. On closer inspection he made out that the bashed in face was Gail's!

The Jesuits had killed a Gail look-alike, almost a clone, for the photos. Gail's genetic profile seemed resistant to cloning technology, and the best the Jesuits could do was produce temporary clones of Gail. Most clones of Gail would not submit to the Jesuits, and would jump off cliffs and kill themselves rather than be a Jesuit. Perhaps, the Jesuits used one of these "suicides" and cut her up and made photos of her for Brent.

He looked at Loree in rage. "Did you kill Gail? But I just heard her crying on the phone!"

Loree smiled, her venomous smile, and just continued flipping through the album, showing one photo after another of a dead Gail, so mutilated, he hardly recognized her. The body looked like butchered steak, blood was spattered everywhere. In each photo, the head was decapitated and all her limbs mutilated, cut off, or missing. Loree smiled at him as she flipped each page, gloating in her power to control the famous Star Trek star.

He got up and paced, feeling like he needed to vomit. "If you kill her, I'll kill myself, so you won't win, you bitch."

So while Gail cried her eyes out in Webster, Texas, after she read about the birthday bash in the Houston Chronicle, even gagging and vomiting a bit into her kitchen sink, Brent grasped at straws to ensure his Gail would not end up like the photos he saw of her in Loree's photo album. The Jesuits also had Gail on a psychiatric drug that induced depression, but to learn that her hero had betrayed her with a girlfriend while she risked the streets to write him because of her jealous husband, truly devastated and confused her that dark and confusing summer of 1996.

Loree's laughter cackled to the walls of his house. The spider so poisoned his house, he felt all the walls, the curtains, the shades, furniture, carpet, basement, stairs, doorway and the entire house was poison. His Beverly Hills home, seemed inhabited by Satan himself.

"Okay, if you don't do as I say, next time she goes in her car for a drive, I can always blow up her car." Loree's laughter wouldn't stop ricocheting off his walls, grating on his nerves.

So Brent made appearances on the Late Show with David Letterman and joked about his girlfriend and her two dogs at his house, hoping his actions would save Gail's life. He didn't know how Loree came up with those photos, but Brent had no doubt that Loree could murder Gail and get away with it, and, even worse, make it look like *he did it*. Just like Loree made it appear that he raped Loree in September 1992, rather than that she raped him.

Here it was, 1996, and he began to feel that for the rest of his life, he would be stuck with Loree McBride. His heart sunk into a sewer. If not for Gail's love for him, he would end it all here and now.

With Paramount on Loree's side, he didn't stand a chance. If he lost his job, he'd be on the streets, ensuring that he would be unable to protect Gail from Loree, and could lose his communication with Gail. At least he had enough income to offer Gail some protection now. If he couldn't support himself, he'd lose Gail and lose everything.

Loree enjoyed the power she had over Brent and Gail. So she never killed

Brent's Forbidden Ground

Brent, but just loved to threaten him that she would. Perhaps she also realized that if she killed Gail that Brent would commit suicide, and that would really ruin her fun.

Late August 1996, Gail's husband got the Internet, and Gail then viewed photos of Brent with Loree online. Disgusted and confused, she lost all romantic feeling for Brent. At the end of August 1996, she viewed Franco Nero as he played Lancelot in the musical *Camelot* on her videocassette player, to view a man who appeared to have the manliness that Brent lacked, eventually replacing Brent with Franco as her dream lover.

She couldn't go back to her husband in her heart.

Because of her relationship with Brent, she had learned writing skills and had evolved into a person totally incompatible with her shallow husband, who had no appreciation for the fine arts. The artist in Gail raged for expression. By mid-September 1996, she transferred her romantic feelings from Brent to a man she felt more worthy—Italian film star Franco Nero.

Brent felt that Franco was certainly a good man, and liked him as a friend and had no problems with Gail going to him, so he allowed Franco Nero to share the wiretap he had on Gail's phone. Brent felt that during this vulnerable time in Gail's life, when Loree so devastated and confused her, that Franco could cushion Gail's heart.

So Brent didn't mind giving Gail up to Franco Nero if it meant she was safer with him. Franco Nero was Brent's friend, and Brent thought Gail would like to meet Franco. He also thought Franco would like to meet Gail, too, and thought the two of them would get along excellently.

But Gail wasn't safer with Franco, because Loree would hit Franco Nero next.

When Gail would learn the truth that Loree was a Vatican agent in December 1999, she would reinstate her old flame Brent as her lover, and this may have inspired Franco to reinstate a woman that Gail often praised to Franco on her phone—his old flame Vanessa Redgrave. Gail felt that Vanessa Redgrave was brilliant and a good and vast person, far above Loree McBride, and often praised Franco for his good taste to be involved with her. Franco Nero married Vanessa Redgrave in 2006, perhaps inspired by Gail's love and forgiveness towards Brent Spiner in December 1999.

Now, hundreds of pages into her novel *Silver Skies*, Gail lost interest in writing it in late 1996. She'd written it to make love to Brent through her writings, to make it up to him that Jesus would not allow her to make love to him. Well, he had a girlfriend the whole time! And she thought he was pining with love for her! He no longer deserved her masterpiece, so she shoved it into the closet and though she told herself to keep writing it, she lost interest in it, and the masterpiece lay in her closet, gathering dust.

Jesuits changed their strategy. Six months after Gail found out about Loree, in December 1996, at Franco's London home, the drug rapist made an attempt on Franco Nero.

In the London December 1996 photos, Loree, in black, with a V-neck to her belly button and no bra, looked dressed to kill. Her eyes, cold and daring, obviously anticipated with relish her encounter with Franco Nero. She wanted to

The Forbidden Abyss

rape him the same way she did Brent. She was going to repeat the same thing all over with Franco and latch on to him instead. So she escaped from Brent in London, while she toured with Brent and Paramount Studios in December 1996 to promote the new Star Trek movie *First Contact*. Loree went to visit Franco with her brain control drugs, which she slipped into his drink.

Franco found her in his London house when he got home one night, and she was sprawled out on his couch wearing lingerie. She was drinking a wine glass with some black wine in it, and when she went to sip it, it turned silver on her lips. He freaked out and threw her out of his house, then, very panicked and stumbling over his words, called Brent.

Brent thought, "He might have only told me the short version. She may have touched his penis at some point. She loves her penis. She's obsessed with men that have big ones."

When Brent confronted Loree about this, her eyes glared in defiance. "He tried to rape *me*, he couldn't *resist me*."

Paramount expected Brent to make some public appearances with his "girl-friend" Loree, to protect their reputations in case Gail's husband gave them bad press about Brent, Loree and Gail. Photographs of Brent, on a Paramount studio's Christmas tour in Europe to promote his new movie, showed him with the drug-rapist by his side, right after Franco reported her attempted rape.

Brent's December 1996 photos, taken in Germany, while he toured to promote *Star Trek: First Contact* in Europe, showed him staring at Loree with disgust and depression. But though he knew she raped other men besides him, he kept her as his "girlfriend", because he wanted to make sure to keep the drug-rapist away from Gail.

In the Germany 1996 photos, Brent's nose almost touched the drug-rapist's cheeks, while his eyes gloomed over her with disgust and depression, with her eyes glaring straight ahead with hate and fire. "How dare that Franco say that about me! He just couldn't resist me and tried to rape me, and knew I'd expose him. That's why he says I tried to drug rape him."

It confused Gail that Brent would not dump Loree as his girlfriend, because the Germany 1996 photos made it obvious that Brent *knew* his girlfriend tried to seduce Franco, and that Loree pretended to be the irresistible seductress that Franco Nero could not resist. Brent heard Gail's reaction through the wiretap he had on her phone. "You're a coward."

When Gail viewed Loree McBride's defiant stare, while Brent's eyes gloomed over her with depression, she guessed the truth that Loree tried to seduce Franco. At this point, she began to realize that Loree could possibly be a criminal. She had no doubt that Loree was wicked and shallow. The woman had to know about her, because Brent spent hours and hours listening to her from her wiretapped phone, and yet she remained Brent's girlfriend. Gail concluded that Brent got suckered into having her as his girlfriend to keep his job at Paramount.

Why does Brent tolerate such an inferior and wicked woman as his girlfriend, Gail wondered. I am so superior to her in character and as a woman, I just don't understand why Brent feels he has to tolerate her companionship all the time, and even worse, why he degrades himself by appearing with this slut in public. Loree's good looks did not phase Gail. She sensed that Loree gloated in her looks as if that was all a woman needed to get a man. "What a wicked fool

Brent's Forbidden Ground

that woman is."

Gail had no doubt that Brent did not want Loree. She concluded that perhaps he was a bit too materialistic for her, because Gail concluded that Loree must have been assigned to Brent by Paramount. I don't want a man who will allow such an inferior and wicked woman to be his companion day in and day out. She's immature, shallow and self-centered, and *vastly inferior to me!* She thinks her youth and looks will win her Brent and I know he's deeper than this.

Apparently, Brent is a coward and not as manly and heroic as I originally thought. At this point, Gail lost so much respect for Brent because he tarnished his manliness by associating himself with such a shallow and vulgar whore, that she lost all romantic interest in him and stopped dreaming about making love to him. He had become a wimp to her, and Gail never found a wimp attractive.

"What's the matter with you? I know you don't love Loree. You must be a coward. I cannot dream about making love to a coward! I'm the woman who sustains you and makes you happy, and yet you hang around with this showgirl, who even tried to rape my Franco and even *after this, you still keep her as your girlfriend. What a coward.*" So while I have kept secret my love for you, this woman, who is obviously enamored with your celebrity status, jumps at every chance to appear with you in public. What a shallow farce of a woman she is!

Gail had no respect for a man who was more worried about public opinion, than in authenticity and genuineness in relationships.

What had happened to her deep and manly Brent, the man who sang to her with such depth and breadth in *Ol' Yellow Eyes Is Back*? Oh, what a disappointment Brent turned out to be!

But, Gail reasoned, even though Brent is no longer my hero, he's superior to my husband and deserves my friendship. I won't kick him off my phone's wiretap and I won't let my husband know that Brent is on the wiretap. Gail was confused, so much of this made no sense, and though she racked her brains trying to figure out the *real reason* Brent had Loree as a girlfriend, she remained confused. Brent must be a coward, she thought, and since Franco seemed like a man who would never stoop so low as to have a woman like Loree for a companion, Gail transferred her affections to Franco, who seemed more manly than Brent. She adored Franco's manly performance as Lancelot in *Camelot.*

No, Franco would never stoop so low as to have such a shallow woman like Loree for a companion. Franco once had the brilliant Vanessa Redgrave, and Gail was so proud of him for this, and told him so often. "I know you would never be like Brent and stoop so low to have such a shallow and flaky woman like Loree McBride! You have my heart. You are *manly.*"

Because the Franco Nero rape plot failed, Jesuits removed the December 1996 London and Germany photos of Loree from the Internet. Yes, Gail smiled to herself, I'm so proud of Franco. I knew Loree couldn't get him, like she has Brent!

Gail didn't know that Brent never attended the June 26, 1996 birthday party for Loree McBride, and that Loree, not his mother, wrote the damning article. Of course, Loree neglected to mention in the article that she stole Brent's credit cards to stage her own lavish birthday party at Spago's. Lying, she claimed Brent hosted the party for her. The world also didn't know that Brent wasn't there, because he wasn't invited! He so longed to call Gail and explain every-

The Forbidden Abyss

thing to her then, but Loree threatened to kill Gail every day at that time. Brent had no doubts the drug-rapist would carry out the murder. She had almost murdered him many times!

He waved to his drug-rapist the white flag of surrender. After Franco Nero replaced Brent as the man of Gail's dreams, Brent let the drug-rapist live in his house—she always broke into his house any ways. New locks, new keys, nothing worked. To stay alive for Gail, he wore bullet-proof vests, football helmets, penis protectors.

He felt it far better to know Loree's location (in his house), than have her lurk in the streets near Gail. Therefore, he allowed Loree free reign in his house from 1996 to 1999.

Loree, free inside his house, decided to quit chain smoking from her mouth, a means to fill the air he breathed with brain control drugs and nicotine. She stated with triumph, "Chain smoking's not hardcore enough for a true Jesuit." Her laughter cackled to the walls. Soon she shoved entire packs between her legs, and smoke billowed from her vagina.

Loree stole cigarettes from him, overwhelming him with nicotine withdrawal symptoms, then stuffed cigarettes into her vagina, smashing his face into her smoke-filled orifice. Laughing, with legs apart, she flaunted cigarettes from her clitoris. Like an automaton he sucked in fluids from her nicotine-laden cesspool, his cravings satisfied. Brain control horror.

The smoke he smelled from her vagina was laced with brain control drugs, which overwhelmed Brent giving him nicotine cravings. Loree would steal his cigarettes, and wait for him to suffer the horrible withdrawal symptoms, then he felt helpless as she grabbed his head and shoved his face into her orifice, smothering his nose with her vaginal fluids. In a trance, his mouth sucked her fluids, tasted the nicotine, felt gratified. To his horror, she had lulled him into nicotine heaven. When her brain control over him wore off, he dry heaved with guilt and tears. Loree laughed and jumped around his room. "Ha! You just can't stop making love to me, can you?"

Over the years, Jesuit press created photos of Brent with Loree, for functions he never attended with her. They made Brent appear happy with the drug-rapist, brushing over Loree's obsessive and crude self with a carefree and happy expression. What could he do? Jesuits practically owned the press.

If not for Gail's vastness, he knew he would have gone mad. Despite everything, he always worshipped the ground Gail walked on.

But each new day with Loree made him feel so filthy and dirty, he felt more unworthy of his awesome Gail. Even if Gail wouldn't take him after Loree polluted him, he felt it his fault that Gail had feelings for him. He had introduced the romance between them in 1991. He'd made love to her on the phone and though only she and he and his close friends knew of it—he had a conscience. To shush the guilt, so he could sleep at night, he had to protect her, even if it meant living with a murderer.

If he ousted Loree from his house, he knew she'd head straight for Gail. Far better him than Gail. It seemed Loree never tired, never gave up. Though she admitted her Catholic religion and Jesuit loyalties, he at first just thought her a horrible Catholic, who belonged to some cult off-shoot of the Catholic faith, and that it was mainly her and Paramount that worked together to oppose his Gail.

Brent's Forbidden Ground

But when he read Jack Chick's *Smokescreens* in 1996, he began to realize that Loree was part of the larger Jesuit and Roman Catholic conspiracy. However, he still wondered if the Jesuit Order was, in fact, part of the mainstream Catholic Church. It was hard to imagine that the Catholic Church could have survived if it was truly guilty of the Nazi holocaust and concentration camps.

Yes, Loree was a Jesuit, but did the Vatican itself sponsor the Jesuit Order that Loree belonged to? Or did Loree belong to a strange, illegitimate version of the Jesuit Order divorced from the main Jesuit Order? Was the pope himself attacking Brent and Gail? Brent struggled with questions about the Roman Catholic Church and its involvement with him and Gail, but had no doubts that Loree and the Jesuit Order *she* belonged to, were monstrous and very powerful.

From 1996 onwards, he realized that whatever conspiracy Loree belonged to, it had to have greater power than Paramount Studios, because Loree had power like God. He wanted to learn more about Gail, to determine why the Catholic Church had such an obsession with her. He began to suspect that there was more to Gail than just being the woman he was in love with. . .

Catherine the Great and King David
1040 B.C. to 2013 A.D.

Jesuits wrote at their website orderofthejesuits.com in 2011: "Gail was born September 15, 1957 to a divorced single mother in Cutler Ridge, Florida. Shortly after the birth, our genetic profiling teams were made aware of a dangerous combination of genes in infant Gail—60% Catherine the Great and 50% King David. To make matters worse, her great uncle was none other than the great Howard Hughes himself. This was a sure recipe for disaster. Since 1957 we have fought to hide her powerful genetic past from society.

"We first tried to kill her by giving her an allergy to baby formula."

Brent recalled that Gail's belly button was protruded, possibly from vomiting so much her first month of life. Gail's mother told Gail she almost died her first month of life because she was allergic to her formula.

"When that failed we started the Cold War in order to keep Russia and the United States distracted so that we could continue to weaken her quietly. It was a success.

"Our current methods of control include sabotaging her own brain, family, friendships and most importantly her love lives with the famous and powerful men that seek to be with her.

"In order to keep Gail from destroying our mission for world domination, society must never find out who she really is.

"We have successfully hidden Gail's power from the world by rewriting her entire genetic profile and fabricating a diminished societal image of Gail. To the ordinary person, Gail is nothing more than an average looking, middle-aged, divorced single woman. She suffers from paranoid schizophrenia. This angle is particularly clever since we are then able to have our agents in the medical field administer psychiatric drugs that keep her further under our control. Anyone that meets her will only see a crazy woman with poor self esteem, who has built a rich fantasy life to fill her deep emotional holes."

Jesuits discussed Gail's genetic profile from their Wiki page entitled "Genetic Profile" in 2011: A person's "genetic profile" refers to the genetic makeup of a person that goes beyond simple DNA and inheritance. A person can have actual genes from both of their biological parents but also have a full scale genetic profile that speaks of something entirely different. Gail is sixty percent Catherine the Great and fifty percent King David (the extra ten percent comes from her being more Catherine the Great than King David). While Gail's biological parents are neither of these people, this genetic profile in essence makes her a reincarnation of both of these historical figures. Jesuits scan the genetic profiles of every baby born on earth using remote satellite computer brain reads in order to determine who will become a possible threat to their plans.

Gail played for Brent and Franco Nero a movie she received from her mother in 1997 on her wiretapped phone. "Franco darling, I just got this from my mom and want you to hear this great saga. It's about my ancestors, the Oshu Fujiwara family. They were a royal family in Japan a long time ago, around 1000 A.D."

What Brent and Franco heard was a Japanese production, which Jesuits banned from the United States, in order to cover up Gail's Catherine the Great ancestry. The production opened up with a swell of music, grand and heroic, capturing the epic scale of the production and the epic family it depicted.

This NHK Taiga drama aired between July 1993 to March 1994 in Japan and was based on the novel (written for TV) by Katsuhiko Takahashi. The eleven and a half hour production was entitled 'Homura Tatsu', which means 'On Fire' or 'Fire and Honor'. It was about the Oshu Fujiwara clan, 140 years in the late Heian era (about 900 to 1100 A.D.). This royal family built a city made of gold, called Hiraizumi, a true splendor in northeastern Japan. Hiraizumi rivaled Kyoto (the capital of Japan at that time) in size and splendor.

The Heian period was the last part of classical Japanese history, from 794 to 1185 A.D. This period was named after the capital city of Heian-kyo, or modern Kyoto. During this time, the imperial court was at its peak, and this time in Japanese history was noted for its art, especially poetry and literature. Although the Imperial House of Japan had power on the surface, the real power at this time was in the hands of the Fujiwara clan, a powerful aristocratic family who had intermarried with the imperial family. Many emperors had mothers from the Fujiwara family. Heian means "peace and tranquility" in Japanese. The Heian period was considered a high point in Japanese culture that later generations admired. During this time, the samurai class rose in power, eventually taking power and starting the feudal period of Japan.

In the Heian period, though sovereignty lay in the emperor, the Fujiwara nobility had the real power. The Fujiwara and other noble families protected their interests with guards, police and soldiers. The warrior class made steady gains during this period.

Taira no Kiyomori revived these Fujiwara practices by placing his grandson on the throne to rule Japan by regency. The Kamakura period began in 1185 when Minamoto no Yoritomo seized power from the emperors and established a shogunate in Kamakura. The only part of Japan that this Minamoto leader had not conquered in 1185 was the north, where the Northern Fujiwara clan (Gail's ancestors) reigned.

The Heian period was preceded by the Nara period and began in 794 after Kyoto became the capital. The early Heian period (784-967) continued Nara culture. The Emperor was Kammu, and though he abandoned universal conscription in 792, he still waged major military offensives to subjugate the Emishi (among whom Gail's ancestors from Russia would choose to live around 1020 to 1030 A.D.).

The Forbidden Abyss

By 801 the shogun had defeated the Emishi and extended the Imperial domain to the eastern end of Honshu (the main Japan island).

Imperial control over the provinces was tenuous. In the ninth and tenth centuries, much authority was lost to the great families. Though succession was ensured for the imperial family through heredity, power became concentrated in the Fujiwara noble family. By the ninth century the Fujiwara had intermarried with the imperial family, and the Fujiwara became very powerful. Central control of Japan through the imperial family continued to decline, and the Fujiwara, along with other great families became wealthier during the early tenth century. Because of this, people and lands became beyond central control and taxation.

By the year 1000, Fujiwara no Michinaga could enthrone and dethrone emperors at will. With little authority left for traditional officialdom, the Fujiwara family's private administration handled government affairs. Despite their usurpation of imperial authority, the Fujiwara had great interest in poetry and literature, creating a time period in Japanese history known for its artistic and cultural flowering at the imperial court and among the aristocracy. Gail's ancestors the Oshu Fujiwara created an artistic masterpiece in their Hiraizumi, which contained great and valuable works of art.

Local power holders became the primary source of military strength. Lack of food, population growth, and competition for resources caused the gradual decline of Fujiwara power, giving rise to military disturbances in the mid-tenth and eleventh centuries. The Fujiwara, Taira (Heishi), and Minamoto (Genji) families—all descended from the imperial family—attacked one another, conquered land, set up rival regimes, and upset the peace. The Fujiwara controlled the throne from 1068 to 1073. In 1159, the Taira (Heishi) and Minamoto (Genji) clashed, and for twenty years after this, the Taira gained in power. But the Taira, seduced by court life, ignored the problems in the provinces. Finally, Minamoto no Yoritomo (Genji leader) defeated the Taira (1180-1185) with the help of his brilliant younger brother, Yoshitsune, who was his main general. Towards the end of this five year war, Yoshitsune joined up with his older brother Yoritomo, leading a major sea battle at Dan-no-ura, in the Shimonoseki Strait off the southern tip of Honshu. On March 24, 1185, the Genji (Minamoto) clan fleet, led by Minamoto no Yoshitsune, defeated the Heike (Taira) clan fleet, in a half-day engagement.

Yoshitshune was born during the Heiji Rebellion of 1159, in which his father and oldest two brothers were killed. His life spared, he lived at the Kurama Temple, nestled in the Hiei Mountains near Kyoto, while his older brother, Yoritomo, was banished to Izu Province. Eventually, Yoshitsune came under the protection of Gail's ancestor, Fujiwara no Hidehira, head of the powerful regional Northern Fujiwara clan in Hiraizumi, the Mutsu Province.

Yoritomo turned on his younger brother, after Yoshitsune's brilliant military prowess gave Yoritomo the shogunate, and Yoritomo became jealous and fearful of Yoshitsune's brilliant military power. Therefore, Yoshitsune fled to the Northern Fujiwara family (Gail's ancestors) for refuge.

When Fujiwara no Yasuhira became the Northern Fujiwara leader, he did not shelter Yoshitsune adequately, leading to the alleged suicide of Yoshitsune. Traditional history records that Yoritomo strongly pressured Fujiwara no Yasuhira to arrest Yoshitsune, and that Yasuhira did this, against the will of his father

Hidehira.

However, the film *Homura Tatsu,* lays the blame for the death of Yoshitsune on Yasuhira's maternal grandfather, Fujiwara no Motonari, who secretly conspired with Yoritomo against Yasuhira, to destroy Yoshitsune. The grandfather, under Yasuhira's nose, secretly ordered 500 soldiers to attack Yoshitsune in a surprise attack, which allegedly led to Yoshitsune's death. Some believe that while Benkei defended his lord Yoshitsune, and died standing up, pierced with arrows, that Yoshitsune secretly escaped, headed north and became the Genghis Khan. Many Japanese believe this because Yoshitsune is one of the most famous warriors in all of Japanese history.

Nobody knows when or where Genghis Khan was born, though it is guessed he was born in 1162, three years after the birth of Yoshitsune in 1159. Genghis Khan reigned from 1208 to 1227. This would place his reign abut nineteen years after Yoshitsune escaped from Hiraizumi in 1189. Yoshitsune was thirty when he allegedly died in Japan. Genghis Khan had sons and grandsons when he died in 1227.

Traditional history further states that on June 15, 1189, Yasuhira led 500 soldiers to attack Yoshitsune and his entourage of servants in the Koromogawa no tachi residence, where Yasuhira defeated Yoshitsune and his compatriot, Saito no Musashibo Benkei. Throughout the battle, Benkei defended his lord Yoshitsune, where Benkei died, standing up, his body pierced with arrows. Yoshitsune, allegedly, committed suicide at the end of this battle.

The decapitated head of Yoshitsune, which Yasuhira offered to Yoritomo, did not pacify Yoritomo and, Yoritomo attacked and conquered the Northern Fujiwara family (Gail's ancestors) in 1189 to consolidate his control over Japan, no longer fearful that the Oshu Fujiwara could defeat him because they harbored Yoshitsune.

Some believe that the legendary warrior, Yoshitsune, secretly escaped, while Benkei was defending him, and he fled north, and became the Genghis Khan. The Yoshitsune head that Yasuhira offered to Yoritomo was soaked in sake, and stunk so much, that Yoritomo could not endure the stench. Some believe this may have been done on purpose to make it hard to identify the head, thus paving the way for Yoshitsune to escape to the continent (via Hokkaido island) to become the Genghis Khan.

This epic film *Homura Tatsu* depicted the downfall of the great Northern Fujiwara family. The Oshu Fujiwara family established their domain in the Touhoku area (northeast area of Japan), independent from the rule of the Minamoto clan. The Japanese film starred Ken Watanabe, who would become famous in Hollywood.

Watanabe tackled a dual role in this grand scale epic. The film showed the insane glory of the Fujiwara clan who built a mighty kingdom in northeast Japan and how their kingdom became threatened from the royal court in Kyoto. The climactic finale depicted the downfall of this family, showing the swell of history related to Minamotono Yoritomo (the first official shogun of the Kamakura Shogunate of Japan) and Yoshitsune (a heroic and epic warrior, who some believe may have feigned his own suicide and then escaped to the mainland to the west of Japan and became Genghis Khan).

The Forbidden Abyss

Towards the end of the twelfth century, two samurai clans, the Heishi and the Genji had a large battle. The Genji clan, led by Minamoto no Yoritomo, demolished the Heishi, making Yoritomo a Shogun. Though Yoritomo was not the first Shogun, he was the first to organize his own government, called a Shogunate. This started the age of the samurai.

Gail informed Brent that she had samurai ancestors, and Brent found it fascinating to study the origins of this fascinating woman whom he had dreamed about day after day since 1990.

Yoritomo had a younger brother named Yoshitsune, who became one of the most popular samurai heroes of Japan—a great commander in chief and brilliant military strategist. Once Yoritomo established his shogunate, he suspected Yoshitsune of planning to use his brilliant military prowess to overtake him.

However, Yoshitsune was an honorable man who admired his older brother, wanting desperately to reconcile himself with Yoritomo. Yoshitsune was forced to escape from his jealous brother with a few vessels to the north, finding refuge with Gail's ancestors, the Fujiwara clan who ruled northern Japan. Yoshitsune remembered that the Fujiwaras had protected him when he was a boy from the Heishi clan.

Yoritomo sent a party to find and kill Yoshitsune, and also ordered the Fujiwara clan to give up Yoshitsune to the Shogunate.

Orthodox history claims Yoshitsune killed himself in the Koromogawa area of Hiraizumi located in the present-day Tohoku area of Japan, that he committed suicide after having nowhere else to run after his plan to hideout with the Fujiwaras in the north of Japan fell through.

There is an extensive history that claims Minamoto no Yoshitsune and the great Mongol conqueror, Genghis Khan, are one and the same. Though this theory has been debunked, there are a couple of reasons to believe it could be true.

First, Yoshitsune was not only a samurai, but one of the first Ninja. He wrote the first book on how to be a Ninja. History claims Yoshitsune committed suicide after being backed into a corner, with his right hand man Benkei guarding the entrance, that Benkei lost his life so that his master, Yoshitsune, could have an honorable death—suicide—and not death at the hands of lowly soldiers.

But Ninjas don't follow this code of honor. Even if Yoshitsune was not the Genghis Khan, it doesn't mean Yoshitsune didn't devise a plan to escape, so that he could see another day.

Second, both Mongol warriors and ancient Japanese warriors used mounted archery. In fact, mounted archery was part of the Japanese warrior tradition even before Mongolia became a nation. Genghis Khan, a Mongol, conquered lands on horseback using the same type of guerilla tactics that made Yoshitsune an unconventional general of his time. So perhaps, even if Yoshitsune was not the Genghis Khan, perhaps he did escape to the Mongols and taught them mounted archery. But many believe Yoshitsune became the Genghis Khan, simply because Yoshitsune had great renown and fame in Japan, becoming a historical and legendary figure.

In Russia, Gail's ancestor, Vladimir the Great, (980 to 1015 A.D.) or grand prince of Kiev founded the Russian Orthodox Church. He is believed to have descended from the Germanic tribes that migrated into Russia at this time. A handsome man, he had a few hundred concubines in Kiev and in the country residence of Berestovo and many wives. From his many children, Gail was descended. For this reason, when Vladimir Putin would fall in love with Gail after 2001, Gail encouraged Vladimir Putin to join the Russian Orthodox Church, to honor her ancestor Vladimir the Great. Vladimir the Great was very devout in his religion. He was of Germanic bloodlines, and became the grand prince who ruled Russia, establishing a precedent for those with Germanic bloodlines to rule over Russia, like Catherine the Great.

The same Germanic ruling tribes that produced Vladimir the Great and his children, also produced Catherine the Great. Some of these Germanic people settled in Russia and some went to Germany.

Among Vladimir's children were Boris and Gleb, favorites of Vladimir—destined to be next in line for the throne. After Vladimir died, Sviatopolk, was blamed for Boris and Gleb's assassination (1015 to 1019 A.D.), because Sviatopolk aspired to the Russian throne and saw Boris as a rival to the throne, even though Boris had no such ambitions. Because of how Boris and Gleb died, they were both canonized by the Russian Orthodox Church. Like his brother Boris, Gleb urged his company not to offer armed resistance, because they were outnumbered and all would perish. He voluntarily accepted his fate in the understanding that the voluntary suffering of the innocent was a direct imitation of Christ.

Though the details remain unclear, from this royal family, Gail's ancestors came. Some of the children of Vladimir the Great, from whom Gail was descended, escaped Russia and headed towards the vast East, so that they would not suffer the fate of Boris and Gleb. Among those who escaped were children of Vladimir the Great that had the same Germanic ancestors who produced Catherine the Great—perhaps children of Vladimir's German wife Anna.

This Germanic family produced children who were willing to die for their country, like Boris and Gleb and Yasuhira of the Oshu Fujiwara family, who died like a martyr in Japan.

Around 1015 to 1019 A.D., at the time of Boris and Gleb's murder, some children of Vladimir the Great trekked across the great Eurasian empire and ended up in Hokkaido island, the northernmost island of Japan, just south of Russia. When they arrived, they found refuge among a race within the Japanese that were Caucasian in appearance—the Emishi. They married into the Emishi or Ainu clans of Japan. The fact that they were royals was known among the Emishi, but kept secret from those outside the Emishi in Japan, to protect them.

If any of the ruling royals of Japan knew that a royal family from another land had taken refuge inside Japan, they could be destroyed, so the Emishi kept secret the royal bloodlines of these Russian/Germanic royals who had escaped death in Russia to live among the Emishi as secret royals. Only those inside the Emishi families knew of these royal Russians of Germanic origins, who had escaped to Japan and who married into the ruling Emishi families. Because the Emishi were a Caucasian looking race, these royals from Russia chose to intermarry and live among the Emishi to hide their true identities as Russian royals.

Before the Russian royals arrived, the Japanese had subjugated the Emishi in 802 A.D. But, though subjugated, the Emishi in Japan still existed as a clan in 1020 to 1030 A.D., the time when the secret royals from Russia intermingled

The Forbidden Abyss

into the Emishi bloodlines. The Emishi were honored that royals from another land wanted to become one of them and much intermarriage between the Emishi and these Russian royals occurred. These marriages occurred at the highest levels of the Emishi, to ensure their leadership would be filled with strong genes. Perhaps this would produce a new generation of leaders who could reclaim Emishi power in Japan.

This turned out to be true, because the children of these Emishi and Russian royals who had arrived in Japan from 1020 to 1030 A.D., became part of the regional framework of government in the Tohoku which became the Northern Oshu Fujiwara regime. This regime, along with the Abe and Kiyohara, formed regional semi-independent states based on the Emishi and Japanese people. In fact, if not for Yasuhira, the last leader of the Oshu Fujiwara family—whose other half was a mother from Kyoto with Japanese blue blood—the Oshu Fujiwara family may have survived way past Yasuhira. Once the Germanic/Russian royal blood or the "Catherine the Great" genes got diluted with Japanese blue blood in its leadership, the Oshu Fujiwara family lost its effective leadership and went down.

Since a number of Japanese Abes served as shoguns and governors of Mutsu (where the Emishi lived), there may have been political bonds between them and the Abes may have granted permission to the Emishi (especially those of royal descent, like the German/Russian royals) to use the Japanese Abe name.

Though the Emishi and Ainu were supposed to be separate, Gail's mother has clearly stated to Gail that she has Ainu blood, which explained why Gail, despite her Japanese mother, did not look Japanese, but Caucasian. The physical appearance of a number of the Ainu who were first encountered by Europeans in the nineteenth century were similar to Caucasians. The Chinese describes the Emishi or Ainu as a "hairy" people with long beards, unlike the Japanese who have smooth chests.

The Northern Oshu Fujiwara were a Japanese noble family of Emishi and Japanese blood that ruled the Tohoku region in the eleventh and twelfth centuries. They succeeded the semi-independent Emishi families of the eleventh century (who had intermarried with Gail's royal Russian/Germanic ancestors around 1030 A.D.). The Emishi honored these royal Russians by allowing them to intermarry with their leaders, thus these Russian/Germanic royals had children who ended up as Emishi leaders, who then married into the Japanese Fujiwara family, to become the Northern Oshu Fujiwara family.

Kiyohira Fujiwara (whose mother was a beautiful Russian/Germanic royal disguised as an Emishi) was born in the Fujiwara family in the middle of Zenkunen-no-eki (9 Years War from 1051 to 1062 A.D.). He led a severe tough life. He was the sole survivor of the war from both the Abe clan and the Kiyohara clan. As Kiyohira established his power in Mutsu province he pursued an alliance with the Kyoto nobility under the protection of shogun Yoshiie Minamoto. Kiyohira Fujiwara moved from Toyoda-no-tachi (now Esashi City in Iwate Prefecture) to Hiraizumi.

During the twelfth Century, at the zenith of their rule, the northern Fujiwara clan governed a fertile land yielding a variety of products that included gold and horses. With this rich environment and affluent economy, Hiraizumi enjoyed a peaceful and stable culture. However, because of the discord between Yoritomo

Minamoto and Yoshitsune Minamoto, and a series of national upheavals, Hiraizumi and the Fujiwara clan disappeared into history.

The Oshu Fujiwara clan started with Kiyohira Fujiwara, the child of a Tsunekiyo Fujiwara of Japanese royal blood and a beautiful Abe Emishi woman (the daughter of head of the Emishi's Abe clan, Abe no Yoritoki). Abe no Yoritoki had Germanic/Russian royal blood. Abe no Yoritoki's beautiful daughter Toyo (Gail's Germanic/Russian ancestor) had strong Russian/Germanic royal blood, from the Russian royals that had escaped from Russia to live among the Emishi.

Fujiwara no Tsunekiyo (Kiyohira's father), the founder of the Northern Fujiwara dynasty, was from a local ruling family in the Watari region in the current Miyagi Prefecture. Tsunekiyo, a deputy governor, was given an order by Fujiwara no Naritoh, the governor of the Mutsu Province, to become part of the central government's army, which opposed the Abe Emishi in northern Japan. Because Tsunekiyo was married to a beautiful Abe Emishi wife (Toyo, who was actually a Germanic/Russian royal), he didn't join the central government's army and, instead, joined the Abes, and the war went in the Abe's favor.

Eventually, the Abe clan was cornered by the Kuriyagawa no Saku (Morioka) and lost. Most members of the Abe clan (among whom were Gail's ancestors) were killed, including Tsunekiyo. This was the end of the Nine-Years war (1051 to 1062 A.D.).

Beautiful Tsunekiyo's wife Toyo (now a widow) was forced to marry the man who killed Tsunekiyo (her husband). This man she was forced to marry was of the Kiyohara clan. For this reason, the son (Kiyohira) she had with Tsunekiyo, survived and grew up within the Kiyohara clan.

Kiyohira would have to fight for succession, and survive the infighting in the Kiyohara clan to become the ruler of Oshu, which was the start of the powerful Oshu Fujiwara family.

Kiyohira's son Motohira, also married an Abe woman who had the Emishi bloodlines of the Russian/Germanic royals, giving birth to their son, Hidehira. The beauty of these Russian/Germanic royals and their children, as well as their royal bloodlines, made them desirable as wives for the royals.

During Hidehira's reign, Yoshitsune, the legendary warrior took refuge with the Oshu Fujiwara family. Hidehira's son Yasuhira became the last ruler of the Northern Oshu Fujiwara family.

When Hidehira died, Yasuhira gave in to pressure from Yoritomo, betrayed his father's will, and allegedly drove Yoshitsune to suicide. Though the film *Homura Tatsu* depicts Yasuhira's maternal grandfather as a traitor who sent a group of men to secretly assassinate Yoshitsune against Yasuhira's wishes. However, Yoritomo accused Yasuhira of giving refuge to Yoshitsune, as a pretext for war, because Yoritomo lusted for the city of gold, Hiraizumi.

Now one hundred years had passed and three generations of Fujiwara rulers. It was 1189 and Hiraizumi was about to be attacked in a war that Yasuhira knew he would lose.

He walked the stone steps up towards the pagoda to offer prayers to Buddha for wisdom on how to deal with Yoritomo. A deep mist encased the surrounding mountains, he felt he could lose himself into the mountains where his ancestors

The Forbidden Abyss

lived. Yoritomo must not desecrate these sacred grounds, Yasuhira knew he must burn these peaceful buildings to spare this heaven from the corruption of Yoritomo. Yes, to burn this city of gold before Yoritomo's arrival would please his ancestors.

Perhaps those of his family who could escape to the mountains could still eat their mochi, root vegetable soup with sliced black mushrooms and drink their sake though sake cups, though they would need to become Emishi to disguise their Oshu Fujiwara heritage. Fortunately, the Oshu Fujiwara had incorporated much of their Emishi heritage into their Fujiwara lifestyle, like eating of gourds and fresh water fish. Yes, perhaps some of his family may survive to carry on the royal Emishi name.

No longer would they hear the clack of wooden sandals on the floors. No longer could they view the waterfalls tripping over rocks in the Genbikei Gorge, or the high cliffs of gray, broken rock dotted with pines submerging down into a placid lake.

Instead they would hide in caves in the mountains, grow their beards long and become again the Emishi. Perhaps their home would be a cave like the Yugendo, long, sprawling and deep into the mountain, with its stalactite and fossil walls of white gray, going deep, deep, deep into the mountain. Only the Emishi knew all the caves, and kept them secret from the government. Here the Emishi hid their royals, until the royals could blend in as them. The cave's underground lake would give them water, but how different from Hiraizumi.

But the Emishi lived off the land, and with the Emishi his family could survive, where the splendor and glory of Hiraizumi would be replaced with a Buddhist peace. Royals in heart, even if not royals in palaces. The Hagi bush clover, delicate white blossoms, or the cherry blossoms would still be there.

This land of Pagoda wood temples covered with gold, the pine trees, the swirling mountains covered in mist, the stone walkways and steps and the grand family that lived, laughed and cried here would go on into Emishi reincarnation, a transformation into a higher, better life; and perhaps all will meet someday in heaven.

Yasuhira gazed with longing at his Hiraizumi home, of ponds and lakes, and pagoda temples with roofs of gold, and red wooden planks lining white squares, formed the house below. The lakes had the stillness of a Buddha heaven, what Yasuhira longed for his Hiraizumi. Here the souls of friend and foe, human and animal, could find peace and consolation. He thought about his ancestor Kiyohira, who lost his father, wife and at least one son in battle and treachery to become the supreme ruler over this place. But rather than strengthen his military forces, Kiyohira chose to embrace the Buddhist principles of peace.

Using wealth from the area gold mines, Kiyohira created temples and gardens, which symbolized the Buddhist Pure Land with Chuson-ji Temple with its Golden Hall. His son and grandson continued his work on this utopian paradise, constructing a massive temple called Motsu-ji, as well as other temples, pagodas, gardens, making Hiraizumi the jewel of the orient. On the lake surfaces reflected the long, sprawling trees with pine needles afloat with stillness and pagoda roofs a picture on the lake top.

So Yasuhira ran to the north, to Hokkaido island, with Yoritomo on his tail, to give his family time to escape to the mountains, and his retainer to kill him on the island of Yezo (Hokkaido), so that his death would earn for his family a Buddha heaven, and time to run to the mountains, to his ancestors, to live on in another life.

Yoritomo's chase after Yasuhira, distracted Yoritomo away from Yasuhira's wife and children and others of his family, giving them time to run to the mountains and disappear into the long secret caves deep, deep, deep, far from danger. But, Yasuhira's wife, upon learning of her husband's death, killed herself, leaving behind Yasuhira's children and kin to live on as Emishi in another life.

They started that other life by fleeing to the mountains, running into the caves, where Emishi smiled and embraced them, welcoming them home.

Yasuhira did not realize that no utopia on earth can happen without Jesus Christ, so Hiraizumi was attacked in 1189 by Minamoto Yoritomo, who would seize power and establish the shogunate government in Kamakura in 1192. Over the years Hiraizumi would lose most of its treasures through fires, but shoguns and feudal lords preserved the Golden Hall and other buildings, so that the world would remember and respect this attempt at utopia for one hundred years, between 1089 and 1189.

In 2011, a few months after the Great East Japan Earthquake, Hiraizumi's treasures were declared a World Heritage site, giving meaning to the devastating earthquake and tsunami, which hit very hard the Iwate Prefecture where Hiraizumi resides. Amazingly, Hiraizumi was untouched.

The Golden Hall is awe inspiring and an impressive work of art, but visitors leave this site with their hearts stirred more by what Hiraizumi tried to be—an attempt at utopia, a testament to the Fujiwara's vision of Hiraizumi as a land of peace and purity from 1089 to 1189. This is what leaves the greatest impression.

Hiraizumi, an unpretentious town of 8,400 residents, not your typical tourist trap, could well be one of the most important places you ever visit. For here were the beginnings of Gail Chana, who would be Jesus Christ's favorite in the twenty-first century. Gail would be a reincarnation of Catherine the Great and king David.

If there was no Oshu Fujiwara family, then Gail Chana would never have existed. Yasuhira's dream lived on through his children. His children through many generations would carry his spirit forward in temples not made of stone, but in bodily temples containing hearts that longed for peace and purity. Yes, the longings of Catherine the Great. The victors always rewrite history to make their victims appear evil, and Yoritomo has been painted as a great man, but one wonders if Jesus wrote the Hiraizumi story, how He would see the hearts behind the fall of Hiraizumi.

Like Catherine, the Fujiwaras collected great works of art and displayed them in their palaces. The longings of their Emishi and Russian/German royal ancestors for beauty, tranquility and meaning lived on in the genes of Catherine the Great in Gail Chana.

The poet Matsuo Basho saw the state of Hiraizumi in 1689 and penned a famous haiku about the impermanence of human glory:

Ah, summer grasses!

The Forbidden Abyss

All that remains
Of the warriors' dreams

Yoritomo sent troops from Kamakura to attack Yasuhira at Hiraizumi. Yasuhira, a devout Buddhist, did not believe in war and had not built up his military, so he was pretty defenseless and a terrible military strategist when Yoritomo attacked. The "Catherine the Great" in Yasuhira was weakened, apparently, by the Japanese blue blood from his mother and maternal grandmother who were nobles at Kyoto.

Though Yasuhira had given shelter to the brilliant military leader, Yoshitshune, he did not make Yoshitsune a commander or leader in any military operations. Yasuhira was so opposed to war, he was willing to die himself, and to abandon Yoshitsune, rather than have a war with Yoritomo.

In this respect, he was much like Vladimir the Great's children, Boris and Gleb, from whom he was descended.

In 1189, Yasuhira burned the Hiraizumi House, his royal residence, by himself, an act of defiance against the encroaching Yoritomo, and escaped to the north, the land of his ancestors. However, he was killed by Jiro Kawada, his retainer.

Following this incident, some members of the Fujiwara clan, which had governed Oshu for 100 years, ceased to exist openly, but went into hiding, allowing the world to believe that they had all been massacred by Yoritomo.

It served them well that they had kept secret their Russian/Germanic royal bloodlines and relatives among the Emishi. These Oshu Fujiwara royal family escapees fled to the mountains of northern Japan, where their Emishi Germanic/Russian royal relatives lived. These Russian royals, to this day, never revealed their Russian royal ancestry, but remained in hiding and disguised as Emishi. The Emishi welcomed the Oshu Fujiwara escapees, had them change their garbs and appearance into Emishi clothing and appearance, and hid the royals from the world. The Emishi clan had become expert at protecting those among them who were royals.

Disguised as Emishi, the surviving Oshu Fujiwara clan, after Yasuhira's death, lived amongst the remaining Emishi or Ainu in hiding, further intermarrying into the Russian/Germanic royal family bloodlines, so that by the time Gail's mother was born, enough of this Russian/Germanic royal bloodline had survived, that Gail at her birth got half the genetic profile of Catherine the Great. The Russian/Germanic royal bloodlines remained pure for many generations, because it was necessary for these royal Emishi members to only marry Emishi to keep their royal secret from escaping to the world. Thus the Catherine the Great genes remained strong within the Emishi and later the Ainu for many generations.

The Emishi became the Ainu about 1264, and some of these Russian/Germanic royals missed their Russian homeland and moved back to Russia on Sakhalin and the Kurile islands. Many of these Russian Ainu assimilated into the Russian culture and their children became ethnic Ulch with partial Ainu ancestry, or ethnic Nivkh, Slav or Uilta. The northern Kuril Ainu spoke Russian fluently and became Russian Orthodox in religion. By 1264, the royals had become so integrated into the Ainu culture that they decided they would no longer be considered a threat to any Russian royals. They incorporated aspects of Russian culture into the Ainu culture, like bear worship.

Many Ainu eventually assimilated into mainstream Japanese society and adopted Buddhism and Shinto influences, while those with strong Germanic/Russian royal blood remained in the north of Japan and honored their ancestor Grand Prince Vladimir of Kiev, the founder of the Russian Orthodox Church, by becoming members of the Russian Orthodox Church.

American anthropologist C. Loring Brace, University of Michigan, described the Ainu as being lighter skinned, having more body hair, and higher-bridged noses than most Japanese. After studying the skeletons of 1,100 Japanese, Ainu and other Asians, concluded that the samurai of Japan are actually descendants of the Ainu, not of the Yayoi from whom most Japanese are descended. He said, this explains why the facial features of the Japanese ruling class are often unlike those of typical modern Japanese. The Ainu-related samurai achieved such power and prestige in medieval Japan that they intermarried with royalty and nobility, passing on Jomon-Ainu blood in the upper classes, while the rest of the Japanese are mostly from Yoyoi.

Gail's mother admitted to Ainu blood, which explains why Gail does not look Japanese. She also said she had royal blood from several clans: the Genji, the Oshu Fujiwara, and others. She said there were many samurai ancestors. It appears the royal Russians who emigrated to Japan and intermarried into the Emishi became the Ainu.

There has been much speculation about where the Ainu came from, but Gail's ancestors chose to live among the Emishi/Ainu because the Emishi looked so Caucasian. Many early investigators into the Ainu proposed a Caucasian ancestry. It has been scientifically suggested that the Ainu may be distantly related to some form of Eastern European subpopulation, because some of their genes matched the populations of this area! One thing is for certain, Gail's Catherine the Great genes come from her mother, who has strong Ainu or royal blood.

If the Emishi and Ainu are truly separate races, as some believe, perhaps it is because the Ainu race came into existence when the royal Russians intermarried into the Emishi clan. The Ainu are the children of the Russian Caucasian royals who married into the Emishi clan. The Catherine the Great genes were passed down to Gail's mother through the Ainu.

This Germanic royal family existed in northern Europe prior to 1000 A.D. and spread to Russia and Germany and elsewhere. In Germany, it produced Sophie Friederike Auguste from Anhalt-Zerbst in 1762, who traveled to Russia to become Catherine the Great.

In Russia, it produced Vladimir the Great in 958 A.D. whose children emigrated to northern Japan and married into ruling Emishi families who then married members of the Japanese Abe clan. These ruling Abe clan members married into the royal Fujiwara family, forming the Oshu Fujiwara royal family, from which Gail's mother was descended.

Because Gail and Catherine the Great came from the same Germanic bloodlines, when Gail was born in 1957 her genes lined up half Catherine the Great, even though she is not directly descended from Catherine the Great.

The Forbidden Abyss

One of Gail's great-grandparents on her mother's side was invited to attend a royal Japanese wedding between an emperor and his empress. Invitations such as these were only given to members of Japanese royal families.

On Gail's father's side, Brent discovered an equally fascinating history. In the late 1800s an orthodox Jewish woman descended from king David disgraced her family by having a baby out of wedlock with a Gentile man named Howard R. Hughes Sr. (the father of Howard R. Hughes, Jr.). This disgraceful baby was Robert Chord, born August 22, 1898.

Robert Chord was Gail's paternal grandfather. This same orthodox Jewish woman descended from king David had a second child with the same Gentile man. This child was Howard R. Hughes, Jr., who would become the famous aviator and billionaire.

The Jewish family and the Gentile family did not like each other. They finally came to a compromise. After having two children out of wedlock, the orthodox Jewish woman had to get married. The orthodox Jewish family was in disgrace. No honorable Jewish man would marry the poor Jewish woman, who loved and wanted to marry the disgusting and immoral Gentile Howard R. Hughes, Sr. who disgraced this Jewish family's honor.

An honorable Gentile man named Chord was willing to marry the Jewish woman and to become the step dad to her first son Robert. This Jewish woman would have other children with Mr. Chord.

But Howard R. Hughes, Sr. was allowed to keep his second child by the Jewish woman, Howard R. Hughes, Jr.

The Jewish woman who fathered two sons of Howard R. Hughes, kept and raised her first son, Robert (Gail's grandfather).

Howard R. Hughes, Sr. married another woman of royal descent Allene Stone Gano (a descendant of Owen Tudor, second husband of Catherine of Valois, Dowager Queen of England). She became the step mother who raised Howard Hughes.

So the two genetic brothers were raised in two different families.

Robert Chord married Verla Chord (Gail's grandmother), who fathered Robert Jr. (Gail's father) an airline captain. Funny how genes seemed to determine one's occupation. From her father (who carried king David genes) came Gail's king David genetic profile, from that disgraced orthodox Jewish woman who lived in the end of the 19th century.

Though Brent did not learn about Gail's Catherine the Great genes until Vladimir Putin uncovered it around 2006, he did learn that the woman who he so loved and who occupied his heart and soul since 1990 had royal bloodlines from both her father and her mother. "Yes, this explained why the Jesuit Order attacked him with Loree McBride."

The Vatican Agent
1998 to 1999

Both Gail and her son suffered debilitating allergies in 1998. Gail became nauseated with diarrhea around February 1998. Her doctor told her it was the flu and she needed bed rest and liquids. The treatment plan didn't work and Gail returned to her doctor. She convinced the doctor to do a stool culture and he informed her that her gastrointestinal symptoms, diarrhea and nausea, were caused by Clostridium Difficile, and that she would need bed rest and antibiotics just for Clostridium Difficile for around a month. After around a month of treatment with metronidazole and good bacteria (probiotics), she lost her nausea and diarrhea. But she laid in bed for almost two months, groaning with nausea and diarrhea. To make matters worse, the doctor's wife became jealous of Gail, assuming that because Gail liked to practice Italian with her Italian American doctor, that Gail was after her husband.

The doctor, because of his wife, almost dropped Gail as a patient, when Gail most needed him. It seemed to Gail, that Loree managed to poison the minds of those who cared for Gail to turn them against her. It took the doctor one month to diagnose her correctly with Clostridium Difficile, thinking at first she had a stomach flu, so until he diagnosed her correctly, she did not improve. Gail wondered why she picked up such a powerful germ. She learned that Clostridium Difficile is a serious germ, with an alarming death rate and often requires hospitalization, which did not surprise her, because it seemed the powerful germ would not leave until she remained on metronidazole for about six weeks. Nauseated for months, she wondered why her body couldn't throw off the "flu", despite bed rest, good nutrition and liquids.

Despite her ill health, she managed to home school her son and make meals, while she dragged through her days.

About June and July 1998, someone started making thumping noises around her mobile home at night, dumping her garbage all over her yard and setting the garbage on fire. Every morning she'd wake up to a new surprise. Often her deck porch would be a mess, because someone appeared to have trashed it overnight while she slept. More work for her to do. She had to go out and clean the mess.

The police for her area, the Berkeley County Sheriff's Department, just showed up and did nothing. They only patrolled the area, then they said, "Maybe you should stay up all night and see if you can catch them."

She concluded that the Berkeley County Sheriff's Department worked for Loree McBride. She thought, "Boy, this woman's good. I mean, she's good. What kind of connections does she have?" She told Brent on her wiretapped

The Forbidden Abyss

phone, "You need to do something about that girlfriend of yours. Man, she's really getting out of hand."

Gail sensed Brent deplored the situation his girlfriend had placed him in, that Loree disgraced and angered him. Gail felt that he agreed with her that Loree had something to do with this.

That was very stressful. Gail and her son were getting very severe symptoms from the mobile home that had a high formaldehyde concentration in the kitchen area, and the off-gassing became unbearable in the summer heat, so in the hot summer months both she and her son were dizzy. Once, with the temperature inside at around 90 degrees in the house, her son said, "Mom, I'm freezing." She piled one blanket after another on her son, and took him to the emergency room. No one could explain it. She decided he was experiencing a strange allergic reaction to something.

It made it hard to home school and clean house, because she felt ill all the time. She suspected that Loree McBride was somehow behind this and marveled at her power, abilities and connections. Then on top of all that, Gail's church turned against her. The police department was against her. Whoever her enemy was, they appeared to hire juvenile delinquents to dump her garbage all over her yard and set it on fire, and she had to go out there and clean it up.

Then she noticed when the preacher from her church came over to mow her lawn (because her husband was out to sea, and needed her lawn mowed,) that he snubbed her, treating her like a mental case, as if she was demon possessed scum.

Gail concluded, "Wow, that girlfriend of Brent has got some connections. She even put this preacher on my phone's wiretap, and he's brainwashed his whole church against me." Gail could tell by the sermons this preacher preached that he somehow got added to her phone's wiretap, and apparently did not approve of her conversations with Brent and Franco. She decided to only speak Italian on her wiretapped phone, so that the preacher could not understand what she said. That King James only church, with around twenty members, adopted an intolerant, self-righteous spirit around Gail, treating her like a hypochondriac, demon possessed lunatic, because she bought air purifiers to deal with the dizziness from the formaldehyde in her mobile home during the hot summer months. She thought, "Loree McBride got the county Sheriff's Department against me, and this church."

Gail called up an engineer, "I want to order some formaldehyde test kits."

He said, "They cost six hundred dollars."

"Six hundred dollars? To get a formaldehyde testing kit? I think I've got extra formaldehyde in my kitchen. It can't cost six hundred dollars!"

He said, "Oh yeah, it costs six hundred dollars."

"Forget it. Isn't there someplace where I can get it cheaper than that?"

"I don't know. . ."

She thought, my gosh, this woman's really good, she even got the engineer. She looked all around to try to find a formaldehyde testing kit, finally locating a cheap testing kit on the Internet, but it wasn't easy. When she used it, she discovered her kitchen had formaldehyde—a pretty high exposure. But then she concluded, "Who's going to believe me?" They'd probably think I made it all up or that I'm not a scientist, so, therefore, I'm not suffering from formaldehyde

Brent's Forbidden Ground

exposure in my kitchen. She could tell that somebody was out to get her, and they also wanted to make her appear hypochondriac and crazy.

And whoever they were, they were good. She figured it was Loree McBride and her friends. She thought, "Those Hollywood connections she has, she's got some powerful friends, that they can do this. Boy, things can't get much worse than this. I'm allergic to my own house!"

Her son almost flunked fourth grade, because of illnesses, though she and her son made the deadlines for fourth grade, just in the nick of time. The A Beka home school video school curriculum had deadlines for submission of tests and final exams. Her son listened to teachers on video from Pensacola Christian Academy, and then Gail would administer the tests and assist her son with assignments and homework. The coursework was rigorous and demanding and she had to spend time with her son helping him prepare for tests.

When she homeschooled her son in both fourth and sixth grades, she had no time to write. Therefore, her writing came to a standstill when she homeschooled her son for the 1997/1998 school year, the first half of the 1998/1999 school year, and again in Seattle for the first half of the 2000/2001 school year. Her son maintained an A average while in home school.

In the month of August 1998, she started thinking about studying law. She told Brent on her phone, "You know what? With all the problems that I've had, dealing with police and corruption—I think I want to be a lawyer. I don't think these people, whoever they are, are going to leave me alone." She started thinking about law.

Around November 1998, her family learned their next duty station would be Seattle. So she wrote to the University of Washington Law School and asked for their bulletin. Thinking perhaps she'd study law in Seattle. With all the trouble she got, she may as well become an attorney.

She told Brent and Franco Nero on her wiretapped phone, "I think I want to become a lawyer." That was November 1998. She was home schooling her son, in the fifth grade. Her husband out to sea, as usual, she was by herself. She got the most lovely Christmas present for December 25, 1998.

In November 1998, Gail's dizziness made her trip and fall over a dog gate at her bedroom's doorway. Her knee landed hard on something sharp (on the top of the dehumidifier) that cut her to the bone on her left knee. "Son, go get the first aid kit now. I'm bleeding bad and have hurt myself. I'll need stitches. Blood's coming out fast." Her son rushed to get the first aid kit. With lightning speed, she put pressure over the wound, because blood was gushing out, and wrapped the gauze securely around her left knee. It was only her and her son. Her husband was out to sea. She limped to the phone, and asked one of her church friends (a warrant officer in the Coast Guard) to take her to the emergency room. The preacher of the small church her family attended had brainwashed everyone in that church against her. So, this warrant officer, took her (the lunatic, demonic woman) to the emergency room. She received nine stitches and a tetanus shot.

A month after she decided to become an attorney, only with her son in her double-wide mobile home, her son said, "Mother, there's a fire outside

The Forbidden Abyss

our kitchen door." It was Christmas Day 1998.

It was about a waist high fire, maybe about three feet away, like a little bonfire. "Oh, put it out."

So, her son got a bucket of water and he put it out. Then there was another fire by the front door. And, did you know, somebody was setting fires, and so they put out the one by the front door.

Then there was another fire by the kitchen door. As soon as they put out a fire by the kitchen door, then there was another fire by the front door. So they went from one end of the house to the other, putting out fires. Gail was filling up buckets with water, handing them to her son, plopping on her crutches from the front door to the back kitchen door and back. They must have put out about twenty fires.

In between breaks, she said, "I'm going to call the police. We've got to find who's doing this." So she called the police.

After three hours, they showed up, while Gail and her son went from door to door, putting out fires. Gail thought, "Good grief, this Loree McBride, she's going too far. They need to put her in jail. She knows I'm in crutches and can't move fast. If not for my son, these fires would burn down my mobile home!"

For three hours they dealt with a blitzkrieg of fires. One by the front door, one by the kitchen door. They were all by the doors. And they put them all out, just in time, just before the flames could catch onto the outer walls of her mobile home. Exhausted and stressed, finally the police showed up, with black heaps where the fires had been...

Gail lived in a mobile home. She knew how quick a mobile home could burn down, and the fires were close to the outer wall of her mobile home. Her son was good. By the time the police showed up, the criminals vanished and the fire emergency had abated.

She did not know it then, but she'd learn in 2012, that the Jesuits used teleportation technology to cause the fires. Just like in Star Trek, you could teleport a person from one place to another, so the Jesuits had teleported a look-alike of her son outside her mobile home, who then bounced from door to door outside Gail's mobile home setting fires. They used her son's look-alike, in combination with their teleportation technology, to teleport the fires to start near the doors to Gail's mobile home and made sure all the fires landed by the doors right as the look-alike was there to make it appear that her son did the fires. Unable to make a clone of her son, Jesuits were able to make a convincing look-alike, and used him when needed. Brilliant Jesuits! The brazen look-alike actually set the fires in front of Gail's neighbors, and then the Jesuits took pictures. Like they did with Loree on Brent, they set up their victim, then used their agents to take pictures to "seal the evidence".

Though the clever Jesuits fooled just about everybody, they never fooled Jesus Christ and up in heaven He became quite angry over their antics. Jesus Christ knew that someday Gail would expose the brilliant and evil Jesuit Order with her testimony and writings, and felt some resolution then. Never in a hurry, things were going according to His plan. Someday, He would use Gail and Brent to bring down the Jesuit Order.

Because Gail was in crutches, without her son's help, she would not be

Brent's Forbidden Ground

here writing this story. She believed that Loree McBride, who's a pyromaniac, used Jesuit teleportation technology to try to kill Gail, but wanted to frame the murder on her son. Her husband was out to sea. This would also serve to remind Loree's captive Brent Spiner that she meant business.

So the police showed up. She got asked the same question, "You must have made someone awful mad, that they'd set all these fires around your house. Do you know who they are?"

She said, "I have no idea." No way was she going to give away that Brent and Franco were on her phone. She knew Brent and Franco didn't do it. It was Loree McBride and she wasn't going to help her one bit. She knew that Loree was trying to kick Brent and Franco and her family doctor off her phone. Brent decided to put her Italian American family doctor on her phone, because he was a nice guy and liked Gail. So Gail said, "I don't know..."

He said, "Those fires were only about waist high. We've had a lot worse cases than that in our police department. This really isn't that big of a deal."

She looked at that man square in the face. "Who's paying you to do this?"

He got real huffed up. "Nobody."

"You're telling me that waist high fires, we just had a blitzkrieg of fires. And you're telling me that this is not a big deal? Our house could have burned down."

"We get fire reports like this all the time."

"Who's paying you to do this?"

"Nobody, ma'am."

Gail, despite her crutches, held her ground. "I want to study to become an attorney and I can tell by the way you're behaving there's something fishy about you. And if I was a lawyer, I'd probably drag you into court. Who's paying you, officer, to try to frame me with these questions? You shouldn't treat these fires so flippantly. This could be very serious, officer."

Irritated, he said, "Nobody's paying me to do this." He then left.

Gail told Brent about that incident.

She decided that for future problems, she wouldn't mess with the Berkeley County Sheriff's Department. She called the fire department next, and the man came over and listened to her story and observed the black heaps where the fires had been. "I'm very disturbed to hear this. The Berkeley Sheriff's Department behaved disgracefully. I recommend you get flood lights for your home and leave them on every night, that should discourage these criminals. No one likes to be seen."

So Gail bought flood lights and put them on every night. That seemed to solve the problem, and the criminals left her alone after that.

When her husband returned from sea duty, all her neighbors said Gail's son did those fires. But he was with her putting them out and she knew he didn't do those fires! Her husband believed the neighbors over her. This made her so angry, that she threatened to end the marriage.

Finally, the stitches came off, and after a month, she could walk. Her family doctor took the stitches out for her, upset this happened to her. He was Italian American and she enjoyed practicing the Italian language on

The Forbidden Abyss

him, that she had learned for Franco Nero. He was a nice guy.

The Jesuits didn't want the marriage to break up. They decided they pushed her a little too far. So, since her son wasn't punished, she decided she'd stay in the marriage.

And her family got ready to move to Seattle.

As a result of the medical problems Gal and her son had in the summer of 1998 with allergies, she started seeing a specialist in Allergy and Environmental Medicine in South Carolina.

She thought they tested her for formaldehyde and found a sensitivity, but were kind of reluctant to divulge it. Apparently, it wasn't severe.

From her mobile home's kitchen, she felt very dizzy and spaced out. She thought it was formaldehyde. It was getting kind of scary to her at this point. She thought, "This Loree McBride. . .she's just too good."

And then another strange thing happened to her. Right after the fires, her psychiatrist called her. He said, 'I got an E-mail from your husband. I'd like to see you. He's concerned about you."

After the fires, Gail went into the book room to split her books from everybody else's books. She was ready to end the marriage over this. To protect her son, she said, "Brent Spiner's girlfriend did those fires."

At her psychiatrist, she said, "What did you get an E-mail from my husband about?"

"We can discuss that when you come into my office." She thought, "Oh, no, what has that Loree McBride done?"

So she went to her psychiatrist's office and this psychiatrist who she'd had a pretty good relationship with before, she had told him all about her Italian cooking and he was telling her about his cooking, he was a cook, too. All of a sudden, it seemed like he changed. The Jesuits had replaced her psychiatrist with his Jesuit clone, though at this time she did not even know clones existed. She just felt that Loree McBride had incredible power for a mere celebrity girlfriend. And she knew Loree was a killer. It puzzled Gail that Loree had such an obsession with her, because she had dropped Brent as a lover and Franco Nero had taken his place. She just presumed Loree raged with jealousy because she couldn't stop celebrities from falling in love with Gail. And though Gail dropped Brent as a lover, she knew he still had feelings for her. She figured this was the problem. Though she couldn't understand why Brent kept her as a girlfriend. She could only conclude that he was a coward, and she never found a coward attractive.

So her psychiatrist said, "Here's the E-mail that I received. I'm concerned that you believe that Brent Spiner's girlfriend. . .set fires. . .around your mobile home. . ."

She said, "Why would that concern you?"

"You really believe that Brent Spiner's girlfriend set fires around your mobile home?"

"I really don't care to discuss this. I don't want to talk about my private life. This is not something I want to talk about."

"We have to talk about your private life. That's how I do my job."

Brent's Forbidden Ground

"I don't want to talk about this. This is not something I want to discuss with you."

"I'm afraid you are exhibiting psychotic symptoms and we need to put you on stronger medications."

She said, "I refuse. I will not go on those medications. I'm not psychotic. And, furthermore, I think I was misdiagnosed with manic depression and that I never had it in the first place. I believe my problems have been nutritional deficiencies and allergies, and that's why I've had trouble sleeping. I don't think I ever was a manic depressive, and I'm not going to be put on anti-psychotic medications. I refuse."

He said, "I can't make you. I'm very concerned about you. I think you should be put on stronger medications."

"What medications?"

"Would you at least please consider this?"

"What medications do you want to put me on?"

So he gave her the names of the medications and Gail said, "I'll go home and think about this, but I'm pretty sure I won't change my mind."

Gail went home and looked up the medications and found out they had some pretty nasty side effects, and would have really messed her up. At this point, she was starting to explore natural medicine. No longer convinced she was a manic depressive, she determined she must get off those psychiatric meds, because she concluded that was a way for her enemies to manipulate and control her. She was on Tegretol, which was very bad for her. She was also on lithium. Tegretol was the bad one. She made up her mind. I'm getting off of this stuff, as soon as possible. I don't want to be at the mercy of these psychiatrists who want to get me all doped up and admit me to a mental ward, when I know I'm not crazy.

To protect Brent Spiner and Franco Nero, she didn't want to discuss her private life with this psychiatrist. To discuss Brent or Franco, could mean they would get kicked off her wiretapped phone. She didn't want this.

In a bad situation, in order to protect her privacy over Brent and Franco, she decided to wean herself off the psychiatric medicines by herself. She had been weaned off before by a psychiatrist in Miami, and pretty much knew the procedure. She knew she had to gradually decrease her dose, or she could suffer bad withdrawal symptoms.

After this, she tried to find another psychiatrist. So she called around to try to find another psychiatrist. All the psychiatrists covered by her insurance were not available. The only ones that could see her were the ones she couldn't afford. So Gail thought, "Loree's really good. She got all the psychiatrists in Charleston. All the ones that I can afford with my insurance are not available. Boy, does she got a conspiracy against me. Well, I'm going to get off this medicine. I'll just do it by myself."

But Gail needed some refills. She came up with a game plan. She knew she could decrease the dose so much every couple weeks and by about May 1999, she'd be off everything. She had enough lithium, but needed a little bit more. She needed a refill.

She called up the pharmacy and asked them to give her a refill of tegretol or lithium. She knew she needed to gradually wean off, because if she did it cold turkey, she'd get those horrible withdrawal reactions—she'd been through that before. Her plan was to get enough refills so she could stock up on the medicines and wean herself off. A little short on one of her medications, she needed some more. She called up the pharmacy and they were having a problem filling her prescription.

Apparently, her psychiatrist had contacted that pharmacy and told them not to give her any refills. She said, "Why can't you give me a refill? It says I have refills on my prescription."

They said, "Well, your doctor just contacted us and said you can't have any refills unless you come back and see him."

She thought, "What? This is ridiculous." She said, "Alright." So she went back to see him.

He said, "Have you thought about getting on those medications?"

"I thought about it. I looked them up and they have terrible side effects. I'm not going to take them. I don't think I'm psychotic, and I don't think I'm manic depressive."

"Well, I'm very concerned about you."

"I need a refill on some of my medicines. Will you give me one?"

He reluctantly gave her a refill. It was barely enough. He gave her a refill to last her about a month and a half. She didn't tell him this, but in her mind, she was planning on decreasing. He gave her just enough of a refill. So she put her game plan into action. In January 1999, she started gradually decreasing her psychiatric meds. She never went back to see him or any psychiatrist again, until Jesus put Gail on Seroquel in 2012.

She did suffer some withdrawal symptoms, which gave her some insomnia, because she didn't have enough refills to space it out as much as she wanted. She figured if she decreased the psychiatric meds and increased her vitamins and calcium and magnesium, that she'd be alright. She believed the reason she wasn't sleeping was because she wasn't getting enough nutrition, which was correct. So she started taking enzymes, and increased her calcium, magnesium and vitamins. It worked. Her sleep actually improved.

Though she suffered some withdrawal symptoms from getting off the psychiatric meds, which she expected, because she had to get off them faster than she liked. She didn't have enough refills. She told herself, "Just go through it, because once you get off, it's going to be better."

By the time her family got to Seattle in May 1999, she was off of all her psychiatric meds. She's never been on them since, except in 2012 when Jesus would put her on a psychiatric medication called Seroquel, mostly to treat her systemic yeast infection. She got off the medications by herself, because she couldn't find any psychiatrist to assist her, that she could afford.

About this time (fall 1999 in Mukilteo, Washington) her son was having trouble in school. He was coming home with viruses—about two a week. And Gail was catching every other one. One week it would be a stomach bug. The next week it would be, maybe one that hit the nervous system. She was putting him on echinacea, all sorts of good stuff. He'd get over it, then he'd come home with something else. Always sick. He said, "Mommy, the kids are making fun of me at school."

And he looked like he was getting really stressed out. He was missing a lot of classes. His grades weren't doing well, which was unusual for him because he was normally on honor roll. She thought, "Oh no, now they're hitting me at the school!" He was out half of the fall school year—out sick.

Then he told her that all the kids in the neighborhood and all the kids at his school were teasing him. He told her, "You have no idea how much stress I'm under."

She told him, "I could imagine." And she thought, "Boy, that Loree McBride is good."

Gail was getting it from her doctors, getting it from her son's school, getting it from the neighbors, getting it from the credit card company. A mountain of stress. Getting it from her family, getting it from that South Carolina preacher. The church in Lynnwood was alright.

When she went to church in Lynnwood, Washington, she had to be careful when she backed out of the parking lot, because there were always people trying to trick her, to hit her car from the rear. Like one time she backed out of the parking lot at Open Door Baptist Church, and a car just sped out of nowhere and just missed hitting her, maybe by five inches.

They were trying to get her in wrecks. She would go out on the road and drive, and there would be ten police cars, hidden, waiting around the corner, hoping that she'd be speeding so they could give her a speeding ticket. She thought, "Boy, this Loree is good."

She made sure she never went over the speed limit anywhere she went. Half the time she was driving she had a fever from one of the twenty viruses she caught in the fall of 1999 that her son brought home from school. It seemed like the pressure was ratcheting up and getting worse and worse. She told God, "I don't know how much more I can take."

So many things happened to her, she was feeling very overwhelmed, like she was in a war. And she was.

Gail told herself, "I am not going to let that woman win. I don't care if she kills me. I'm not going to let her win. This is disgusting. She's evil." She just made up her mind that she would do what's right, even if she went down in her own blood. She would stand by her friends.

But boy were they putting the pressure on her. Probably the greatest stress for her in the 1999/2000 year was to see what they were doing to her son.

Her son started having terrible problems in school (sixth grade) and she couldn't get him out of bed to attend classes. The kids made fun of his clothes, picked on him, and bullied him. He became stressed out and didn't want to go to school, was always sick, and said he was too sick to go to school. He'd bring illnesses home and Gail would catch them.

She caught about six or seven viruses a month from her son, who brought home everything. He wasn't handling the Jesuit stress as well as Gail. She tried to explain to him that it was the Jesuits. She thought maybe if she let him know what was going on in her life, it might help. It didn't work. It just made it worse. He thought his mom was crazy.

She told him, "You know, I know this is rough. I don't think you're imagining any of what you're going through at school, and I believe that you're being harassed. I don't think you're faking your illnesses. And I wish I could do some-

The Forbidden Abyss

thing to make life better for you."

"My life is so bad, I wish I was dead." As if he whined for his last breath, his voice whined with pain, "I can't go to schooool. . .I feel teeeerrible. . ."

"Oh come on, you can't be sick this much."

"But I aaaaam. . ." And he'd roll around in his bed and whine and cry like a helpless and depressed worm. "I have a stomachache. . .I can't go to schoool."

Gail tried everything. He was almost a teenage boy. The only way she could get him to go to school, was she'd have to pick him up. So, she couldn't make him go. Most of the time, he didn't want to take the bus, because he said the kids on the bus made fun of him. So, when she could get him out of bed, she drove him to school half the school year, to protect him from the kids that were harassing him.

That was probably the worst part about the 1999/2000 year, to see what they did to her son.

As if that wasn't enough, he was flunking sixth grade.

In January, she got a letter from the school. "Your son is charged with truancy, because he's missed so many days of school. We're concerned about this and we want to meet with you."

So she met with the principal, and they were playing all these dirty tricks on her, where they'd send her these letters in the mail and she was given one or two days to respond. She thought, if I don't respond, then they'd consider me in default and I'd need to go to court, and have my son with me for truancy in court. That would kill him!

She always met the deadlines. It's a good thing she checked her mail every day.

The only mistake she made from a legal standpoint was that she should have insisted that all the promises she got from that principal about not taking her son and her to court, should be *in writing*.

They played dirty tricks on her. The principal of that school was very friendly toward her, which was kind of deceptive. Apparently, they knew the school might be blamed if Gail's son flunked sixth grade, and they wanted the blame to rest squarely on Gail and her son.

Gail met with her a couple times and she said, "I'm very concerned about your son because he's missing a lot of school."

It eventually got to a point where they tried to get her son to appear before a judge on truancy charges. Gail figured out why they were doing this. It was because of the fires in South Carolina. They had to blame her son for the fires, to cover their butts. That really made Gail so mad. She threatened to go to the news media over this and also got a letter from her son's psychologist stating that for her son to appear before a judge would devastate his mental health, and so her son never had to stand before a judge for truancy. But her son did fail sixth grade, and her son was brilliant.

An extrovert, his friendships meant everything to him and he had no friends, only Jesuit kids, who were bullies that tormented him, trying to taunt him into criminal behavior—a Jesuit attempt to make her son into a juvenile delinquent, the kind who might set fires to a mobile home.

Brent's Forbidden Ground

When Jesuits attack their victims, it's like a blitzkrieg from twenty different angles.

In July 1999, Gail began seeing a naturopath in Seattle. She struggled from day to day, overwhelmed by problems, with deteriorating health, deluged with a morass of complications and treachery.

Gail complained of heartburn to her new Seattle naturopathic physician in June 1999. This naturopathic physician that Gail saw in Seattle (summer 1999) for digestive problems, actually had a fixation that Gail had weaned herself off psychiatric medications and suggested she get back on a small dose, though Gail told her she was sleeping fine and didn't understand her concern.

She then changed the subject and suggested that she could do some chiropractic type manipulations (spinal extremity corrections) to cure her stomach problems (heartburn).

But when Gail went to her, she jerked her neck back several times (as part of the manipulations) and (after Gail's second or third visit with her) damaged her neck so bad that she couldn't sleep and became very nauseated.

The naturopath expressed concern that Gail was totally off psychiatric meds and thought she should start a small dosage and go back to a psychiatrist, even though Gail told her that mentally and emotionally she was great, her sleep was good, and that she was more concerned about her stomach. She talked Gail (a reluctant patient) into trying spinal extremity correction (similar to chiropractic adjustments with some physical therapy).

"I'm doing this mainly to help with my stomach," Gail said.

"Well, this will help you with your stomach. . .and it probably will help with other things, too."

The naturopath manipulated her spine, and then she grabbed Gail's head and kind of jerked it back.

Gail noticed she was feeling a little stiff in her neck, but thought, "Oh well. . .that was kind of a weird treatment that she grabbed my head and jerked it back like that."

She jerked Gail's head straight back several times, as well as worked on her lower spine. Her heartburn improved, but she began to develop a new symptom: insomnia. She started losing a little bit of sleep, but didn't worry about it too much. It came on gradually, getting worse each time the naturopath pulled back Gail's neck. Gail did notice some minor sleep loss after her first spinal adjustment with her, but shrugged it off as normal, because the manipulations she did to her lower spine helped her stomach symptoms.

Though Gail began to get suspicious, she still was not convinced the naturopath assisted Loree McBride. So she continued the spinal extremity correction.

So she went back to her. But after about the second or third visit, she realized that what she did to her neck, sabotaged her sleep and mental health, and gave her neck spasms that kept her up all night. She couldn't understand why she manipulated her neck for stomach problems.

Gail went back for about one or two more treatments. After the second or third treatment, when she went home, the muscles in the back of her neck were having spasms. She was in so much pain, she was up all night. Oh my God, she thought, Loree McBride got the doctor to try and induce psychosis in me using

The Forbidden Abyss

that spinal extremity correction.

Up all night, she had a headache, was nauseated, and was actually getting mental symptoms because of the manipulations done to her neck.

After the damage was done, furious, Gail realized the naturopath deliberately manipulated her neck to try to induce psychotic symptoms (and insomnia) in her through her neck manipulations. She did notice that the manipulations (especially after her second and third visits with her) seemed to bring on some psychiatric symptoms, such as depression and anxiety. She never went back to the naturopath again. Loree got this doctor somehow.

But she thought, "I bet I know who can fix this—a chiropractor."

So she called up a chiropractor and made an emergency appointment. "I need to see you right away. I'm really in distress. I feel lousy."

This is the first time she'd ever been to a chiropractor.

Gushing with friendliness, he said, "I need to take x-rays." After x-rays, he said, "Ahhh. . . yeah. . .we need to manipulate your C2." Grasping her head with both hands, he jerked her head to the side.

Gail felt better, but it didn't last.

So she had to go back to see him again. Now her bills were really piling up. The second time the chiropractor gave Gail an adjustment, she felt worse than she did when she went to the naturopath. She thought, "Oh no! They got the chiropractor!"

Exhausted, she called him up and said, "I don't know what you did to my neck. But I want you to fix this. I'm going to show up, and whatever you did—you did something bad to my neck, and I know you didn't do it right. Now, you fix it." She went to him and said, "I want to be able to function and I don't know what you did to my neck, but I want you to fix it."

He didn't fix it too good.

Eventually, her neck muscles became so spasmed (and she'd never had these symptoms before in her whole life) that she was up all night with nausea and mental and emotional irritation. The Jesuit naturopath used the neck jerks to induce psychosis on Gail under the guise of spinal extremity correction treatment for her stomach.

"Forget that doctor, man." What am I going to do? She realized her insurance covered physical therapy.

"He's no good." She gave up on both the chiropractor and the naturopath.

Let's quit paying out of my credit card, she thought, and go with something that my insurance covers,

She went to a physical therapist, who happened to be a Catholic and was really nice. Her name was Donna (she was heavy with brown hair, but not obese).

With an office in Mukilteo, the HealthSouth physical therapist was right down the road from Gail. She used some muscle manipulation that helped the muscles in the back of her neck to relax. "Your C2 is in a bad position. It's lying flat up against your skull, and that's why you're having trouble. I'm going to work and see if I can get it to go down a little bit more."

Gail learned some exercises from her to help bring her neck back into a more correct position, and went to her for two months of physical therapy. The physical therapist helped her enough that Gail could sleep for about six hours a night.

Brent's Forbidden Ground

But she certainly wasn't getting beauty rest.

Finally after about two months she did all she could, and Gail felt so much better. Donna and her assistant treated Gail with kindness. Finally, Donna said, "I've done everything I can with physical therapy to get your C2 to go down, but it is just so stubborn, I think you're going to need to see a chiropractor."

Gail told her, "Oh boy, my insurance doesn't cover that."

"I talked with a chiropractor that's down the road from here. And I hear he's really good. You may want to try him. It may only take one or two visits and you'll be fine. You may want to try him and see if he can help you, because I've done everything I can with physical therapy to get that C2 to go down, and it won't."

Because Gail had faith in Donna, she went to visit the chiropractor down the road. He was a blonde, trained at a Los Angeles chiropractic school, and Gail was very impressed with him.

"I'm going to make a special arrangement with you where you can visit me as many times as you want in a month, and you just pay a monthly fee of sixty dollars." Gail strongly suspected that Brent had struck a deal with this chiropractor. The chiropractor used a ping machine on Gail's neck, and she got really good help from him. "Your C1 is way up there, but I'll keep working on it and we'll get it to go down where it needs to go."

She ended up going to him for a year, and had him do her entire spine. She ended up taking her son to him. Eventually her neck problem got fixed. She had never had neck problems before in her life.

After several months, a good chiropractor and physical therapist fixed her. But the total charges to fix her neck problem were very expensive and didn't help her rising debt.

Gail fought for months to get those criminal medical charges off her credit card. It seemed her certified, return receipt letters never made it to the credit card company until about three weeks after she mailed them. And then, once they reached the credit card company, they somehow got lost.

She decided to dispute the charges from that naturopath and the chiropractor that ruined her neck. She refused to pay for their charges. What happened to her letters was unbelievable.

She wrote a letter to the credit card company, First USA Visa. She sent it certified, return receipt and made copies of it. She didn't get her return receipt card till about three weeks after she mailed the letter, and she got no response regarding her letter.

The second letter she sent to them certified, return receipt got lost, and they didn't know where it was. On the third try (certified, return receipt), finally the letter made it to the right department.

But for each attempt, it always took two or three weeks for it to get to the credit card office. Finally, after making all sorts of copies and making about 11 or 12 letters, (three of them certified, return receipt), she finally got a response.

They said, "There's nothing we can do for you about this because the chiropractor and naturopath deny that they gave you bad services."

She thought, "Alright, just forget it." She wanted to dispute the charges because she was mad at that chiropractor and that naturopath, and wanted to make it plain that they should probably be sued for malpractice. But, she got the run-

The Forbidden Abyss

around, because the Jesuits protected them.

Gail told Brent to bring Loree McBride to court for more charges.

After Loree tried to burn down Gail's mobile home in 1998, he took Loree to court to try her as a criminal against Gail.

After several rounds of physicians, chiropractors and physical therapists, Gail found good practitioners (B. Scott Jones, chiropractor, Seattle, Washington and physical therapist Donna of Health South) who fixed her neck, so that she could get her rest.

During conversations with Donna (who was Roman Catholic), Donna said, "Oh, I loved *The Thornbirds*, but that Ralph was certainly not a very good example as a priest."

These crimes against her health cost a lot of time, money, and harassment—along with the discomforts of sleep loss and nausea (from a maladjusted neck).

Her debts piled up. She'd started using credit cards (with no job) for the first time for her health expenses, because her ex-husband refused to pay for any of this, and much of this (chiropractic and natural medicine) was not covered by her military health care coverage. She was getting ripped off by criminal (though licensed) health practitioners.

During this time period, when Jesuits deluged her with viruses, her mother paid for her to study for the Washington state real estate salesperson's licensing exam. She passed it on the first try (October 1999). Though the law interested her, she had no interest in working as a real estate salesperson, especially when she heard about real estate agents murdered while showing people houses.

In December 1999, Gail went for her mammogram, like most women do every year or so.

The radiologist's face in his dimly lit office, his x-ray equipment off to the side, reminded her of a phantom in a haunted house. His whole demeanor gave Gail the spooks. "It's not an emergency, but you have calcium deposits in your right breast. You shouldn't sit on it too much. It could possibly be breast cancer. We just need to do a breast biopsy under general anesthesia, to get a sample of your breast tissue. We can schedule the surgery within a week."

She didn't like the way they were trying to rush her into general anesthesia. "I don't think this is such a big hurry. I don't want general anesthesia." After the criminal naturopath and chiropractor, Gail had a strong distrust of doctors. I wonder what they plan to do to me under general anesthesia? Gail was more scared of what the doctors would do to her under general anesthesia, than the possibility of breast cancer.

That scene with the radiologist she played over and over in her mind.

It was a dimly lit room and the radiologist came in looking really somber and serious, along with his nurse. He said, "Can you sit down, we need to talk with you about something..."

She sat down.

"We found some calcium deposits on your right breast. We don't want you to worry about this. In ninety-five percent of the cases, it turns out to be nothing to worry about. But, however, this is something we don't want to totally ignore.

Brent's Forbidden Ground

We want you to get this checked, because there's a slight chance this could be breast cancer or a precursor to breast cancer. The good news is it looks like we caught it early, and if it is cancer, you're probably fine. We want to do a biopsy, a needle guided biopsy on your right breast."

"What's involved in a needle guided biopsy?"

"We'd have to put you under general anesthesia and you'd have to go in the operating room."

"Why does it have to be so complicated? Why do I have to be under general anesthesia?"

"Because that's the way it's done."

"Can't it be done any other way?"

"No," he said. "That's the way we do biopsies."

"I don't know. I have to think about this." There was something about him. She felt he was spooky and creepy. She was at the point in her life, where she sized up people and tried to determine if they were her friend, or working for Loree. She went home and thought about that thing. She just got the spooks thinking about it. She thought, "What are they going to try to do to me in general anesthesia?" Loree and her naturopath friend had already messed with her neck, so Gail didn't trust the radiologist. Something about him did not sit right with her. He was in too big a hurry to put her under general anesthesia! She decided to abandon him as a physician and told the radiologist she would get a second opinion.

She thought about that radiologist and how spooky he looked. She thought, boy, this Loree McBride is good.

Overwhelmed and exhausted, around December 10, 1999, she awakened from her sleep around two in the morning in her Mukilteo apartment. She lay in her bed in the darkness, with her eyes wide open, and heard a sentence in her mind that said, "Your enemy is the Roman Catholic Church." As she thought about her life and what had happened to her and Brent, suddenly it occurred to her that if the Roman Catholic Church was her enemy, then perhaps Loree McBride was an agent for this church. She recalled that she'd read on the Internet (around 1996) that Loree was Roman Catholic. It seemed odd that when Brent brought her to court, she mounted a granite mountain against Gail and Brent, so that the case dragged on and on and on and the attacks against Gail (because of her) worsened and worsened and became more and more complicated, convoluted and devastating. It seemed she controlled the doctors, the pharmaceutical companies, the school districts, the governments, the airplane industry, economics, and the environment. Gail couldn't believe the power this woman had! She felt as if her ship sunk further with the endless storm surges from Loree's cannon. How did this woman have so much power? On the Internet, she did not look capable of mounting such brilliance and power in law, medicine, and politics. Gail always wondered why, even after she tried to rape Franco Nero, Brent kept Loree as a girlfriend.

Gail figured it all out in 1999 when her God told her in December 1999 that Loree was a Vatican agent. Her brilliance always amazed Brent. He'd learn later that she was half king David and half Catherine the Great.

December 1999 she said Jesus spoke to her in a still, small voice in her

The Forbidden Abyss

mind, around 2 a.m. "You're enemy is the Roman Catholic Church." Jesus also told her if she'd start writing again, He would remove a breast cancer that she had in her breasts. Gail started writing for Jesus and her two biopsies for breast cancer in 2000 came back negative. In 2005 she would finish her novel *Silver Skies*.

In horror, that December 1999, her confusion about Brent vanished. She read Brent's heart with brilliance. She realized that he allowed a woman he hated, Loree, to be his constant companion, only to protect his Gail. Then Gail reinstated Brent back onto the throne of her heart, and decided that his love for her was as high as the heavens, or he would not have allowed a killer to live in his home, only to protect her.

What love he had for Gail, to allow a murderer to live in his house, so he would know where the murderer was at all times, in order to protect Gail! Gail realized this in 1999, and yearned again to nurture her Brent. She figured out that he only lived for her, so she reinstated him back to the throne of her heart, believed again in his greatness, cried for hours begging his forgiveness for calling him a wimp over Loree.

She told her long distance lover Franco Nero that night when Jesus spoke to her (December 1999), that she must marry Brent, because he'd gone through hell for her. Brent felt reborn, he no longer contemplated suicide. He kicked the drug-rapist out of his house, his way of reinstating Gail as the wife of his heart.

So on this cool, brisk winter evening at 2 a.m. in the middle of December 1999 in her Seattle, Washington apartment, as Gail pondered over the granite mountain of Loree McBride and her "friends", suddenly, everything made sense, when God told her in His still, small voice: "Your enemy is the Roman Catholic Church." Gail didn't know exactly what happened to Brent to cause him to acquire Loree, but she knew if she was a Roman Catholic agent assigned to break up her relationship with Brent, that she received brilliant directions from a brilliant church, and that she used criminal means to acquire her girlfriend status with Brent. A flash of insight glared through Gail's mind, she realized Brent could not give her up as his girlfriend, because whatever type of extortion she used on Brent (for he'd hinted to Gail that she got her relationship with him through some kind of extortion) that it must have devastated Brent—that he strived to overcome the devastation, but was no match for the granite mountain of the Vatican (under Jesuit direction). Loree McBride, through a brilliant and diabolical plot, obtained girlfriend status with Brent, because Brent felt that by maintaining her, he could protect his communications with Gail.

Gail felt now that Brent kept Loree for one reason only, in order to keep his relationship with Gail in the only way he knew how, because he worshipped the ground Gail walked on. That he never wanted her, that he only kept her for Gail, that he put up with the constant companionship of a woman he couldn't stand— just for Gail. She could only imagine what it must have been like for him to have to endure the companionship of Loree McBride who, after Brent made love to Gail on the phone (July 1993), called her to scream at her (midnight) with spite and venom in her deep, lacerating voice: "Hey bitch, what the *fuck* are you doing to my boyfriend!"

She knew now that he allowed a criminal to be his girlfriend, that he loved Gail so much, he put up with the company of a woman he couldn't stand, just for her. That he adored Gail so much, he was willing to have this criminal for a girlfriend, so that he could continue to hear Gail's voice, her thoughts and to have what little presence of Gail in his life that he could have. Someway, somehow, Loree had weaseled and extorted herself into Brent's life, so that Brent felt that the only way he could protect or continue his relationship with Gail, was to go along with this criminal Roman Catholic agent, that he despised. But he did not realize that she was a Roman Catholic agent, because the Roman Catholic Church targeted Brent and Gail behind the scenes.

Recalling the Roman Catholic Church's brilliance (from the publications of Jack Chick), Gail felt she'd been too hard on Brent about Loree, because Brent fought, not a woman, but an empire. That he maintained her just so he could keep his communications with Gail, made him seem heroic in perseverance. Gail realized that she'd horribly misunderstood him, that he did have greatness as a man, that he had the greatness and courage to take on an empire, in order to try and acquire Gail as a wife. Gail knew he must have wanted to marry her, or he would not have allowed this horrible woman to remain in his life. That he somehow had to keep her, in some sort of dirty deal with Paramount, so that he could maintain his communication with Gail, and that it was awful for him, but what he felt he needed to do to maintain his communication with Gail, because he loved Gail and wanted to marry her.

Gail ran to her light switch and switched on the light, rubbed her eyes and glared, as if in a daze, at the rows and rows of books in her room. She had nearly a three thousand volume library, that filled all the walls of her Mukilteo bedroom. A little over half the books were hers, and one whole shelf was all writing instruction books, including her course from The Institute of Children's Literature, with notes from her instructor Jim Murphy.

Brent tried to fight off an empire, because he adored her, because he worshipped the ground she walked on, because he wanted to marry her more than anything in the world.

Gail had had more dealings with Loree McBride since 1998 (who seemed to possess extraordinary wealth, power and brilliance—that didn't match at all her appearance in the Internet) and began to realize just how difficult and impossible it was to deal with this woman and began to get an inkling of what Brent suffered over the years with this woman, and that the reason she maintained her public girlfriend status with Brent, was an empire financed and supported her. Her brazenness and deadly actions made sense. She was just like the powerful and brilliant Church who directed her. She, a criminal, a pawn, cooperated with a dangerous and brilliant organization (the powerful Roman Catholic Church); and though Brent wanted to give her up, the Catholic Church made it that if he did this, he would lose Gail as well. So Brent must have gone through the scourges, fires of hell, and pestilences with this woman just so he could keep Gail in his life.

This realization of how Brent suffered and endured because of Loree McBride, backed by the Roman Catholic empire, who forged her way into his life, hit Gail like a tidal wave in the wee hours of that December morning.

One may wonder how Gail could so readily forgive Brent for having Loree McBride as a girlfriend after he had propositioned Gail on the phone in 1991. It was because, when she discerned in December 1999, that he was the victim of

The Forbidden Abyss

Vatican targeting—Gail realized (for the first time) that he had strived heroically to protect her from the harassment and targeting of which he'd been a victim since around 1992. But despite his monumental efforts, the Vatican outsmarted him, and they commenced with their attacks on Gail and her family, working through every loophole they could find and manipulating Brent (like a pawn on a chessboard) into a favorable position on which to launch their (hopefully) decisive and fatal thrusts and machinations against Gail and her family.

Gail reasoned that Brent never told Gail about Loree McBride, because he never wanted her, and probably thought he could get her out of the way (through his own efforts), and so felt Gail didn't need to know about her, because Loree wasn't that important to him, and he didn't feel that Gail's knowing about Loree would be of any help.

Unfortunately, Gail thought, he never figured out that she was a Vatican agent and he greatly underestimated how dangerous she was, and what a formidable player had just encroached into his life.

Therefore, because he did not know who she really was, and because he did not know that when he took her on, he was taking on the Vatican—he only saw her as a hell raising woman, obsessed with him—and the sly Vatican played on this to the hilt.

Gail concluded that Loree McBride was the smokescreen. She was instructed to become a nuisance (privately with Brent) and in public, to play the part of the celebrity girlfriend. The Jesuits wanted to use her to play on the public stereotypes about celebrity girlfriends and she was to be as opposite Gail as possible to create the impression that Gail would never be a woman that Brent could be in love with.

Around the public, she played the celebrity girlfriend role and made sure that her lifestyle, attitudes and views would fit the typical stereotypes that the public has about Hollywood stars and their girlfriends, with maybe a little added emphasis in the areas where she differed from Gail in appearance, attitudes and lifestyles.

The Vatican realized that Brent might get mad enough to drag Loree to court and they were prepared for this eventuality.

She received expert legal counsel from Vatican lawyers from the very beginning of her "romantic" relationship with Brent. Brent was duped.

He thought she was just a hell raising drug rapist that he could get rid of eventually. Therefore, she was never a woman that he desired romantically.

Because Gail believed she blackmailed him under the guidance and advice of her Vatican legal advisors, they wanted to make sure that if all this ended up in court, they could come up with a strong case for Loree McBride. Loree's encroachment into Brent's, and eventually Gail and her family's life, was very meticulously planned to deal with every possible contingency.

The Vatican must not be exposed and Gail Chana must never be in a position where she could influence public opinion.

Apparently, the Jesuits knew all about Gail and determined she was a serious threat to their goals, and Gail must never become famous through her writings or her love life. Gail and her family must be destroyed. This was Loree McBride's job, to assist in this effort.

So how did Gail believe Loree had sex with Brent? Gail thought, "Brent drinks alcoholic beverages. I believe she spiked an alcoholic beverage which he drank. When he was knocked out, she raped him, took pictures of the incident, and when he awakened he had no idea what happened to him.

"She then furnished him with the 'proof' that she and Brent had had sex, and held it over his head constantly to 'maintain' her girlfriend status with him. The reason the Jesuits spiked an alcoholic beverage is so that if all this ended up in court and Brent claimed his drink was spiked, they could say he lied, and that in a drunken state he raped Loree and that she graciously forgave him for it and kept him any ways.

"That's why she often dressed seductively (to make her appear like a woman Brent would not be able to resist if he was drunk) and she was very physically attractive (the Jesuits didn't miss a thing).

"Of course, Brent would never want me to know about this, and that's part of the reason I only found out about Loree as Brent's girlfriend from Brent's mother via the Houston Chronicle's society page in June 1996."

But why would Loree McBride insist on maintaining a relationship with a man who listened to Gail every day on the phone for hours, and did this for years from 1994 and onward, and who voraciously read all Gail's letters to him? He was very interested in hearing from her and Gail could tell he read, heard and saw her at his every opportunity.

Gail never suspected he had a girlfriend because he was giving her too much attention.

That's why she was so confused when she found out about Loree in June 1996!

But—if she was a Vatican agent—everything made sense.

Why was she so obsessed with appearing with Brent in public?

Why was it when Gail dropped Brent as a romantic interest (because of her) that she targeted Franco Nero next?

She may have tried spiking Franco's drink, too, and (who knows?) maybe Franco was her next rape victim?

Why couldn't Loree be content with Brent alone? Why was Gail's home almost burned down in December 1998 (when she wasn't interested in Brent romantically and was no threat to her)?

If she claimed she did this because Brent had a sick obsession with Gail and she wanted to take care of his obsession, why would she desire to marry a man who was afflicted with so many hang-ups?

If she was a Vatican agent—it all made sense.

Loree would admit in the Quebec trial (2011) to Gail that she was the woman who called Gail around the third week of July 1993 and said in a vicious alto voice, "Hey bitch, what the fuck are you doing with my boyfriend!"

If Brent had sex with Loree, he was raped. Just because Loree was very attractive physically did not mean he desired her.

These conclusions about Brent's drink being spiked were Gail's guesses and theories—if she was right, she was a genius at reading people.

Gail perceived all along that he was intimidated by her.

She always knew he didn't love her, but couldn't understand why he kept her as a girlfriend for so long. . .

That is—until she figured out she was a Vatican agent.

The Forbidden Abyss

The Jesuits have made deep penetrations into Hollywood. They know how Hollywood influenced (influences) public opinion.

So she ran to the cordless phone in her dark living room, and rushed it back to her bedroom and sat up in her bed, dialed her own number to create the "blank" she used to talk to Brent, and then cried her heart out to Brent for three hours at least. Her husband was out at sea on a deployment. Brent listened to her at every hour of the day or night, Gail believed he carried the device that he used to listen to her everywhere he went. She broke into wails on her phone, which she rarely did, because she's a strong woman.

Gail pondered over all the pain and suffering Brent endured because of his love for her, because of the treachery that the powerful Roman Catholic empire committed against his love for her. She began to realize that he had adored her since 1990, had always adored her, that he always wanted to marry her, and that he pacified and maintained Loree and endured the suffering of seeing Gail drop him as a lover for Franco, as he attempted to fight off an empire, in the vain hopes he could still retain his relationship with Gail—only because he wanted to marry her and because it meant (more than his life) to keep Gail's presence in his life. He felt that in order to maintain his communications with Gail he had to retain Loree. Now she realized what pain she brought into his life because, when she found out about Loree McBride in 1996, she allowed Franco to replace him.

She realized that she almost allowed a brilliant and powerful empire to manipulate her to destroy the love of her life, because she'd fallen for their diabolical plot against her lover.

In between sobs and sniffles, she told Brent what God told her, and asked Brent to forgive her, that she now understood what he'd gone through for her. So she cried for hours on the phone to Brent (from about 3 a.m. to 5 a.m. in the middle of the morning on that December 1999) and asked Brent to forgive her for taking Franco in his place, that she felt that the Roman Catholic empire used Loree McBride to cause problems between Brent and herself, in order to destroy their love for each other. That they somehow extorted him into a relationship with Loree and interfered with his relationship with Gail, that Gail had no doubt that he loved Gail as much as his own life. She knew he had to love her supremely, in order to put up with all this pressure (and to put up with the company of this awful woman, even after he knew she tried to seduce Franco), so that he could keep his communications with Gail on her phone.

All doubts about Brent's commitment toward Gail as the love of his life—vanished. He was so committed to Gail that he risked all he cared about, to maintain his communications with her.

Then she said: "I offer you my hand in marriage. I will end my marriage, because my husband opposes natural medicine. So now I have Scriptural grounds for divorce, because I need natural medicine to stay alive and to function, and my husband opposes it, so I can't stay in this marriage any ways. When I'm free, I'll marry you."

Brent would accept her offer, she had no doubt, because she had him all figured out now. Gail realized that he had adored her since 1990 and that he'd never stopped adoring her since then and that the only reason he put up with Loree McBride was because he felt this was the only way he could maintain his communications with Gail, so that he could one day marry her.

She told Brent, if her husband refused to support natural medicine, that she had scriptural grounds to end the marriage, because that was desertion, and so now her conscience was at rest about ending the marriage. Brent sacrificed his time, money and emotions to deal with this powerful Jesuit empire for her, and so now she no longer had moral scruples about marrying Brent. And she had no doubts at all about which man deserved marriage to her. She had no doubt now that Brent loved her far more than any man ever did, than any man ever could.

God also revealed to Gail as she prayed and read her Bible in that December 1999, that if she did not end her marriage, that the Jesuits would kill her and/or her son within a few years. She sensed the Jesuit noose around her neck tightening and tightening (like a boa constrictor), and she knew that the Vatican would use her husband as the Vatican agent to promote her death. God told her to get out of the marriage now and not to delay anymore ending her marriage. She got a distinct impression from God that it was His will for her to now leave the marriage, and that if she failed to have the courage to end the marriage now, that she would be dead within a few years.

God said to Gail distinctly in that December 1999, that she must end her marriage and do it now, if she wanted to stay alive. And as she viewed her life around her, she perceived her life in grave danger, and knew that God had spoken to her about His will, and that, indeed, if she did not end her marriage immediately, that she would be dead within a few years. So, despite the $40,000 divorce, and despite the tidal wave of pressure the Jesuits mounted against Gail as the divorce case went forward, she went forward with the divorce.

Now that Gail knew who her enemy was, she was furious. Furious, because they almost allowed her to devastate a man who loved her from the depths of his heart, and furious, because they had ruined her health and used her husband to try to destroy her.

Loree McBride would not easily give up her publicity boyfriend or her undeserved reputation as the Hollywood glamour queen, and she had the backing of a Roman Catholic empire (with wealth far more vast than Brent or Gail would ever have) to support her, in her attempts to control and takeover Brent Spiner.

But you can live with someone in their house, or at their workplace day by day, and still not know them. These, like Loree, are obsessed with illusions, with impressions, with appearances, with falsehoods, with lies, with delusions.

Such was Loree with Brent Spiner. She didn't love him, but only wanted to use him to promote Jesuit agendas. She never gazed into his eyes to explore his manliness, courage, or honor. She could care less about this. These traits got in the way, they were useless drivel

Brent, not a romantic interest to her, was a conquest for the Jesuit Order, a star she could shine with.

Her relationship with Brent was a career, not a matter of falling in love, but a matter of serving the interests of the Jesuit Order to ensure that Gail Chana would never have a famous man for a lover or a husband. Ever aware of impressions, she'd use her knowledge of press and public relations to manipulate and extort herself into girlfriend status with the nice and "easy" Hollywood star.

With Brent as her perfect sucker, she knew he'd do anything to protect Gail. Yes, he'd do anything, even take Loree as a girlfriend, if she set up conditions so

The Forbidden Abyss

he'd have to do this, to protect the woman he adored. So she set him up and raped him, and shoved herself into his life and into his relationship with Gail. She got between Gail and Brent, to try to break them up, to have Brent all to herself, to ensure that Brent Spiner would never marry the Howard Hughes/Catherine the Great woman, and thus destroy the goals of the Jesuit Order.

She knew the complications in their relationship. She knew Brent was helplessly in love with Gail, and discerned that she could manipulate these complications to her advantage. She could take care of his infatuation with Gail, because she knew enough about Christians to know how to make him nauseating to Gail. Once she got her title: the girlfriend of the famous Brent Spiner, she had the clout she needed to win her war against the nobody housewife (with stars in her eyes about her hero) that Brent wouldn't give up on.

But to remove Gail from his heart became a tougher obstacle than she anticipated. No ordinary housewife, shrewd Brent discovered rare traits in Gail that he could find in no other women. Loree began to realize that her sparkling good looks and cruelty towards Brent and others, paled in comparison to Gail's penetrations into Brent's heart and soul, and her extraordinary courage, devotion, and passion in the way she loved him.

Gail's soul and spirit left such imprints in Brent's heart, that Loree could do nothing to remove Gail from his heart—so that he idolized Gail day in and day out, no matter what Loree did—so that one day Loree called Gail up like an earthquake, and screamed with venom, "Hey bitch, what the *fuck* are you doing to my boyfriend!"

She appeared with him in public as much as possible to irritate Gail. But Gail ignored her, to her irritation. And she never could get in the way enough to cause problems, until Loree printed a lying Houston Chronicle snippet that claimed that Brent's own mother announced how Brent gave Loree a birthday bash at Spago's in L.A. on June 26, 1996. Loree stole Brent's credit cards to give herself that birthday bash as the "girlfriend" of Brent Spiner. Brent was not there, because he was not invited. Besides, who'd believe a Hollywood star could be so noble in love, that he'd adore a poor, nobody homemaker?

What a perfect scenario, a genuinely nice Hollywood star who adores an honorable, but naive, woman, who won't go to bed with him, but talks or writes love nonsense to him all day!

So, as Loree observed Brent Spiner, she plotted and schemed a way to weasel this man into marriage with her, to trap him into a relationship with her that would ensure Brent Spiner would never marry Gail Chana. She used her good looks and public relations savvy (to the fullest) to accomplish her objective. A rape would be the perfect way to gain entrance, because with her good looks, who'd believe Brent, if he claimed that she raped him?

Brent would be so devastated by the rape (which he was) that he'd lose his head, so that he wouldn't lose the love of life. Loree would take full advantage of his emotional devastation to trap him into a relationship with her. This evil woman, fully aware of stereotypical public perceptions, used this knowledge to the fullest advantage.

Yes, she didn't have stars in her eyes about Brent, because her only feelings and goals for him were to enjoy and use him for the Jesuit Order, not to nurture

Brent's Forbidden Ground

or support him as a soul-mate or a husband.

While Brent's heart withered in despair in September 1992, when Loree somehow managed to obtain his sperm as evidence of his sex with her, as he contemplated that he could lose the woman of his dreams forever—Loree bided her time, to go in and "make the attack", in order to promote her Hollywood romance career, to ensure her name blazed besides his in all press releases. She planned associations with him as much as possible, to create the impression that he could find her attractive and that he had an authentic boyfriend/girlfriend relationship with her that included regular sex.

The Jesuits used Paramount to give Loree the legal and financial backing she needed, so they could use her to blackmail Brent's love for Gail. When Brent eventually signed his contract with Paramount to allow his extortioner to enter his life, Loree McBride floated in dreamland. Her brilliant Hollywood romantic career as the destroyer of the love between Brent and Gail had begun!

The Jesuits never expected Gail to figure out as much as she did. But God told her in the wee hours of that December 1999, that her enemy was the Roman Catholic Church.

By 1998, after Franco rejected and exposed her, Loree felt threatened that she would be exposed as the fraud and rapist she really was, and she realized that she had failed utterly to stop Brent's love for Gail, and that he loved her more than ever, and that the Jesuits would kill her for this. She had failed in her assignment, an assignment that cost the Jesuits *and Brent* millions of dollars! Even worse, because of Franco, her reputation as a nice girl was about to be demolished. Her Hollywood romantic career as the girlfriend of Brent Spiner was ruined.

All she cared about had burned up in a vast bon fire. Already, all the Hollywood men labeled her as the dirty whore who tried to seduce Franco Nero (while she paraded as Brent's girlfriend). Her reputation as a "cute Hollywood blonde" (which was her obsession) was ruined, because of Franco Nero. Even her two dogs could not overcome the damage.

All of Hollywood knew she was a cold-hearted, calculating bitch, who only owned dogs to create the false impression she was an animal lover and, therefore, had to be "nice" and cute and friendly, and never one to use drug rape to extort Brent Spiner into a boyfriend/girlfriend relationship with her. How could she convince the world that Brent had willing and knowing sex with her, when it's obvious such a nice guy would never want a woman as vulgar and vile as her, who tried to rape Franco Nero, like she raped Brent Spiner?

Is it any wonder that Brent stared at her like she was a viper in all the Germany photos of her taken in December 1996–the time when she tried to do a repeat performance on Franco Nero, like she did to Brent in September 1992, when her actions caused Brent's heart to wither in despair?

The Jesuits wasted no time to doctor up her Internet photos (taken of her London visit to Franco in December 1996), to cover up more of her breasts (and bring the V-neck on her seductive dress up higher), create a more angelic look to her face, minimize her purple and seductive lipstick, and make her look less like the murdering whore she was and is. She was dressed to seduce, but instead repulsed the Italian film star, who had the gall to expose her rape attempt to Brent Spiner, who stared at her like she was a viper (in the photos taken of Brent and

The Forbidden Abyss

Loree together in Germany in December 1996). These photos show that Brent hated being with her and hated the game Paramount extorted him into, that he'd rather have just about any woman in the world for a girlfriend or constant companion than this cruel and lying viper.

Even if Franco rejected her, he didn't have to tell Brent and the whole world about it. Her expression in the Germany photos indicated she wanted to kill Franco Nero and Gail for how they ruined her life.

Loree McBride (or her clone) would now impregnate herself with Brent's sperm in September 2001, after the Jesuit 9/11/2001 plot to terrify Gail with the World Trade Center attacks had failed, causing Gail to transfer her desire to marry Brent to Russian President Vladimir Putin.

So the Jesuits, realizing Gail had become enamored with Vladimir and had somewhat put Brent aside, would use semen they had stolen from their September 1992 rape of Brent, to impregnate Loree McBride through artificial insemination. The Jesuits, who created clones of just about everyone on earth, could easily steal any man's sperm without his knowledge or consent and use it to destroy any relationship (like the relationship between Brent and Gail) that threatened Jesuit goals.

But before 9/11/2001, when Gail first realized that Loree McBride was a Vatican agent, she wailed on her wiretapped phone to Brent, "Oh Brent, I'm so, so sorry that I kicked you out of my heart as a lover. I will dream about making love to you again. In fact, because you have put up with so much for me, to protect me, I will marry you." Gail sniffled and cried for some minutes, then got herself together.

"I will lay down an ultimatum with my husband and tell him that if he won't pay for my naturopathic medicine that I will divorce him. He's so stingy, I know he will not help, and then I will have Scriptural grounds for divorce. Desertion, because he refuses to pay for the medical care that will keep me alive."

Gail forgave Brent Spiner in December 1999 and fell in love with him again, all because of a thought that came to her mind as a still, small voice. It was God. God spoke to her at 2 in the morning, while she lay on her bed in her Seattle apartment.

Gail Divorces Her Husband
2000 to 2001

Once Gail realized that Loree McBride was a Vatican agent assigned to Brent to destroy his love for Gail, Loree got a lot worse, because she was furious. She bought Brent and herself a membership to the zoo and got a fish tank full of eels (possibly to stuff eels down the head of Brent's penis, like she did in 1992). She invested in more lingerie, like she was planning another rape.

Brent just bolted from his Beverly Hills house and fled to live somewhere else. He wasn't even afraid anymore, because he had Gail back, and was so happy.

He did manage to save enough at this point in his acting career, that he could survive without his income from Star Trek, by living off of investments, though he certainly would not be living with the income of a typical Hollywood celebrity. Because of Loree's embezzlement into his finances, he didn't have nearly as much income as everyone thought he did. Loree had spent millions of his income from Paramount, by embezzling his credit cards from 1993 to 1999.

When he confronted Loree about her embezzlement, she threatened to kill Gail. "You dare tell that Gail that I steal your credit cards, then I'll kill her!" Loree would then flash photos before him of Gail mutilated, with Gail's head chopped off and body pieces and blood scattered everywhere.

Because Brent had started legal proceedings against Loree around 1998—going after Loree for trying to burn down Gail's home, for poisoning Gail's medications, for bribing the police and Gail's doctors against Gail—so that by the time Gail took Brent back as a lover in December 1999, Brent was able to convince Paramount that he could no longer have Loree as his girlfriend.

He went to the Paramount executives and presented his case to them. "This Loree is a criminal. I've tried to tell you this, but you wouldn't listen. I have gotten a court order for her to leave my house. She attacked Gail and harmed her physically, tried to burn down Gail's mobile home and I am sure you don't want to be associated with her anymore. That is, unless you want the world to think you support her criminal activities!"

Brent glared at the Paramount executives. "She could kill Gail and we all could be blamed for it." Brent put his fist down. "She is not my girlfriend, anymore. Gail is also divorcing her husband to be with me, and I have never wanted Loree from day one. In fact, Gail has figured out that Loree is a Vatican agent. My brilliant Gail has figured out this evil Loree McBride, even though she has never met her, like you all have." Brent glared at the Paramount executives in disgust. "I can tell you myself, that Loree is a killer, because she has nearly

The Forbidden Abyss

killed me many times, and she has threatened to kill Gail from the first day that I met her. I can also tell you that the only reason I have put up with this bitch as my girlfriend is because she has threatened to kill Gail if I don't."

The Paramount executives looked at Brent with blank faces. Brent knew they would not want it to be known that they extorted Brent to have a murderer for a girlfriend. "What does Gail do for a living? Never heard of her."

Brent smiled with pride. "She's a writer, a brilliant writer."

"We're sorry that things didn't work out for you and your publicist." The executive seemed apologetic. "Perhaps a writer is more to your liking."

"She doesn't write for the money. It's a passion for her. You may never hear of her. Fame is not necessarily an indicator of worth, or even of talent." Brent looked each executive square in the eyes. They looked at him like he was a lying fool. "I know she'd love me, even if I lost all my fame and became a nobody. There aren't many women I can say that about." Brent snarled in disgust. "I can assure you the only reason Loree got girlfriend status with me is because she threatened to kill Gail if I wouldn't let her. Loree's only famous because of being associated with me. She has no worth or talent, except to be a lying and murdering bitch who wants to kill Gail for the unpardonable sin of being the woman I dream about." Brent headed for the door and then turned to face the executives once more. "Oh, by the way, I just found out that Gail is the great niece of Howard Hughes. I believe you've heard of him." Then Brent shut the door behind him and never turned back.

He left the executives behind, not at all certain he had a future left with Star Trek or Paramount, or even Hollywood, because Hollywood is a small town, and he had just "told off" the Paramount big wigs. Paramount seemed a bit concerned over Brent's anger towards them and offered years later to let him help write the script for their 2002 movie *Star Trek: Nemesis*, since he was in love with a writer.

But, Jesuits, nervous as hell over Brent's adoration of the great niece of Howard Hughes, made sure that *Star Trek: Nemesis* flopped at the theatres, and that Brent had a pitiful career as an actor. Jesuits ensured that Brent's fame as Data of Star Trek would dwindle down to nothingness.

However, in the twenty-first century Brent would find fame again as the husband of the great niece of Howard Hughes! Gail would end up having an entire cable news channel created about her in 2012, called the Gabrielle Chana FOX News channel.

Brent managed to get a court order for Loree to leave his house in 1999, but did not expect her to obey it. Therefore, he just packed his bags and left his house, and went to live elsewhere, away from Loree. He didn't care if he had to sleep in a trailer, because he was so happy to have Gail back.

Though Brent didn't believe in Jesus in December 1999, it all made sense to him what Gail told him, "Yes, this Loree had to be a Vatican agent." She had even told him in 1993 that she was a Jesuit. He didn't know what a Jesuit was in 1993, but after reading Jack Chick's *Smokescreens* and after his experience with Loree, he knew now that they had to be behind the Nazi holocaust, just like Jack Chick said. Only a brilliant organization, with genius political sense, could commit the atrocities of the Nazi holocaust and manage to pin all the blame on the Germans. Only a brilliant organization could use drug-rape to extort him into have the girlfriend from hell from 1992 until now.

It seemed that he and Gail were up against an empire. Later, in 2011, when Brent would accept Jesus Christ as His Saviour, he would believe that it was Jesus who spoke to Gail in that still, small voice at 2 a.m. in Seattle and said, "You're enemy is the Roman Catholic Church."

Though Brent didn't believe in God, he knew that when Gail told him that Loree was a Vatican agent, whose job was to sabotage his love for Gail, she was right. He came to the conclusion that Gail's own brilliance put it together. Either way, he had no doubt that Loree was a Vatican agent assigned to him to sabotage his love for Gail, and he wasn't playing the Paramount Studios girlfriend game anymore.

At this point in his life, he had put some of his acting earnings from his years working for Paramount into annuities and other investments, and was able to live off of these. He wanted his money "tied up" too, so that Loree could not go to town with his credit cards anymore.

Loree had often stolen his credit cards and went on shopping sprees at the mall, buying tons of clothes or other things, and had reduced him from a millionaire to one who had an income like a physician, not like a Hollywood star. The world did not realize what a spendthrift Loree was with his money. Confronting her about it did no good, "Well, I am your wife, so I'm entitled to use your credit cards!"

It seemed that once she managed to plaster her photos next to his in the press and the Internet, her next step was to steal his credit cards at every opportunity and spend all his money. The Brent Spiner fans often commented how Loree seemed to live at the mall spending money. If only they knew how she did it, by stealing Brent's credit cards!

Therefore, Brent felt he had nothing to lose to kick Paramount in the rear about Loree, because, if he kept Loree, he'd lose so much money because of her, that it would be the same as not having his Paramount job any ways. Now that he felt he made Gail safer by letting the world know that he wanted Gail, and not Loree, he finally felt free to kick the bitch out of his house.

Possibly because Gail had taken back Brent, he thought, and because the Jesuits at Paramount were worried about bad press, they would allow Brent to kick out Loree from his house. But even if they would not, he'd had enough.

But Brent had no power to stop the fake photos that Jesuits posted everywhere online and in the tabloids that made Brent and Loree appear to be a couple. Now that Brent had officially kicked Loree out of his house, the Jesuits flooded even more fake photos of Brent and Loree together—a form of damage control.

He decided that because he had dared to rebel against Paramount, that his Hollywood career was finished. He began to make plans to go to medical school. Even if they don't destroy my acting career, he thought, which they will, because I'm not playing their game anymore, I'd like to study medicine to help Gail, because those Jesuits are always attacking her health. She needs a doctor for a husband.

Brent had considered medicine for a career as a young man and practically had a degree in pre-med studies. He would enroll in U.C.L.A. medical school and graduate as a physician in 2006.

The Forbidden Abyss

When Gail asked Brent (January 30, 2000) on her wiretapped phone to expose on the L.A. news that he had taken Loree McBride to court, the Jesuits crashed Alaska Airlines Flight 261 head first into the Pacific Ocean right off the coast of Los Angeles on the next day, the day the news was to air. That day was January 31, 2000. The horrific jet crash, head-first into the Pacific killed all onboard, so it eclipsed any news coverage that Brent had taken Loree McBride to court for her crimes against Gail.

Because this crash happened in Southern California, it would definitely eclipse any coverage of Brent's case against Loree McBride on L.A. news. Apparently, Brent tried to go public over his case against Loree and the Jesuits decided to create a major news story to eclipse any coverage of Brent taking Loree McBride to court.

Alaska 261 was a scheduled international passenger flight from Lic. Gustavo Diaz Ordaz International Airport in Vallarta, Mexico to Seattle-Tacoma International Airport in Seattle, Washington, with an intermediate stop at San Francisco International Airport in San Francisco, California. Jesuits used their space age technology to accomplish the crash, making it appear to be caused only by inadequate maintenance due to in-flight failure of the horizontal stabilizer trim system jackscrew assembly's acme nut threads. Because of the crash, Brent's story about taking Loree to court never made it to the front page of any paper in the Western United States, and the Jesuits knew, because of their crash, that this story would not go any further than California (where Brent and Loree lived) or Washington (where Gail lived at the time).

Jesuits loved to crash jets, and this would not be their first attempt to use jet crashes to accomplish their purposes against the famous men who loved Gail. They would do it again on September 11, 2001 to deter Brent Spiner and with the November 12, 2001 American Airlines Flight 587 crash in Queens, New York to deter Vladimir Putin.

Jesuits started setting wildfires all over the country, probably to make it appear that the fires Gail put out at the mobile home in South Carolina were just random incidents. All of a sudden, everything all over the country became contaminated.

Gail knew it was the Jesuits. And she knew they were trying to frame their crimes on somebody else.

Both Brent and Gail's mother wanted Gail to get breast biopsies, so she found other physicians who did two biopsies (Feb. 2000 and Oct. 2000) for her, using local anesthesia. However, before the February 2000 biopsy, the Jesuits contaminated something she ate or ingested with blood thinners and she lost so much blood from the biopsy she couldn't get out of bed for two weeks. She went to God in prayer. He told her she had cancer, but He'd take it away if she'd write for Him. So she wrote *Emerald Towers,* and God blanketed her heart with peace. She never worried about the cancer, she knew God would keep His end of the deal. Good news, both biopsies turned out negative for cancer.

So in January, February and March 2000, she started writing again. She had laid aside her *Silver Skies* and hadn't written a thing since 1996, because she only wrote to make it up to Brent that she couldn't give him her body.

She worked on a short story called *Emerald Towers* in the spring of 2000, and ordered some books from her Writer's Digest Book Club about short story writing. *Emerald Towers* became her victim impact statement, because that person in that story was Gail. The only thing about the story not true was that she was not diagnosed positive for breast cancer. But everything else about that story is true about the emotions and what she went through as a result of the Jesuits sabotaging her love for Brent Spiner.

So she worked on *Emerald Towers* from February to April 2000, and in April 2000, she mailed it to the Writer's Digest Writing Contest. When she went to the Post Office to mail it, there was a very long line. Jesuits always flooded her life with their agents whenever she did anything to promote her writings.

It was January 2000, when Jesuit contamination of her supplements became brazen. Now that she knew the Vatican was her enemy, the pressure just got stronger. Her son was ill all the time, and missing a lot of school.

After a lot of harassment and mess with her son's school and after threatening to call KIRO news and expose this conspiracy against her son on television, and then making personal visits to the courthouse and complaining to the principal and basically making a big stink, she prevented her son from having to appear before a judge, by the skin of her teeth.

She also got the help of his psychologist, who did not recommend that her son appear before a judge, that it would be bad for his mental health.

That was very stressful for her. Because of the harassment her son got at his school, he failed sixth grade, when he was normally an honor roll student. And he was sick all the time. Part of it was stress induced. Part of it was germ warfare launched against him and his mother. They were catching all sorts of things.

They had a drought in the fall of 2000 and the winter of 2001 *during Seattle's rainy season.*

Gail went through a very expensive divorce from August 2000 to May 31, 2001. Her Jesuit husband disputed about everything, not about to relinquish his control over his wife without a fight. A pretty nice guy when she first married him in 1985, Jesuits replaced him bit by bit with his Jesuit clone, so that when Gail decided to end the marriage, he was a cold and cruel Jesuit.

He forced Gail to go to a guardian ad litem because he expressed concern over Gail's effect on their son, claiming she was not mentally fit to be a mother. So Gail visited a clinical psychologist, who acted as the guardian ad litem for the divorce, and he asked Gail all sorts of nosy questions about her personal life, that she really wanted to keep out of the divorce. Gail just wanted to divorce her husband without complications, so she could be with Brent. The less she had to talk about Brent, the better. She feared bringing Brent into the divorce could introduce complications into her ability to marry Brent after the divorce. But the guardian ad litem asked too many nosy questions, even mentioning Brent and Loree, because Gail's husband brought up the subject, and Gail ended up opening a little bit about Brent Spiner and Loree and she got written off as crazy.

And then September 11, 2001 happened. Gail thought. . .my God, as if they hadn't done enough to me already. . .What more could they do? She could tell that Brent was trying to find a way to use the airlines to meet her. She had made friends with her step-dad's niece, who was a stewardess. Gail sensed that Brent planned to use her somehow to find a way to meet Gail. Gail was just about to

The Forbidden Abyss

get a job at Sears.

So that morning on September 11th Gail had to show up for a medical appointment for Sears to give a urine sample, to determine she wasn't a drug user and as she drove to the doctor's office, she saw this water main, with water just going up like fifty feet up into the air like a geyser.

She thought, boy, something major's happened today. This is really strange. . .with litter all over the road. She learned to feel the mood of the Vatican. She could tell something big had happened. The streets seemed eerily quiet. When she got to the doctor's office, everybody was glued to the news.

Oh dear. . .something terrible's happened. They all looked pale. "What happened?" she said.

"You didn't hear?"

"No."

"Two airplanes hit the World Trade Center in New York City and one hit the Pentagon, and all the firefighters and the police died."

Gail thought, "Oh my God. . . this is World War III. Those Jesuits. . .they never give up."

She was in shock September 11th. She hadn't accepted that they would go this far. . . to keep Brent and her apart. See, he was planning on using the airlines. . .to try to meet her.

They found a way to eliminate that possibility. Besides her dad was a retired airline captain. In rebellion, she just refused to watch the news for most of 9-11-01. She said, "I'm not going to give them the satisfaction of making me miserable today."

I know they're trying to intimidate me. And I know they're trying to intimidate Brent. I'm going to watch *Gladiator* all day.

The spirit of *Gladiator*, especially the beginning battle scene, mirrored her heart on September 11, 2001. She raised her fist in outrage, and dared Loree McBride and her Jesuits to kill her. Gail watched the beginning scene of Gladiator over and over from about 9 a.m till about 3 p.m.

She spoke to the walls, knowing the bugs in her mom's house picked up everything she said and that the Vatican and all the world leaders heard her. "You don't scare me a bit! So you go and kill three thousand people! You scumbags of the earth. You haven't crushed my spirit. Now let's watch the news! I know this is going to be really interesting."

So she turned it on. . .oh yeah. . .ah ha. . .oh yeah. . .She watched the scenes of the Twin Towers crumbling to the ground over and over. Her lower lip scowled, and something inside her refused to cower. Rather, her heart rose up in triumph like a General Patton, and she flowed into the battle music from *Gladiator* as she watched the beginning battle scene of *Gladiator* over and over. Yes, this was her response to 9/11/2001! She would lead the forces of the world into battle against the Vatican!

The next day she drove out on the road, and screamed at the top of her voice, "I know you want to kill me." They had tried to use tricky vehicular homicide methods, using these big Mack trucks, right after Jesus told her in that still, small voice that her enemy was more than just Loree McBride, it was the Vatican. Once she and Brent knew Loree was a Vatican agent, they became more brazen in their attempts on Gail's life, and tried to kill her. . . about ten times. . .

on the road...She decided that when it was her time to go, it was her time to go. God protected her, they didn't get her, though, at times, she missed a deadly accident by a hair's length, it seemed.

There was one time in Seattle (around 2000), she heard a gunshot. She heard the bullet ricochet off the tin roof that was the view from her second floor bedroom window. She was really getting fed up with this Jesuit business. She said, "I know they're trying to intimidate me."

The Jesuits shot the gun in her apartment complex and she heard the bullet ricochet off the tin roof just outside her second story bedroom window. She leaped up from her bed in her bedroom, and spoke to the bugs in her room, knowing the Jesuits and much of the world listened. "Alright, I dare you to shoot me, you Vatican whores. I know you're trying to kill me. I heard that bullet that ricocheted off the roof!" She sniffed to herself in defiance. "Yeah, I'm going to go outside *right now* and take extra time walking my dog! Whoever you are, go ahead and shoot me! I dare you!"

Gail rounded up her collie, and then she went out the door with the dog. They didn't shoot her. She returned after a prolonged walk with Henry, their collie.

Whenever Jesuits tried to intimidate her, she'd just go out and dare them. She'd say, "Go ahead and kill me."

September 12th, 2001, she screamed from the bottom of her lungs, "I know you want to kill me! Why don't you do it, so you'll quit killing everybody else. Maybe if you kill me, you'll quit killing everybody." Gail always became furious anytime Jesuits killed people. September 11, 2011 made her steam like a volcano. She was outraged. "I just want to go out and move into an apartment, because I know that when I'm by myself, that you're going to try to kill me. Why don't you just get it over with, so you'll quit *killing everybody*!"

By 2000, all December 1996 photos of Loree's cold, defiant stare as a depressed Brent stared at her, vanished from public view, creating the illusion that in 1996 Brent had sexual heaven with the woman who made him want to kill himself. Those rare photos of him with her showing his disgust and her defiant, hard eyes, disappeared. Around this time the Jesuits decided to change her image from publicist to filmmaker. They created a movie called *Real Doll* and listed Loree as its producer.

Oh my God, Brent thought in 2000, *that* woman, a *producer?* He laughed so hard at the thought, that his stomach hurt. The extent of her conversations with him were, "I want to suck your dick" or "Time to make love!" while she pounced on him like an animal. But as crazy as he knew it to be, he also knew how brilliant Jesuits were with propaganda. Yeah, that woman will get credit for being a legitimate producer, while they'll make sure my brilliant Gail's writings will go nowhere. They have to turn Loree into a producer, because too many know I'm in love with a brilliant writer.

Some producer Loree would make! If any movie came from her that the audience wouldn't boo to death at the theatres, it would most certainly not be *her work*. Some Jesuit did all the work and gave her credit for it to boost her image, to make her believable as Brent's wife. The Jesuits just wanted to slap a more respectable title onto her than that of "publicist" to give her credibility as

The Forbidden Abyss

Brent's "wife". After all, Loree was competing with a brilliant writer—Gail.

So the Jesuits needed to beef up Loree's image, make her believable as the wife of Brent Spiner. At the same time, they would portray Gail to the world as a middle-aged crazy woman that Brent would never desire, and ensure that Gail's writings would go nowhere.

The world must never see any undoctored photos of Brent with Loree, or they'd know how nauseating he found her. The world must believe he found his drug rapist so irresistible, he married her! So, of course, all the December 1996 photos of him staring at her with revulsion vanished.

The Jesuit fabrications about his love life on the Internet disgusted him. But at least, Gail still loved him, and understood his predicament.

Jesuits upped their game, and unleashed all hell against Gail as she started divorce proceedings against her husband, so that she could be with Brent. In amazement he saw this shy, devoted Christian housewife and mother transform into Catherine the Great and king David. Though at that time, he just saw a woman hold up against an empire that would have made a lesser woman insane.

Though he had plunged from major star of a major television series in the 1990s, to an actor lucky to land bit parts in the twenty-first century, he would not give up his love for Gail. Jesuits punished him for this. But hang all else. His love for her, he'd die for her.

Gail, after a long and expensive divorce, defended Brent against Loree with some of the legal statements or forms that became part of her divorce legal paperwork. However, when she mailed her statements to her attorney, Brent received what she wrote, but her attorney received a Jesuit counterfeit version that made her appear crazy.

After Jesuits caused her son to flunk sixth grade (1999/2000) in the public schools, Gail pulled him out of the public schools to home school him for the 2000/2001 school year. But Jesuits used her ex-husband to stress out her son, so that he became ill from stress, and unable to concentrate on his schoolwork, screaming at his mother when she tried to force him to do schoolwork.

Because Gail believed that she and her son were victims of a Vatican conspiracy, her ex-husband was able to get custody through a clinical psychologist he hired to evaluate Gail during the divorce process. This psychologist concluded that Gail suffered from persecutorial delusions and paranoia, and that because she shared these delusions with her son, she was unfit to be his parent.

Gail did not want to discuss Brent Spiner or Loree McBride during the divorce, but was forced to, because her ex-husband brought up Brent and his "girlfriend" in charges he brought against her, that alleged Gail lacked the mental health needed to be her son's mother. Her ex-husband did this so that he could get custody of Gail's son and force Gail to pay him child support.

Therefore, the divorce judge felt that Gail was so mentally ill she should not have custody of her son, but he concluded that she had enough mental health to get a job and support herself! And so, Gail, who had not worked her entire marriage, but stayed home to care for her child, was thrown out into the world to fend for herself after the divorce became final on May 31, 2001. Even worse, she was expected to pay her ex-husband child support, starting in 2003.

Ironically, the Mukilteo school the Jesuits used to torment Gail's son was in a top rated school district. Jesuits left no stone unturned in their campaign to

Brent's Forbidden Ground

discredit Gail and her son. When the dad put her son in the Lake Stevens School District in early April 2001, her son, apparently, did well there and Gail was so glad to hear that her son did well in school under his dad. So, the combination of Gail's homeschooling and the Lake Stevens School District worked, and her son passed sixth grade this time with flying colors.

From then on, he was an honor roll student. The Vatican left him alone, while he was with his dad.

Once the divorce became final, Gail was not allowed, under court order, to meet with her son, unless the dad was present. Gail decided to sacrifice her time with her son, to protect Brent. Therefore, Gail never saw her son again until 2010.

However, Russian President Vladimir Putin had custody of Gail's son from December 7, 2003 to around 2009. Her son became very close to Vladimir's two daughters during this time. When Gail reinstated Brent as her main lover in February 2006, her men eventually decided (around 2008 or 2009) that her son needed to go back to the dad, so that Gail could see her son again.

When they returned her son to his dad, all memories of his time with Vladimir were removed, and false memories of his time with his dad (from 2003 to 2009) were inserted in place of his real memories with Vladimir. Vladimir used to joke with Gail brain to brain (2003 to 2006) that perhaps he would allow her son to marry one of his daughters. Her son was especially bonded to the younger of Vladimir's two daughters.

Her son had only stayed with Vladimir, because Vladimir planned to marry Gail. Now that it looked like Brent would marry Gail rather than Vladimir, Gail's son needed to go back to his father, so that he could see his mother again someday. This happened around 2008 or 2009.

Forced in early 2001 to document her work search (because she had no job except that of wife, mother and teacher to her son), to home school her son, and to visit a psychologist who assessed her mental fitness to be a mother, Gail's schedule barely gave her room to breathe. Perhaps Jesus allowed her son to be removed from home school, to give Gail a break.

When her divorce was final, she lost custody of her son. Jesuits arranged for her son to fail sixth grade (1999/2000) to ensure the dad would get custody, because he was always out to sea and Gail spent the most time with her son. So though she fought for custody, she almost felt relieved that she lost it, because she felt so helpless trying to protect her son against the almighty Jesuit empire. Perhaps with his dad, Jesuits would lose interest in him, and leave him alone. She knew they overwhelmed her son to discredit her as a possible wife for Brent.

The divorce final on May 31, 2001, Gail waited for her Brent to come and claim her as his bride.

In July 2001, Loree blew up her clone in a car. She wanted to show Brent that she would make good on her threat if he tried anything. She told him it was Gail at first. And then after he broke down about it, she laughed and told him it was a clone of hers.

Brent remembered that momentous day when he almost boarded a jet to meet Gail. Right before he boarded his jet to go to her, Jesuits crashed jets into

The Forbidden Abyss

the World Trade Center towers and the Pentagon. That day was September 11, 2001. His flight was cancelled. While the World Trade Towers crumbled to their death, so did his hopes for a marriage to his Gail.

Gail, in fury, raised her fist to heaven and screamed from her car in Florida, her new home, "I know you Jesuits want to kill me. Why don't you just kill me right now and get it over with, so you'll quit killing everybody else!"

On September 25, 2001 Gail decided she needed a President in her life and fell in love with Russian President Vladimir Putin, who happened to be Brent's favorite politician.

Brent liked Vladimir Putin, he was always his favorite world leader. He figured maybe he would be able to go see Gail and satisfy her, since Brent wasn't able to. He didn't have a Loree McBride to contend with, but then, well, Lyudmila happened.

Nine months after Brent dared to claim his Gail, nine months after September 11, 2001—the Jesuit press reported in June 2002 that Loree McBride gave birth to Brent's son. To ensure that Brent would never dare marry Gail, Loree impregnated herself with Brent's stolen semen. With the birth of Brent's son, Loree had recouped her losses. Even though Gail reinstated Brent in December 1999, because Loree now could claim to be the mother of Brent's child, Gail didn't stand a chance in hell of marrying Brent Spiner. Loree laughed, gloating in her victory against Brent and Gail.

Brent felt Loree's noose tightening again around his neck. He wanted to gag to get his breath.

Even worse, Gail was all wrapped up in Vladimir Putin, too poor to have the Internet as she struggled on food stamps in Tallahassee, Florida, waiting for Vladimir to marry her.

Perhaps if she knew that Loree had impregnated herself with Brent's semen (from semen Loree obtained during her drug rape of him in 1992), Gail may have retained Brent as her primary lover in 2002. Gail never really abandoned Brent. She just got discouraged about him after 9-11-2001 and figured she'd have better luck with a President.

From 1994 to 2011 Jesuits denied Brent his Gail, while he longed to write, call or feel her. Because Gail so longed for her Brent in 2006, Vladimir allowed Brent to share the brain-to-brain loving that he had discovered with Gail in 2003.

Brent Spiner Returns
2006 to 2011

In February 2006, Gail challenged Vladimir to give her some much needed financial support, to show that he was willing to stick his neck out for Gail and not be so obsessed with his public image. When Vladimir failed to come through, Gail decided that at least Brent was willing to talk to her on the phone; Vladimir wouldn't even do that, so Gail reinstated Brent as her main lover again.

Brent jumped at this, thrilled to have his Gail back, and Brent and Gail's minds and bodies mingled and caressed each other, with flesh and flesh and spirits and thoughts swirling together. They called it "brain-to-brain loving". But was it real or a long winded fantasy of his insane mind? If it was a fantasy, it was his only reason for living, and it made both of them feel married to each other forever. At this point, Gail only felt morally comfortable with loving one man at a time in "brain to brain loving", so Vladimir got scuttled aside until 2010.

In 2010 Gail got the Internet, after not having it since 2001. When she did a Google search on Loree, her heart went out to Brent. Loree claimed to be his wife and to have fathered his child! Only Gail knew his heart. She tried to reinstate in him faith in his manhood and created a website to present him to the world as a man with depths and breadths. He yearned to be all that Gail believed about him.

In 2011, Gail sang "Moon River" from her new YouTube channel, with an expression that rivaled Audrey Hepburn. How that voice soothed Brent as he embraced his sheets for her. While she whispered her songs into his ears as he clutched the dummy he had of her, he felt reborn. In ecstatic embraces with her as his pillow, her voice swam in his heart.

Ah, those fantasies of her as he rolled in his sheets. That year, Gail's "Moon River" drifted through his consciousness, in and out like a dream. He'd often clutch his pillow, his Gail, and surge his dreams of manhood into her. Her voice resonated throughout his days, overpowering him; his desire for her overwhelmed him. That voice believed in him and made him want to live. That voice, which he heard for the first time in 1990, when he dreamed of her each night in his bed.

His longings for Gail and for love and honor had overwhelmed him with each passing year. Then hearing her voice again in 2011, he could stand it no longer. It seemed 1990 had resurrected into his heart, and Loree had never raped him. Those happier days returned, when he worshipped the very air Gail breathed, when he kissed her footsteps with delight and adoration.

The Forbidden Abyss

By June 2011, he could stand the decades-long charade no longer. He imagined Gail bent over her computer, getting a back and shoulder ache from arguing too much with one of her book reviewers. Most labeled her as paranoid schizophrenic.

While she made YouTube videos to defend Brent, people under Jesuit mind control, posed as book critics, and labeled his Gail as crazy. After all, why would big-shot star Brent want the nobody Gail, who, despite winning secret Nobel Prizes and Academy Awards, could only land a clerk's job. Gail, outraged over Loree, dared to expose Loree McBride as the fraud who drug raped him in September 1992, and that he never married the drug-rapist, his rapist and stalker.

June 2011, he looked over his shoulder and out the bedroom window of his Malibu home. Jesuit agent Loree McBride did not lurk about his shadows. Loree seemed nowhere in sight.

Brent heard no steps in the grass, and shut the window until it clanked. For the first time in twenty-one years, he felt he could reach out and touch Gail. Hearing her voice over and over through her new YouTube channel, his longings for Gail overwhelmed him.

He scanned his surroundings. Thank God, Loree seemed nowhere in sight. Loree had denied him his dream woman for decades, long enough. Time for things to change. Though Loree threatened Gail's death if he dared one step in her direction, he felt he had to go forward with his life. So he created a YouTube channel for her, to reach out and touch that soul that returned him to light and happiness.

He could stand it no longer. To Gail, he sent off a "friend" invitation through her YouTube channel, then returned to his computer. He felt bad for Gail, who suffered because he allowed Loree, a criminal and murderer, to have public girlfriend status with him. From 1993 to 1998, he felt it better to have Loree in his house, rather than away from him, maybe breaking into Gail's home or planting a bomb on her car.

Now he dared to contact Gail and hoped and prayed his stalker for nineteen years, Loree McBride, would ignore the move.

Even in her fifties, he felt Gail a ravishing beauty; his heart and eyes seeing her through a heart deeply in love. But how his nerves rattled him, as they often did, whenever he made any bold move to claim his Gail.

Thoughts of Gail made his heart float in the clouds. He much preferred floating in the clouds with Gail to nightmares about Loree. His dreams of Gail shushed the nightmares, so he finally wrote her.

But if Loree won, he'd end it all the next day, and snuff his existence into oblivion. Better to die, than to go on without Gail—his life had become a fragile shell enclosing torrents. Oh, how he longed for Gail, to hear her voice, that voice that made him walk the clouds in 1990.

Gail floated in his arms, he soared in ecstasies, his one finger, pecking at his computer with rapid fire strokes, dancing to the beats of his heart. That mid June 2011, he braced in anticipation, while Gail defended Brent online against lies that crushed his heart. A month later, she checked her YouTube inbox and noticed his friend invitation.

Brent's Forbidden Ground

"Brent, I don't check my YouTube messages very often. . .My God, you're so brave."

"Indeed, you are correct. I don't wish to have many people know about this channel. I would go to the ends of the earth to protect you my dear, don't worry what a few childish Internet goons think of me. I invite them to say what they will, I am not afraid of their words and neither should you be."

"Oh, Brent, some Jesuit is after you already. Just because we're writing each other."

"You die, bastard Brent Spiner! The Jesuit Order is onto you and your days are numbered." Reading the Jesuit words at his YouTube channel, he winced.

Of course, the Jesuit drug-rapist never missed a beat. She wearied and depressed him, making him need Gail more. But did he jeopardize the woman he adored, just because he couldn't stand it and had to write her?

Gail, finally able to write her decades-long lover, seemed to float in the air and swim over the threat. "I don't think you're trying to win friends and influence people with your latest Recent Activity. A bit of a perverse sense of humor there, hey? But then, it doesn't appear that most people even know about your YouTube channel. Sixteen views? I suspect you like this."

He saw that his courage to write her set her face aglow in her videos. The glow on her face made his dreams of her seem more real as he made love to her in his sheets. He saw that glowing face now as he moved over his sheets for her. "That last Jesuit attack gave me a startle." If he pulled back now, that radiance would vanish. "And I can already feel the tensions growing around us. But I'm not going to let that scare me away from finally writing you so directly like this."

Gail seemed excited about her newfound way to communicate with her brain to brain lover. "You think we could communicate through Skype, face to face?"

Brent shuddered to think what could happen if he used Skype with her. "Should the Jesuits get too close and try to do something terrible, I can always claim this channel's a fabrication, whereas if there were any videos of us face to face, that could be devastating. This world's not a safe place for you and I. Even as I write you now, I have to watch my back. At any moment, a Jesuit could seize my Internet or hack into my computer and this could all be for naught." Brent dared to hope his courage would not endanger Gail. "I must admit, I rather enjoy seeing you make public videos about me. The fact that you are able to bear yourself openly in front of everyone and tell the entire world how much you love me, something I wish I could desperately do for you, shows so much courage and sincerity in your feelings. Although I enjoy our personal intimacy throughout the days and nights in brain to brain loving, sometimes I wish we didn't have to be so secret."

If only she lay right next to him in his bed, his dreams of her would become more vivid, the brain to brain lovemaking would burst with excitement. "On to other matters. . .I had a very vivid dream about you last night. I will just come out and say it. I was wondering if I could get a video of the 'spicier' variety from you." He just had to get something more intimate from her, to help him hold on. "Your workout video was adorable, but this time. . .I want to see you in your nightwear. In bed, if possible, maybe with a few candles lit, playing one of my songs for you." Perhaps, within a month, the Jesuits would cut off his com-

The Forbidden Abyss

munication with her. "I just want to see you, and be able to do more than just imagine what it would be like if I was there in your bedroom with you physically. I want to see you with my eyes and hear you with my ears. I know the public may not see me as the romantic type, but I would be hopelessly floored to come home and see you in the bed, full out ambience and lighting and everything I could possibly dream of, like something out of a movie made real."

Brent dropped back onto his bed, shut his eyes, grabbed his pillow and dreamed. Dare he say more? The brain to brain loving helped, but he longed to see her, to let her beauty melt his soul before he merged with her brain-to-brain. "I apologize, I bet those cheeks are blushing. I know you are rather discreet about your sensuality and I would never pressure you to do anything you wouldn't like to." Because he often dragged under mountains of Jesuit pressure, he needed to see his "wife" nude for his morale. "If you wish, you can simply bat my hand away from the cookie jar."

"I really don't think you've had much of a sex life, except for our brain to brain sessions, because I really believe you've been loyal to me. I'll come up with something for you in a video."

He couldn't risk losing any more videos, especially nudes from Gail. For the first time in his relationship with Gail, he created an email for her. "I just wanted to let you in on a new email I created for you and I to correspond with."

"It is BrentSpiner@email.com. Rest assured, that it is my private email, and nobody else but you has been informed. You won't have to worry about any public associates of mine destroying your messages or forging my name, as they have done in the past. I just want you to have it as a backup. Missing you dearly, Brent Spiner."

Gail sent him nudes within a week. He was floored. Apparently, she felt that God respected lovers, especially lovers who had vastness, forgiveness, humility; and above all, commitment to protect and honor their partner, even unto death. He soaked her nudes in, famished, absorbing all her curves and movements. How he adored her, not just her body, but all of her, her spirit, her soul, her intellect. To see her nude, with depth of feeling towards him, and a desire to nurture and thrill him, thrilled him to his very core.

So brave. So beautiful. She made him feel like a knight in shining armor, who swayed over and protected his princess. His depression transformed into elation. Addicted to Gail, he needed her for his sanity, and for meaning in his life. "You have no idea how beautiful you are. My lady, you have me speechless! Excuse me, while I climb back into my chair! Right now, I feel like the luckiest man alive. I viewed both of your videos, including the private one you sent to my personal email. I can't decide what I like best, the tantalizing peek at your voluptuous breasts as you strip for me like a vixen, or your adorable, girlish bashfulness in the public rendition for me on your channel. Hearing the warm, melting resonance of your singing was simply icing on the cake. More! Is it my birthday? I feel truly special.

"My Gail, sometimes I don't understand how you could be so shy of your sensuality. You are a breathtakingly gorgeous woman with such class and depth. Of course, I know from our brain to brain that there's quite a bit more behind that shy schoolgirl persona you tried to portray in those devilishly teasing videos. You naughty girl, you. I can only hope that the Japanese side of you will come out to play more fearlessly in the future. Maybe not in public, but in private...well, you know how to reach me.

"Even though I can only have you brain-to-brain, through these amazing videos you make for me, I feel truly blessed to have a woman like you in my life. They say ninety percent of sex is all mental any way, and baby you give me 9001%. How many other husbands out there have timelessly beautiful wives that are devoted and adventurous enough to make them sexy videos? Even after all these years, the passion within your soul is still so powerful for me, and you show me every day that you would do anything to bring me happiness and pleasure. You're every man's dream.

"Oh boy, have you got me riled up like a colt. I will bite my tongue now. Thank you so much again and again for doing this for me. I know it's because you love me, my dear, but I'll never stop expressing my gratitude for everything you do to show me you care. I appreciate you, and I love you. Your man, Brent Spiner."

His telepathic orgasms with her, reached such sublimity and beauty swirling with passion and tenderness, he could live on an orgasm with her for months. Some thrilled him to the core, and sustained him for years.

But because of the brilliant lies in the press about his love life, poor Gail suffered in her courage to try to portray to the world the real Brent. "As you know, the Jesuits have tried to portray me as crazy, claiming that you've never contacted me and that you don't even know of my existence." He knew she sighed in her longings for him, and yearned to feel Brent's skin on hers, to taste his sensitive mouth or feel his loving breath on her face.

He, too, longed to be more real with her, he also longed for her touch, her voice, her eyes.

"Unfortunately," she wrote, "this kind of propaganda against me makes it easier for Jesuits to harm me and frame it on you, so I thought it good strategy to post at my YouTube channel some of what you've said to me. I'm very proud of the articulate and manly way you express yourself to me."

To read her very words right in front of him, thrilled him. He bit into a sandwich, and fired back to his brave Gail. "My dear Gail, whatever you feel comfortable sharing with the world is just fine by me. I don't think you should ever be afraid, or hold back." Brent knew Gail down to her very soul, brain-to-brain gave you emotion and memory reads. He knew that Gail had a mother who screamed at her, "Stupid. Selfish. You will never be any good."

"Why don't you put back up the videos that you've removed in the past? Some of those wound up on Jesuit sites, but why let that stop you? After all, Jesuits aren't the only people out there that may stumble across those sites. Whenever you remove one of your videos, or try to censor yourself, the Jesuits win. Freedom is squashed by the suppression of information." She denied her power and strength, but he fueled it and believed in her power. "Be free with yourself Gail, and show them how powerful you are."

The usurper and Jesuit rapist Loree had reigned over him long enough. She'd posted lies in the press, used fake and touched up photos, to make it appear Brent married the drug-rapist and even willingly and knowingly had a child with her. Time for truth to take a turn. He wanted Gail to stand up to her, to not be afraid to show the world her beautiful and courageous heart. "Do what you feel

The Forbidden Abyss

is right. No matter what, I will always be by your side."

"Something disturbing has come to Vladimir's attention. He didn't want to risk sharing this information with any human translators, so he sat down with his Russian-to-English dictionary for about six hours and tried to do it himself." Brent trembled, thinking of Loree.

He then pasted Russian President Vladimir's message onto his email to Gail. "To Gail, my dear love, I work with my trusted secret agents trying to kill the Jesuits. It has come to my attention that they were very brave. They had a secret, internal website, that they have now made public."

Russian President Vladimir, another of Gail's brain-to-brain lovers, had a worried face lately. Though excited about Brent's ability to write Gail, he warned Brent about this new Jesuit website. It appeared Jesuits wasted no time to retaliate against Brent's courage.

To Brent, it seemed that Loree again breathed down his throat. He loosened the collar around his neck to breathe. "The Jesuits have stepped up their game and it looks like we may have to as well. Just look at what happened to their past targets." Brent sighed in disgust. His stomach turned, he wrote Gail, "I developed a strange headache just looking through this thing and I still can't shake it."

He loved her for over twenty years, and finally created a YouTube channel to write her. Now Loree, with her Jesuit cohorts, threatened death to Gail, just because he dared to contact the only woman he wanted to marry for twenty years. How unjust! Did he endanger her life, because he dared to write her now? God forbid. Perhaps, he should not have? Oh, but how his heart and conscience began to feel free.

A month earlier, Jesuits would never own Loree as one of them, brushing over her hard eyes, giving her a softer image. They now revealed her real eyes to the world, the hard ones—the eyes of the Jesuit drug-rapist. He knew it meant only one thing—they were sure of Gail's death! All those years he feared for Gail's life, and when he finally dared to end the Loree McBride charade, Loree lunged for Gail like a rattlesnake leaping to strike, trying to force him back into submission to her.

He lifted his hands to his face, scraping his fingers down his face in terror. He remembered all those photos Loree showed him of a mutilated Gail, the images flashed before his mind, they exploded into his consciousness. Yes, that Loree was at it again, terrorizing him into submission with death threats.

Brent found the website Vladimir pointed out to him. It divided into four sections: Mission, Agents, Targets, and Log In.

Under Agents for the Order of the Jesuits, he saw a photo of the beautiful, but deadly, Loree McBride—known disgustingly as his "wife" to the brainwashed world. Her brazen, hard eyes laughed at him from her photo. The sight of her jumped at him. He froze in terror, revolting memories leaked into his consciousness. He hushed them away into oblivion—looked away, wouldn't think about her. Would only think of Gail. No, not Loree again! His emotions froze.

Next, came Camila Alves, Matthew McConaughey's Brazilian model "wife", another Loree McBride, a Jesuit, who almost caused Matthew to commit suicide.

Brent's Forbidden Ground

Next on the list, Lyudmila Putina, the demure Russian President "wife". She put Vladimir into clinical depression. If not for this Jesuit agent, perhaps Vladimir could have spared Gail bankruptcy in 2002. Because Lyudmila blocked Vladimir, he could not give Gail any money.

Next agent, Gail's ex-husband, a Jesuit clone, who abused and degraded her during a sixteen year marriage.

Next, her former allergy physician. Using temporary mind control, Jesuits extracted from him her allergy records, causing many allergy migraines for Gail.

Last, her former sleaze psychiatrist, a Jesuit clone, who, in order to destroy her, wanted to put her on dangerous psych drugs.

Under Targets, Jesuits listed photos of Gail, of Brent himself; of Gail's Russian President sweet heart Vladimir Putin. Then underneath these, they had the gall to list Gail's brief brain to brain lover, world famous actor Matthew McConaughey, star of the *Silver Skies* movie made from her book. They also listed as their targets another brief brain to brain lover, the Australian actor who once hosted the Academy Awards, Hugh Jackman; and then her brief brain to brain lover, Scottish actor and psychiatrist, the brilliant and world famous Gerard Butler.

At the bottom of the page, Jesuits showed their trophies, their *past* targets, all *dead*: Michael Jackson, Billy Mays and Princess Diana. All of a sudden, he got a headache.

It seemed that Loree's spirit jumped at him from the website, haunting his house and his life again, staring him down with her hard eyes. He couldn't rid himself of her! Her cackling voice seemed to sear the walls of his house; and memories, like cold fingers, stabbed at his conscience, raging guilt flooded him, so that he could only stop and gasp in horror. It didn't happen, no way would he do that to Gail. Loree's cackle and laughter screamed at him. "If you try to marry Gail, I'll kill her." Her laughter bounced off the walls. "Why would she want you, when you raped me?" He couldn't get her mocking voice out of his mind.

He imagined the next names on the Jesuit death list: Brent Spiner, Gail Chana.

Rage filled his heart, he wanted to twist Loree's neck and throw her into the dumpster all over again, as his friend had done in September 1992. Over his dead body, they would get his Gail!

Oh dear, how he worried over Gail. He must stop it. Now that he contacted her, perhaps he and Gail could work it out together, how to deal with these horrible Jesuits. At least, he felt less alone with these momentous decisions, she could help him decide what to do. Gail seemed a fount of wisdom and surprised him in the past with her courage.

So now they created a website called Order of the Jesuits and listed Loree at the top as their top deadly agent. No shame at all. How brazen and arrogant, advertising to the entire world their need to eliminate "targets".

But he no longer had to deal with Loree alone. After all, he had the almighty Gail on his side. She always amazed him. Yet, amazing as she was, it seemed Jesuits always found a way to stop her, and always killed people in the process. But he would tell Gail and from her response, they'd find a way together to overcome the almighty Jesuits.

VLADIMIR & CATHERINE THE GREAT
2000 – The Kursk Submarine Disaster

The husband and wife shed tears together. "I'm so sorry. I'll be strong for you. I promise you, if you die, I will be Russian President."

His wife died. Overwhelmed with grief, he could only cope by honoring what she whispered to him on her death bed. "Vladimir, for me–to honor my death, become Russian President."

Vladimir became Russian President in March 2000. Each day he battled depression, but overcame it because he honored her death by becoming Russian President. But to be Russian President was not enough. He only took this job for her. She wanted him to become President to save Russia. To save Russia, he must make decisions that would bring on him public scorn. To honor her death, meant more to him than to please the crowds.

World leader now, the U.S. President offered to let him view a woman in love with Brent Spiner, of interest to world leaders because she dared to expose Jesuit treachery because of her love for the world famous Brent. Through the bugs in her Seattle apartment in 2000, he viewed a woman named Gail overwhelmed by an empire, but whose spirit refused to stay down. Like watching a heroine from a movie, he cheered her on and her courage fused with his.

The bitch Loree McBride phoned her, "You *bitch!* Get out of my way. I'll take care of you. You die!"

Gail's back straightened, she gripped the phone and screamed from the top of her voice, so that the walls of her apartment shook. "You don't scare me a bit! Go ahead and kill me, I'll fight you over my dead body. You evil whore. You scum of the earth. How dare you break Brent's heart. How dare you! How dare you! I'll fight you to the end of my days. I dare you to kill me. Go ahead. I dare you, And I'll expose you to the world, you Jesuit whore. *Go ahead and kill me you bitch. You don't scare me a bit. You're disgusting. I'll never desert Brent. God is on my side, not yours. You filthy scum!*" She slammed the phone down, till her apartment seemed to shake, and walked away tall and straight, with fire in her eyes.

Yes, that's the spirit, show that Jesuit bitch what you're made of Gail. I'll make this Gail proud. What heroism she has against tyrants. The Chechen rebels would destroy Russia. Gail replaced his wife in his heart, his wife would want him to deal with them. His wife Gail would want him to be brave. To honor her, he scorned public opinion, he took on the Chechen rebels with fury and valor. "We'll kill them, even if they're sitting on the toilet." His wife would not want him to be a coward. With Gail in his heart, it

Vladimir and Catherine the Great

was if his wife had never died.

But the days dragged on and his new job brought on more challenges. Though Gail helped him heal from his wife and seemed to replace her, he could not carry on ordinary conversation with her. In fact, she didn't even know who the Russian President was, and didn't care.

Face it, she was like a heroine from a movie, a glorious figment of his imagination who gave him the will to live. Strange the effect she had on him, making him feel as if his wife never died. But for a tragedy like the Kursk, he needed a wife he could talk to. He caught himself every day trying to make Gail proud. But, for what? It made no sense, but she healed him from his wife's death. He felt he needed to be heroic for her, nevertheless.

To make Russia strong for Gail, he must strengthen its military. He would make a grand show with the Kursk submarine, so that the world would not dare attack Russia, so that Russia could defend herself. But, to the American Jesuits, this naval exercise in the Barents Sea was at the heart of a strategic operation. One that could lead to a major world conflict involving Russia, America, and China. Vladimir trusted the Chinese more than the Americans and wanted to form a military alliance with them. The Jesuits, with their mind and emotion-reading technology, also knew he was falling in love with Gail, from the bugs the American President had put in her apartment in Seattle.

The morning of August 12, 2000, two American submarines in the Barents Sea, the USS Memphis and USS Toledo, observed the Kursk from a distance. The USS Toledo openly shadowed the Kursk to signify American disapproval of the demonstration of the Russian Shkval torpedo to the Chinese. The Shkval was a weapons system started in the Cold War whose principal purpose was to attack American aircraft carriers.

All admirals in the Northern fleet had memories of the Cold War. The number of submarines at sea resulted in a chain of accidents between Russian and American vessels, causing the death of hundreds of submariners. These accidents remained top secret, although many subs still lay corroding on sea beds with their nuclear reactors and warheads intact. Submarines were the only nuclear weapons in the world carrying nuclear warheads for which no international conventions had been signed.

On Saturday August 12th, 8:51 a.m., the Kursk announced to the control tower of the Russian flagship *Peter the Great* that it would dive sixty feet to periscope depth, to prepare the firing of the Shkval torpedo for the Chinese military observers. At 11:28 a.m., inside the Kursk, the new Shkval torpedo was ready to fire.

Shadowing another sub is dangerous, especially in shallow depths with a great deal of magnetic interference and where maneuvering is difficult. The American Toledo, in its obstruction movements around the Kursk, came too close and collided with the Kursk.

When the Toledo rammed the enormous Kursk, it was as if a fishing trawler had rammed the Queen Mary. The Toledo, badly damaged, limped off. The second American submarine, the Memphis, moved in to cover the Toledo's escape. It detected the opening of the hole in the Kursk, from which the torpedo would fire, hearing the loading of the Shkval torpedo.

The Forbidden Abyss

The Americans knew that the Shkval is so fast, that if fired, the Memphis would have no time to dive or make for the surface.

The Russian flagship *Peter the Great* recorded the collision, while an alarm sounded. The Russian fleet closed in on the Kursk. Russian fighter planes took off from their base.

Fearing retaliation, the American commander fired a Mark 48 torpedo, which cut clean into the Kursk's torpedo department, exploding its particles inside.

The Kursk seemed hardly affected and pursued its route. Then an explosion took place in the front of the Kursk submarine in the torpedo compartment. The general alarm sounded. The breached double hull erupted into a flash fire, detonating the torpedoes on board, including the highly explosive Shkvals.

In peace time, the Russian submarine commander would press the emergency button releasing the air ballasts to send the submarine back up to the surface—but he didn't. Nor did he signal for the distress buoy to be released. All evidence pointed to an attack from another vessel. So, instead of heading to the surface, he boosted the engines to full throttle.

Two minutes and fifteen seconds later, a second explosion, registered on seismograph reports. At least a hundred times more powerful than the first explosion, it tore an enormous breach in the front of the submarine. The Kursk plunged three hundred feet to the ocean floor, while the nearby Memphis, shook and rolled from the shock wave.

The Kursk crews shut down the two nuclear reactors, and twenty-three men out of the one hundred and eighteen managed to scramble to the vessel's rear, where the escape hatch is situated.

The Russians discovered oil leaks on the sea's surface near the Kursk that appeared to come from the escaping Toledo. All the foreign vessels as well as the Russians recorded the two explosions.

Russians easily tracked down the slowly navigating Memphis, which strangely took seven days, instead of the normal two, to reach the Norwegian port of Bergen.

Admiral Popov, in charge of the exercise, ordered the flagship *Peter the Great* to leave the area. He returned to the mainland by helicopter with the Chinese admirals who came to observe the Shkval torpedo, and had a conference with the head of command.

An American submarine had torpedoed the Kursk. Oh, what should Vladimir do? Russia would surely lose a war with the United States. Another factor entered his mind. The American woman he observed through the bugs in her apartment would vanish from his life. She was the only reason he found the strength to be Russian President after his wife's death. If Russia and the U.S. were at war, he would be denied the privilege to view this woman through the bugs in her apartment. Vladimir lost his mind. Should he save these sailors? If they came up and survived, they would tell the world the truth. That would mean World War III.

Jesuit President Clinton offered him a deal. "Make sure no one knows that America did this to you. America will pay damages to the families. Just cooperate with us in the future when we need you—that's all we ask. Another thing, we are aware that you recently lost your wife and extend our sympathies. It must

Vladimir and Catherine the Great

be horrific to take on the duties of the Presidency without your wife. But we don't want you to advertise that you are now single—for reasons we cannot disclose. You did not mention your wife's death in your book *First Person*. We'll keep it that way. To the world, your wife never died. We have our agents lined up to cover up your wife's death. Also, start wearing your wedding ring. Is this understood?"

"Why do you care about my personal life?" Vladimir asked.

"Well, though we can trust you to keep secrets, we are not sure about your future wife. We will be monitoring your love interests for this reason."

So, the Americans knew he was falling in love with Gail! The thought of World War III overwhelmed Vladimir. If war with the U.S. happened, Gail would be cut out from his life. He'd be unable to view her from the bugs in her apartment, and he'd be forced to deal with his wife's death head on. The raw emotions from her death flooded back onto him. Observing Gail in her apartment made it like his wife never died.

He took the path of the coward and agreed to the dirty Clinton deal. This new job had no glamour and try as he may, without a wife, he felt overwhelmed. He made the wrong decision, because he lacked the courage to take on the American government. All sailors aboard the Kursk died, when they could have been saved. He concluded that President Clinton was just like how Gail portrayed his government in her novel *Silver Skies*! Bill Clinton worked with Jesuits to assist them in their takeover and control over the United States.

Vladimir had read Gail's unfinished novel, which his agents obtained from her copyright of it at the U.S. Copyright Office in 2000. Though in her book she implicated Russia as being in league with Jesuits to take over the U.S., she portrayed the main enemy of the U.S. as the Jesuit Order. This book would never make it in America, not with Clinton in power, he thought. But perhaps, one day, he could make Gail famous in Russia! Russians had more respect for writers than Americans. And then perhaps. . .someday. . .his heart would no longer be lonely. He hated the Jesuits as much as she did.

Though Jesuits sent Gail's husband out to sea for nine months, the husband returned in August 2000. So she finally hit her husband with divorce papers this month. Yes, the husband was a bad man. He assisted the Jesuits. This divorce would free her to marry another. Apparently, Jesuits knew Vladimir was falling in love with her. That explained the Kursk incident. It was not certain if she could fall in love with a Russian President, but the Jesuits would take no chances.

Why did they go to such extremes to track and control this woman? His agents discovered she was the great niece of the famous American aviator Howard Hughes. Yet she had no money. Apparently, Jesuits tracked this woman from her birth. There was more he needed to learn about this woman.

Immediately, the Russians sent an ultra secret mini submarine, the AS-15, to inspect the Kursk with a special intelligence unit of deep sea divers. The press later demanded why the mini submarines weren't used for the rescue operation. But to appease Clinton, Vladimir instructed the Russian authorities to remain mute and their investigation remained top secret.

Vladimir discovered that the slow moving Memphis served as a decoy,

The Forbidden Abyss

which enabled the Toledo to escape across the Atlantic undetected to the United States. Russian Secret Service later learned that the badly damaged Toledo had been concealed in a closed dock, where the Americans refused permission to anyone who wanted to inspect it.

Later in the afternoon of the 12th, Russians dropped depth charges around the Kursk. Russians claimed they did this to summon the submarine to surface. But foreign experts knew that Russians did this to warn vessels to keep away from the area.

The Kursk was strangely in very shallow depths for a submarine about to fire a Shkval torpedo for practice exercises. Even as it laid helpless on the ocean floor, observers saw the wreck from the surface. If raised to a vertical position, its tail would have emerged from the water by one hundred and fifty feet, and the escape itself could have occurred well above the surface.

George Tenet, a member of the CIA, secretly arrived in Moscow, three days after the tragedy. Presidents Putin and Clinton exchanged telephone calls. During these calls, Vladimir assured President Clinton he would cooperate, and in all his non-Russian press releases he would pretend his wife never got sick and died. However, he did not change his marriage certificate, because that could raise questions. To explain his lack of appearances with his wife, he would claim his wife preferred a low profile. To seal the deal, Bill Clinton cancelled a Russian debt, and the Russians received a new, ten and a half billion dollar loan.

Mr. Clinton's voice on the phone remained firm. "Remember. No one knows about this agreement between us. If you tell anyone, then you must pay us back the loan at once and you will also owe us the debt that I just cancelled for you. If this deal is found out, you will also be at war with the United States. We also will not guarantee the safety of Gail, if you break your word. We know that as you've spied on Gail in her apartment, you've grown attached to her. Do we have an understanding?"

"Understood." That Clinton would not harm Gail! Vladimir's growing love for Gail and his desire to keep on viewing her from the bugs in her apartment, staved off World War III.

On August 22, 2000 an astonishing article appeared on the PRAVDA website:

On Saturday, August 12, 2000, an incident occurred in the Barents Sea that almost led to the start of a third World War. For several days, world peace hung on a thread. A political faux pas could have led to an exchange of nuclear strikes. Igor Sergeyev, the minister of Defense, informed the President in Sochi of the event. It was decided against his immediate return to Moscow, as his presence at central command headquarters would have indicated Russia's preparation for a confrontation.

Two weeks after the exercise, an American commander admitted to the New York Times that an American submarine, the Memphis, was observing the Kursk submarine at the time and location of the accident.

The lies mounted. The Russian navy declared that it took over thirty hours to locate the Kursk. Two whole days later, when the Russian submariners could

Vladimir and Catherine the Great

have been saved, on Monday, the 14th of August, the tragedy was finally announced on television.

The fax issued to the press by a Navy spokesman declared the first official lies. "Kursk on Sea Bed, Monday, 13th. Minor technical incident. No Nuclear Arms on Board."

But Navy experts argued, "How could a submarine go out to sea, without any of its normal weapons?" They stated that although submarines intend to fire practice weapons as part of their practice exercises, they may be diverted during the exercise to a real incident.

Admiral Motsak, one of the admirals in charge of the exercise, made an announcement reviving hopes. "We know that there are survivors tapping out S.O.S. messages on the hull. These messages inform us that they have enough oxygen for ten days."

Five days after the public announcement of the tragedy, on August 18th, Vladimir addressed the journalists from his holiday resort on the Black Sea. His conscience tormented him, but his heart became overwhelmed with grief over the death of his wife. Without Gail, the wounds would become very raw. One week was lost because of lies, deceit and political negotiations. One week in which the surviving crew could have been saved.

A British cargo plane left the U.K. with the LR5, a highly sophisticated rescue submarine. But because of his deal with Clinton, he couldn't give them approval to enter Russian airspace.

The British actually enlisted the help of the Norwegian army. The rescue vessel from Norway, the Normand Pioneer, took several days to reach the site of the rescue operation. Norway also sent out another vessel, the Seaway Eagle, with professional Norwegian and British divers onboard.

For a whole week Vladimir had his Russians insist that due to poor weather conditions, strong currents, the steep list of the submarine and damage created by the explosion, that evacuating the survivors was impossible. The Norwegians and British began to realize that a lot of the things they had been hearing were not accurate. This made Vladimir nervous, perhaps Clinton would cut off Gail from his life, then he could no longer view her through the bugs in her apartment.

The British and Norwegians discovered there was visibility. The currents weren't too bad, and the attitude or list of the submarine on the sea bed was not beyond the limits for a successful rescue. They realized they could probably assist. Because the press and the families continued to hound Vladimir, he finally accepted the offers of the British and the Norwegians. To continue to resist outside help, indicated there was something to hide. He had to erase this perception.

The following day, the Norwegians and British divers were finally authorized to dive down to the wreck, but not to approach the part of the submarine where the explosion occurred. They took the divers down pretty quick and recognized that the ship was lying there, and there were no currents. So the Russians lied. This leaked to the press. The ring to open the hatch for the rescue operation had been reported as destroyed. More lies. It was not destroyed at all. The Russians had said it was impossible to open the hatches, and yet the Norwegian and British divers managed to open the outside one in twenty minutes.

The Forbidden Abyss

Once inside the submarine, the cameras showed the vessel was swamped, with no survivors. By the time they got there, it was too late. All the submariners were dead.

Admiral Popov said off camera, "I shall spend the rest of my days, searching for who is responsible for this tragedy." The press suggested the real reason the catastrophe was concealed is because possible survivors could have revealed the truth. The Kursk affair became officially classified as a state secret.

Two main theories emerged. The first, given by the Russian admirals, incriminated the British or American submarines in the area. They hinted that a collision or the firing of a torpedo caused the tragedy. Western diplomats, under Jesuit direction, immediately refuted the presence of their vessels on the scene. They offered a second explanation: the accidental explosion of an antiquated hydrogen peroxide fuel torpedo, abandoned fifty years ago by other fleets because of its instability.

Russian people, under the influence of Jesuit brain control, claimed that by accusing the West, Russian admirals threw up a smokescreen, trying to put the blame on someone else.

Ironically, despite accusations that incriminated the Russian government from their own Russian people, the Russian prime minister agreed with Vladimir, that they should opt for the faulty torpedo theory.

Twelve days after the catastrophe, Vladimir appointed one of his men, Vladimir Ustinov, the general prosecutor, to direct the legal inquiry. Ustinov immediately favored the faulty torpedo theory, which became the official version before the inquiry had even begun. But some people asked, "Why would an antiquated torpedo be used in an exercise aimed in Vladimir's own words, 'At proving Russia's naval supremacy' "?

It amazed Vladimir how everyone accepted this explanation, that an antiquated torpedo caused the death of all the mariners. That is, everyone, but the sailors themselves. Under pressure from the U.S., it was the only explanation that allowed Vladimir to dispel suggestions of foreign responsibility and defuse American displeasure.

At about the same time, a team from the flagship *Peter the Great* discovered a foreign distress buoy in the area of the Kursk incident. The admirals also presented evidence on videotape of a collision with another submersible. Tears could be easily discerned in the Kursk's hull as well as a strange hole with the metal turning inwards. The amount of damage sustained could not have been caused by a mere collision. The presence of the USS Memphis and Toledo on the scene could explain the two undeniable impacts on the hull.

Jesuits knew that if the Russians sold to the Chinese the latest model of the Shkval, the Americans could lose their naval supremacy in Southeast Asia. A Jesuit plan for a U.S. takeover was in the wings. Only Gail and those who loved her held them back. Having a weapon like the Shkval would put the Chinese in the same sort of league as the Jesuit-led Western forces.

The Chinese distrusted the Jesuits and the American government. A powerful China would be a real problem for Jesuit-led America. Jesuits knew this.

Vladimir's nerves rattled. He hoped he did enough to hide the truth, so that America would not attack Russia again, under the pretext that he violated his agreement with Clinton. He did not want to give them an excuse to start a war

Vladimir and Catherine the Great

with Russia.

To appease the public, Vladimir allowed the bodies of the submariners to be brought to the surface. Some of the dead sailors wrote notes, and from those notes the press learned that some crew members managed to survive in a section of the Kursk. Vladimir managed to hide parts of an important letter that emerged. Only part of the letter was shown to the press, the other pages were kept secret. Twelve bodies were brought to the surface. The others remain imprisoned in the wreck until the whole submarine was raised.

A second letter was found in Dmitry Kolesnikov's pocket dated August 15th, which was three days after the tragedy. It was addressed to the head authorities and contained information about the accident. But Vladimir's Vice Admiral Motsav had explicitly ordered them not to reveal its contents. The letter was never made public. It indicated that the sailors were left to die.

Families brought a lawsuit against the Russian government, so Vladimir decided to raise the wreck on October 8, 2001. Finally, the Dutch company Mamoet, the only company that refused to raise the torpedo section, raised the wreck. They sawed off the torpedo section and left it on the sea bed, thus carefully avoiding the discovery of the Kursk's hidden secrets. The operation cost one hundred and thirty million dollars, double the yearly budget of the Russian navy for the submarine fleet. This time the whole of the international press was invited, when the submarine, minus its head, was raised from the sea bed to the surface. Hotel rooms, conference rooms, creation of websites, nothing was too grand for this impressive ceremony. Vladimir felt himself such a hypocrite. To protect the American government, his lies broke the hearts of the submariners' families. But the next big lie he would have to perform for the American government, would break *his* heart.

Even though the torpedo section had been sawed off as they raised the Kursk from its sea bed, the hole where the American torpedo penetrated the Kursk glared at onlookers. Vladimir turned pale at the sight. The Dutch had tricked him. It surprised the public to see an obvious round hole in the Kursk's hull. It was obvious it had to be a torpedo strike. The sight of the Kursk with the trace of the torpedo impact, Vladimir quickly shuffled away from the cameras.

A main reason for the recovery of the wreck was to prevent foreign fleets or terrorists from getting a hold of information about the top secret missiles onboard. Vladimir corrected his earlier lie, and finally admitted that there were, indeed, nuclear warheads onboard. Only six of the twenty-four missiles appeared slightly damaged by the explosion. Their nuclear heads were sent to be dismantled by a secret military base.

All the bodies from the Kursk were extricated from the wreck and autopsied. Discrepancies glared and made it to the press. Though Vladimir claimed the explosion pulverized the majority of the crew and they could not have been saved, yet only three, out of one hundred and eighty-eight bodies, could not be identified. And these were found in the torpedo compartment itself.

Vladimir sighed in disgust. Americans had forced him to wait four hundred days (October 8, 2001) to retrieve the bodies of the submariners. Vladimir cooperated with the new U.S. President George Bush to get this issue settled once and for all and to clear the U.S. of any blame—part of his deal with Bush, so he could marry Gail, who declared on September 26, 2001 that she would marry

The Forbidden Abyss

him.

His heart went out to the submariners' families. He paid the families damages, visited them in their apartments, erected monuments to the Kursk, to honor their deaths. But his conscience raged. But if the Americans cut off Gail from his life...

He knew the real reason for the Kursk incident. He kept his word and the book *First Person* that he published in May 2000 would not be updated to reflect his wife's death, it continued to claim his wife never got sick and died. If he ever decided to marry later, he could move up his wife's death date to a future date.

The American President Clinton monitored every inch how Vladimir handled this affair. Therefore, Vladimir in early 2001 had to fire ten of his admirals for openly accusing the Americans in the Kursk affair. Two of these admirals, who he genuinely admired, he gave other comfortable functions. Vladimir then had to fire those in his political cabinet who accused Americans of responsibility. Now the United States was completely cleared of any responsibility, and now Vladimir could completely pursue his new friendship with the next American President George Bush, who seemed better than Clinton. The new American President belonged to the Republican Party, different from Clinton's Democratic Party. He seemed to be a man of honor. Vladimir began to hope that he could eradicate the lie that his wife never died. But he'd soon learn that Americans thrived on lies, that this one big lie would lead to another.

In the meanwhile, in Jesuit laboratories, Jesuits quickly created a clone replica of Larisa, (Vladimir's wife who died in June 2000). Using accelerated growth hormones, the clone baby grew from infancy to adulthood from February to April 2001. Perhaps because the Jesuits were in a hurry, and did not expect the Russian President to notice Gail, they goofed. The clone was not an exact match to Larisa. They got the clone's skin coloring wrong. Larisa, with blue undertones to her skin, looked ravishing in silver. Lyudmila, with orange undertones to her skin, looked drab in silver. Gail would have a hey day with this in the future. But the brazen Jesuits would never fear, because the skin tone differences could be covered up with photographic trickery.

Vladimir learned that because he covered up American treachery with the Kursk lie, Americans would expect more lies in the future. It seemed that to be Russian President you had to be a master of lies. But the audacity of the next lie would devastate his heart.

In 2002, Vladimir created an official two thousand page explanation full of contradictions about the Kursk, which he could easily dismiss for lack of evidence. It amazed Vladimir how easily details were forgotten and lies prospered. Though this Kursk lie pained him, it didn't devastate Vladimir in the heart. The next big lie the Americans would force him into, would almost lead to his suicide.

He transported the wreck of the Kursk to a secret military island where it was dismantled and melted down. The Russian fleet blew up the remainder of the wreck, which was the incriminating torpedo section—and which had been left on the sea floor for months after the accident.

Now any means of knowing the whole truth of the matter was eradicated

Vladimir and Catherine the Great

once and for all. Just like any means of knowing the truth about the death of Vladimir's wife in 2000 would be eradicated once and for all.

This new job had no glamour and try as he may, without a wife, he felt overwhelmed. Gail was not his wife—face it. The Kursk reminded him he must make these momentous decisions alone. If he saved the Kursk by raising the submarine from the ocean bottom, where it lay, it would reveal the hole caused by the American missile. Russians, in outrage, would demand a war with the United States. A war Russia would lose. He knew he made the wrong decision, because he covered up murder, when he should have brought the murderers to justice. But the price for justice, meant more murder: war with the United States.

Threat of war with the United States, would become a key Jesuit strategy to keep Vladimir in submission to the Jesuits.

Vladimir tried to make up for his failure to be great in this Kursk matter, he still tried to shove the Chechen rebels from their holes. The Jesuit-run world attacked him in the press with fury. This made him feel good. He felt he made up for the Kursk. Gail, who took the place of his wife in his heart, would probably have wanted him to save the sailors. This haunted him. But try as he may, she wasn't here. He had no wife. Viewing her in her apartment through the bugs was like watching a heroine in a movie.

Vladimir's Wife Who Never Died
2001 to 2002

A year and a half into his Presidency, a miracle happened. Vladimir watched Gail on September 11, 2001 through the bugs in her room. She was living with her mother and disappointed that Brent had not married her yet.

In outrage, she raised her fists into the air.

Vladimir knew the Jesuits launched 9-11-01 against her because her celebrity lover dared to schedule a flight that day to fly to Gail and claim her as his wife. Though she knew the Jesuits launched 9-11-01 to crush her—rather than crush her, she raised her fists in triumph, "I declare war on the Jesuit Order. Brent, I need to talk to all the world leaders. Tell President Bush that we need to make alliances with Russia and China and work together to defeat the Jesuits. We will declare war on the Jesuit scumbag terrorists. We will *not* be intimidated. Warn the Russian and Chinese leaders to be extra careful for their life, because I know the Jesuits will try to kill one of them and frame the murder on the Americans, claiming some crazy American shot the Russian or Chinese leader, believing them to be behind 9-11. This is a deflection tactic and we won't fall for it . ."

Gail was talking about him! Trying to spare his life. Suddenly, this woman who before, seemed like a fantasy heroic damsel in distress, became real, and reached down to the recesses of his soul and inspired him to heroics. He arranged for her local paper to flash a daring and heroic photo of him. With some hope for his broken heart, still reeling over his wife's death, he chose a photo of himself where he looked especially handsome and manly, knowing from Gail's rants about Franco Nero's manliness, she was attracted to heroics and manliness. In this photo, a scarf whirled round his neck, giving him the appearance of a dashing and handsome war hero, like a Russian Lancelot from Camelot. "Gail's not a politician in heart. She's a true leader, who inspires those who follow her to heroics. I want to show her how she inspires me!" He worried that her perceptions of him may be colored by American brainwashing against the Soviet Union.

He knew from the bugs in her room, she read the paper every day. There was a new President in America, who seemed to have more honor than Clinton. His hopes for his heart soared.

To his amazement, when she read the paper and saw his photo, she brought the paper to her room, plopped on her bed and lay on her back, observing the photo. A strange look came on her face. She just stared and stared at his photo. "I never knew the Russian President was so handsome. How heroic he looks.

Vladimir and Catherine the Great

Just like my Brent, but with more heroics and valor. I don't think the Jesuits will ever let me marry Brent. But now I think I'm in love with a President. With a President in my life, we can defeat the Jesuits. Oh, how heroic and handsome he looks." She smiled. "He's flirting with me in this photo."

She went to bed that night and dreamed about him in the bed with her. Now she was helping him heal from Larisa's death, and made it so that it was like his Larisa never died; and he helped her heal over 9-11-01, so that the Jesuit plot to ravish her heart over Brent, boomeranged.

He recalled how her heart, ravished for a day over September 11, 2001, rose up in triumph with world leaders the world over to declare war on the Jesuit Order. It amazed him the respect all world leaders had for her courage. The entire earth seemed to rally behind her as she defied the Jesuits to keep her down.

Now, fifteen days after September 11, 2001, this woman from the United States, made a statement from her bedroom that he heard through the bugs in her room.

"I'm going to marry the Russian President."

He couldn't believe it. The woman seemed to be Larisa resurrected from the dead. Except this woman had traits that would make her a great wife for a President. She had heroism and valor–a perfect match for him. With a woman like this in his life, if another Kursk disaster happened, he knew he would be a better man next time, he'd have more steel, because this woman had the steel to reinforce him. His heart soared, she was the perfect President's wife!

Before her, he hated the job, and almost resented his dead wife for forcing him on her deathbed into the job that forced him to be a wimpy marionette on a stage. He felt himself a lifeless puppet, in a grand performance, while the puppet master, the evil and ambitious Jesuit Order, guided all his strings.

It seemed the higher up he got in politics, the more strings the Jesuits put onto his marionette. When he tried to escape, to stop being a marionette, the Jesuits began to cut off the strings, leaving him dangling and suffering, like the Kursk disaster, or the bombings in Chechnya, or jets crashing to intimidate him.

Larisa, only had idealism about him as the greatest President, she had no idea how much fantasy and lies controlled a President's day to day actions. If only she knew that no one could attain a high position like Russian President unless they let the Jesuits control the strings.

Now the wife who could sustain him as a leader, to encourage him to break off the strings and perform on his *own stage*, had died. He faced the wolves and spiders, the puppet masters, alone and very lonely.

While the world cheered him on as the great Russian President, the victory seemed hollow to him, because to be a puppet on the Jesuit strings, a cowardly puppet who couldn't break these strings, these strings that strangled all that was honor, manliness, courage and decency—as he sat in his limousine headed towards the Kremlin, he stared out the car's windows, and only saw drabness, dreariness, depression, death, in the sticks of trees and landscape of Moscow nearing the dead of winter—cold, barren, like his heart—like the Kursk sailors who died needlessly to preserve the powerful puppet master, the Jesuit Order. This monster, this puppet master, this puppeteer planned more treacheries in the future, and he knew that as the Russian President, the spider would weave him more and more into her web.

The Forbidden Abyss

And how would he meet the challenge? Like he did the Kursk. He paled at the thought. To do this again made him want to throw himself before a Bengal tiger, let the tiger maul his neck, grasp his jugular vein, and throw him to the woods, because that is where his heart was.

If he couldn't be a man, a real man, he didn't want to live. If he could only be a coward, a wimp, when he viewed himself in the mirror, it didn't matter what the world thought of him. If he failed as a man, and became a shell, a limp puppet on a stage, playing a grand performance as some almighty leader, but was just a limp puppet on a stage—a sham, a worm—let him die!

Vladimir hated the charades and performances, which the American Presidents seemed to love. Perhaps if he had less male blood in his veins, he wouldn't mind the charade, but Vladimir Putin had real manliness, real honor and each time he betrayed that manliness, he longed for the manliness and heroism that stirred deep within him, to rise up and triumph, to shove the spider, the puppet master, to the wall, smashing him until his guts spilled out. Yes, that's what a real man would do!

But every time he tried to rise up, the puppet master grabbed the strings harder, wrapping them around him, round and round like a spider preparing her meal, twirling him round and round in the deadly webs to the death of all that was honor, manliness and truth.

Yes, that was what a President was—a puppet controlled by a spider in its web. There was no glory to this job. Yet, if he quit, he could see that another person in this job, would bring Russia totally under the control of the Jesuit spider. He didn't know how, but he had to find a way to break these strings! Too much of a man to quit, but too much of a man to want to live as a shell of a man.

His sweet wife Larisa, the role model of submission and poise, lacked the steel he needed as a President's wife. He loved her deeply, but whenever he needed steel, she seemed vacant, away. She had died on him! Oh, it was his fault, because the Jesuit doctors fooled him, thought she had breast cancer, so the chemotherapy he used to cure her breast cancer, fed her systemic yeast infection and she died!

He felt himself no match to these brilliant and daring Jesuits, these brilliant puppet masters, who moved each world leader with precision on the Jesuit stage. The puppet master wrapped him tighter and tighter in their web, controlling his doctors, his alliances, the rebels within his own government, his wife. They killed his heart, when they killed his wife! The former Soviet Union must not regain her world power status with a President like Vladimir Putin. If he could not be controlled, he must be destroyed!

He thought he could forge on with her memories alone to sustain him. But after the Kursk, he began to realize he needed real flesh and blood beside him to sustain him. There was no one he could turn to, who could understand the complexities of his job, and could counsel him over how to remain a man and a President at the same time. No easy feat, when a Master Puppeteer determined to eradicate manliness from the earth, to replace it with absolute submission to the puppet master, especially in any man of importance and influence.

Larisa, sweet Larisa, what more could he want in a wife? But he needed steel in a wife, because only steel could break the puppet's strings! Larisa lacked the wisdom and courage to make him that President of steel to run his own stage, to

Vladimir and Catherine the Great

break free from the powerful spider. This spider had reigned since the days of Ignatius of Loyola (1491 – 1556), the founder of the Jesuit Order, and had only increased in power and wealth, rewritten history to make those sympathetic to Jesuit goals the victors and heroes and those who opposed Jesuit goals, traitors and villains. To break free from this spider, who reigned for centuries, with all world leaders inside her web, would require a miracle from God.

Without a wife or soul mate to guide him as a world leader, Vladimir felt himself a shell of a man, putting on a grand performance to placate other puppets on a stage. Though he hated his job, he couldn't abandon it, because Russia had a chance, if he remained. He didn't know how, but he had to find a way to give Russia this chance.

Ah, but his heart reeked with loneliness. How few understood the loneliness of this high office! How few understood how impossible it was to break free of the spider!

All world leaders were puppets on this stage, all rehearsed their lines, put on performances. The public only saw the performances, failed to realize that the true leaders, the Jesuits, pulled all the strings, so that all the puppets on the world stage, danced to their tune, yes, all the puny world leaders danced like marionettes on the Jesuit stage.

It disgusted him! How he wanted to break free of this humiliating performance! But if any world leader dared to say his own lines, the strings would be broken and that marionette would tumble to his death. He had dreams of a free Russia. A Russia free from Jesuit tyranny! The impossible dream, but the only reason he kept his President's job. If he ever decided that dream could not be attained, he would throw himself to the Bengal tiger, and let the tiger maul him to death.

And so Catherine the Great became his secret wife (to replace Larisa).

Gail made Vladimir the President that he was from September 2001 to now. When she stopped making love to him (brain to brain), 2006 to 2009, Vladimir realized how much he had grafted her into his life, he didn't want to live without her love. He didn't care at all to be President anymore without her love in his life. When Gail ignored him, Vladimir became depressed, and entertained thoughts of suicide. Vladimir only became President to honor a great woman, and without her, he didn't want to live.

When, in early 2000, Vladimir's wife, Larisa, died of a systemic yeast infection right after he became Russian President, the duties of President so overwhelmed him, he didn't have time to grieve. So that he could do his job, he suppressed the pain he felt and told himself she was still alive. But when he came home to his house and there was no wife, he was reminded again that she died. The pain was so deep, it overwhelmed him.

Gail took Larisa's place in Vladimir's heart. So much so, that he even denied to himself that his Larisa really died from a systemic yeast infection, because he soon learned that Gail had the same germ that killed his wife.

At first he thought his Larisa had breast cancer, so he put her on chemotherapy—a fatal mistake. Doctors had misdiagnosed his sweet, submissive Larisa. She had no breast cancer. She had a systemic yeast infection.

Chemotherapy for her "breast cancer" so weakened her, that her yeast infec-

The Forbidden Abyss

tion had run rampant throughout her body. The yeast infection inundated her, even attacking her breasts so that they appeared cancerous and deformed. He scrambled to save her, but by the time he discovered Larisa's systemic yeast infection, around May 2000, the yeast had so overwhelmed her body, she was at death's door.

This particular yeast ate its own toxins, so that when it was killed and released its toxins, any remaining yeast would eat the toxins released from the dead yeast and would multiply as if fed yeast fertilizer. The mortality rate for this yeast, when it became systemic, was fifty percent. The best course of treatment was to pass the yeast out of the body without killing it. This required a strong immune system, and chemotherapy weakened the immune system. So putting his wife on chemotherapy cost his wife her life.

When he learned Gail also was infected with the same yeast that killed his wife and that Gail's infection was also systemic or throughout her entire body, it racked his heart with guilt and torment. Gail's infection also was rather advanced, so that even passing the yeast out of her system only held off her death, but could not eradicate the yeast totally from her system.

The Jesuits had created the perfect germ in their laboratories, one not recognized as deadly by the Jesuit-run medical community. Therefore, Gail's brilliant medical management to hold off the yeast made her appear hypochondriac.

Jesuits also knew that eventually the yeast would kill her, and when that happened, they could blame it on the supplements Gail took to ward off the yeast, because the myriad of supplements she took to ward off yeast death were not approved by the FDA (America's Jesuit-run Food and Drug Administration).

Also, Jesuits manipulated the germ within her body remotely, using computer/satellite technology, to make the germ more resistant and deadly. Jesuit science was cutting edge and their cloning technology, brain-reading abilities, super germs, super humans and brain control drugs never made it to mainstream news, medicine or publications. When they created Loree McBride in the laboratory, they gave her and her hundreds of clones the strength of Olympic athletes to make her drug rapes of men possible.

The deadly yeast also had a voracious appetite, feeding on iron, carbohydrates, magnesium, and many of the same nutrients that humans needed for survival. To make matters worse, Gail had developed an allergy to this yeast's toxins, so that the yeast's toxins irritated Gail's bladder, so that she required the restroom at least every hour. Because her yeast infection had spread to her entire body, when Gail fed herself to stay alive, she also fed her yeast infection. To maintain her health, she followed a regimen of vitamin and mineral supplementation, diet management (especially avoiding foods that fed the yeast), and yeast killing medications. But no matter what she did, it seemed that she and the yeast were at a stalemate. The powerful yeast would not leave her body.

In her attempts to not feed the yeast sugars and carbohydrates, one of its chief foods, she abstained from all refined carbs or sugars, and made herself look as skinny as a skinned cat. It gave her a model figure, but Vladimir would much rather she have more weight on her, than for her to be infected with the deadly yeast.

The panic he felt in his heart for Gail, made him deny to himself that his Larisa died of a systemic yeast infection. He told himself and the world that Larisa

Vladimir and Catherine the Great

died of breast cancer. Believing this lie, made him feel the yeast would not kill his Gail. For this particular yeast, he knew there was no known cure. He could only hope to hold it off, and to postpone Gail's eventual death. Petrified for Gail, he told himself and the Russians that his Larisa died of breast cancer (his wife's original diagnosis).

Gail's medical genius and her distrust of Western medicine kept the yeast from overwhelming her body, but she experienced many setbacks with this powerful yeast. With each passing year the yeast seemed to gain more power over Gail's body, so that she took more and more supplements to fight it, but to no avail.

One thing consoled Vladimir, he knew Gail was far too smart to ever allow any doctor to give her chemotherapy. Despite Jesuit attempts to discredit her as a hypochondriac because of her attempts to hold off the deadly yeast, Gail's medical genius at least held off the powerful yeast enough that she could function and maintain a job. But it required the discipline of a soldier for her to maintain her diet and supplement regimen to stay alive and functioning. The yeast wrecked havoc on her immune system and she developed so many food allergies, there was not much she could eat. She experienced negative reactions in her body to just about everything she ate.

After almost having to quit her job (spring 2009) because of reactions to foods she was eating and a yeast-overwhelmed liver and gallbladder, she finally discovered she could sustain herself on a Japanese style diet. She ate raw radish every day to purge her liver and gallbladder, and added liver support nutrients to her regimen, like milk thistle. Her diet became very bland and limited. She staved off hospitalization, which probably would have made her worse, and was able to return to work.

Fortunately, raised on Japanese food, she found a way for this bland diet to work for her. She loved Japanese food. By eating only Japanese food, she sustained herself on a Japanese style diet. Because of her systemic yeast infection, she maintained her strict diet, because she genuinely enjoyed Japanese food. But no matter what she did, she always lived on the toilet.

September 10, 2001 Gail watched *What About Bob?* all day on her mother's videocassette player—her way of honoring the sense of humor that both Brent and she shared. Apparently, the Jesuits didn't like this, because on the morning of September 11, 2001, when she went to a doctor's office, she noticed as she walked into the office that all the radios were on.

"What's going on?" she asked.

"You haven't heard? About forty of fifty firefighters died trying to rescue people in the World Trade Center towers in New York City. We lost just about all the New York City firefighters. Jets crashed into towers at New York and maybe the Pentagon. The World Trade Center collapsed. Everyone in the towers died, when they collapsed.

Inside, she felt white with rage. *Why won't they leave us alone! I'm sick of these people!* After this, Brent will never show up to get me. She knew they did this to stop Brent from coming to her.

She knew the Jesuits partied that day and determined not to give them any satisfaction. She refused to watch the news until at least 3 or 4 in the afternoon.

The Forbidden Abyss

She knew that the tragedy started around 9 a.m. On her way back from the doctor's office, she stopped off at Blockbuster video on September 11, 2001 and checked out the movie *Gladiator,* and watched the opening battle scene over and over from 10 a.m. to 3 p.m. while the rest of the world was glued to the news channels. When she came home to her mother's house, where she lived at the time, she told no one what she knew about the World Trade Center, because she didn't want the news on. In defiance, she wanted to watch the *Gladiator* opening scene battle scene over and over. She told Brent (through the bugs that Brent through President Bush put in her mother's house), "This is how we must respond to these attacks, like this opening battle scene in *Gladiator."*

Because she knew there were bugs in her room, she talked to Brent from her room. Over the next week, she told Brent, "Tell President Bush that I'm worried about Russia. The Jesuits will try to blame this on Russia or China and I know both countries are innocent of this. The Jesuits want a pretext to start a war against the wrong party, because a war between China or Russia against the U.S. would work to their advantage. Tell the leaders of both China and Russia that they need to take extra precautions to protect themselves from a crazy Jesuit-American assassin who may try to kill them (thinking they are responsible for these 9-11 attacks), and then this would create all sorts of complications that would help out the Jesuits." She didn't know who the leaders of Russia or China were, but she knew the Jesuits.

On September 25, 2001 her local newspaper printed an article about Vladimir Putin that featured a photo of him with a scarf that swirled around his neck, making him look especially handsome and manly. It appeared that President Bush contacted Vladimir and let him listen to her through the bugs in her room.

Vladimir appeared to flirt with her in this photo.

She thought, "How I admire this man for his stand against the Chechen rebels. The whole world criticizes him for doing this. And yet, I know the Jesuits are trying to use Chechnya as a base with which to attack and take over Russia. Vladimir is apparently aware of this and trying to save Russia from a Jesuit takeover."

To her amazement, she couldn't get the photo out of her mind and began to dream about making love to him in her bed. "This Russian President is *so* manly, so heroic and handsome. He must be sixty years old. But, my how manly and heroic he looks! He's just like Brent, but with heroism and valor. Why do I dream about making love to him? And I've never seen him before this. I had no idea the Russian President was so handsome. *This Russian President is flirting with me. He was curious about me because I told President Bush to warn him to protect himself and he did some research on me. I don't think he's married, because he's flirting with me.* He makes me feel like we can beat these Jesuits. I think this man will have the guts to show up and marry me." By the end of the day, she made a statement in her bedroom so that all the bugs and Vladimir Putin could hear her: "I'm going to marry the Russian President."

She talked to the bugs in her room, "Tell President Bush to leave Vladimir alone about Chechnya. Vladimir's doing the right thing. If Chechnya becomes a separate state, their goal is to take over Russia. These Chechen rebels are Jesuits. I'm on Vladimir's side. In fact, I don't think Vladimir has been aggressive enough against these rebels. His country will go down, if he doesn't stop these

Vladimir and Catherine the Great

rebels. If Russia goes down, we all go down. Tell Bush to leave Vladimir alone! Vladimir is a hero. He takes a lone stand against the Jesuit Chechen rebels to prevent Russia from becoming the Jesuit-run Soviet Union or a Jesuit-run Muslim terrorist state, even though the whole world's against him. I love him. How heroic he is! The Jesuit-run world makes up lies about him and says he's a bully, just because he won't cave in about Chechnya. This man will have the guts to marry me, if he's like this. He's David against the Jesuit-Goliath. That's all Jesuit crap that he's a bully. He's fighting for Russia's life. Tell Bush to stop criticizing Vladimir's Chechnya policies."

It's funny. After she said this, President Bush changed his mind about Vladimir's Chechnya campaign and quit criticizing Vladimir for Chechnya.

Within days, she heard on the American news that the Russian President planned a pioneer visit to the United States. "He's not married. He's coming here because of me."

So, about a year and a half after his wife's death, Gail came into Vladimir's life (September 2001). She reminded him of his wife that died. He wanted to marry her. Worried that Jesuits might kill him because he loved her, she urged President Bush, who claimed to be a Christian, to lead her Vladimir to Christ. She urged Vladimir to say the sinner's prayer to accept Christ as His Savior. She led her Vladimir to the Lord in 2001, but encouraged him to honor the Russian Orthodox Church, because her ancestor, Prince Vladimir of Kiev (1000 A.D.), founded the Russian Orthodox Church.

The Jesuits wasted no time to sabotage Vladimir's love for Gail. They knew that he had not really dealt with the death of his wife, that he still told himself she was alive, that Gail took her place. They fed on this, and gave him the Lyudmila lie.

Jesuits also wanted to ensure that Gail could not return to Brent Spiner. Using semen they had stolen from their September 1992 rape of Brent Spiner, they impregnated Loree McBride in September 2001.

Loree informed Brent of her pregnancy right away. With Gail focused on Vladimir, it was part of her trying to torture Brent and ensure that Brent and Gail would never get together. Jesuits would use the pregnancy to prove that Loree and Brent had sex.

Brent was mortified, because he wouldn't know how to explain it. It sounded too unbelievable that Loree used semen she had stolen from her prior September 1992 rape of him to impregnate herself.

Jesuits attacked Gail on two fronts. They impregnated Loree with Brent's stolen semen, and then they contacted President Bush and said, "You either cooperate with us, or your wife Laura dies." Bush, who loved his wife far more than Jesus or the Bible, gave the Jesuits no resistance. Though Bush claimed to be a Christian, when push came to shove, he would always honor his wife above the real Jesus Christ. Unlike Gail, who sacrificed Brent on the altar in 1991 for Jesus, and unlike Abraham who was willing to sacrifice the son he loved, Isaac, for Jesus—Bush's wife became his idol, because he always chose his wife over God. Satan, a master at using idols to serve his purpose, found President Bush's idol and tempted Bush with it. Bush failed the test, and chose his idol over Jesus.

The Forbidden Abyss

So like Eve who worshipped knowledge over God, Bush worshipped his wife over God. Jesus tested him and He failed the test. Jesus, at this point, put President Bush on the shelf. But Jesus had plans for Gail, who so far, had passed several of His tests.

Bush even went so far as to choose a name for the Russian President's wife. Her name would be Lyudmila. Idol worship, the sin of the Jesuits, who worshipped Satan over God, would also become President Bush's sin, who worshipped his wife over God. Jesuits, because of Bush's cooperation, had no problems printing an article in *USA Today* (November 2001) that said Vladimir had a wife named Lyudmila.

If Bush had had the courage to sacrifice his wife on the altar for Jesus that momentous day in 2001 when Bush decided to betray his Lord by cooperating with Satan worshippers in the sin of idolatry against the Russian President, Jesus would have surely spared his wife, and perhaps would have made Bush the greatest President in all of American history. But, alas, Bush failed Jesus' test.

Gail's mother (who she lived with when she first fell in love with Vladimir) moved her to Tallahassee at the beginning of November 2001.

Gail did not know it in 2001, but in July 2001 her real mother had been kidnapped, her memories removed and the memories transferred to a Jesuit clone. This Jesuit clone of Gail's mom moved Gail to Tallahassee (Florida's capital) in late October 2001, to keep Gail near the President's brother, who was governor of Florida then. The American President instructed his brother in Tallahassee, Florida to ensure Gail got nowhere near Vladimir while Vladimir made his pioneer visit to the U.S.

Early November 2001, *USA Today,* in cooperation with the American President, printed a short lie that said Laura Bush would be happy to escort Vladimir and his wife Lyudmila around their Bush ranch in Texas.

Bush played that the article surprised him and insisted to Vladimir that to protect his wife Laura against the Jesuits that Vladimir needed to appear with a fake wife. "We found a woman who looks just like your Larisa. Use her."

This confused Gail about Vladimir at first, until she noticed that Lyudmila's name had uncanny similarities to Brent's "cute blonde girlfriend" Loree McBride (Lyudmila—Loree McBride). Vladimir's arrival date was November 12, 2001. Glued to the news that day, an American Flight 587 crashed on take-off from New York on November 12, 2001 as Vladimir's jet flew towards the United States. She fumed, "Those Jesuits did this to intimidate Vladimir from meeting me when he comes over." The jet crashed around 9:15:57 a.m. (her birthday was 9-15-57). Turbulence from a Japan Air Lines jet nearby contributed to the crash. Gail's mother was from Japan.

Jesuits reminded President Bush, "As you can see, we mean business. When Vladimir visits you with his fake wife Lyudmila, inform him that he is to marry the woman we've chosen for him, or your healthy wife Laura Bush, may suddenly become very ill. We killed Vladimir's wife. Perhaps you'll be the next widower." The Jesuits found President Bush's idol and used his sin of idolatry (also the sin of the Jesuits) to crash the American Flight 587 jet to intimidate Vladimir and Bush, because they knew Vladimir came to the U.S. to begin his

Vladimir and Catherine the Great

relationship with Gail. The crash intimidated the American President. The devil worshipping Jesuits got Bush's full cooperation (November 2001 to 2010) and now Vladimir's wife Larisa never died in 2000, and ***got a new name: Lyudmila.***

Vladimir got the news, that the crash occurred at 9:15:57 with a Japan Air Lines jet involved. Gail's Japanese mother had given birth to Gail on 9-15-57. So Vladimir decided to go down the ramp of his Russian jet on worldwide news (November 12, 2001) with his fake wife, Lyudmila, by his side. He met with President Bush at the White House, though he really wanted to meet Gail. He looked so nervous. Gail knew he feared he'd lose her, because he had a wife by his side. As he nervously went down the ramp from his jet, Gail laughed with hysterics for about a half hour. "My. . .my. . .what a performance he can put on with his fake wife. But how can he meet me with a fake wife by his side? How can he explain this?"

When he observed Gail's reaction, Vladimir's nerves settled down, and he now tolerated his wife performance with humor.

But when he arrived at President Bush's ranch in Texas, Mr. Bush took him aside, "Here's how it's going to be, Vladimir. Lyudmila will be your legal wife and you will present her to the world as your wife, or the United States will declare war on Russia."

Vladimir's mouth dropped. "But—"

Just then, Lyudmila burst into the room, giggling and excited, waving a piece of paper, her fat body bouncing and wriggling. "Here is the marriage certificate. Vladimir has married me."

Vladimir turned in disgust, grabbed the forged document, because he had never married Lyudmila in any way. "This signature is forged." He laughed. "Anyone who knows my signature, knows I never sign it like this."

Bush placed his hand over Vladimir's hand, sealing his deal with the Jesuits. "And no one will ever know it's forged. That will be a legal marriage certificate, because you will say it is. I won't let those Jesuits touch my wife. So Lyudmila will be the wife you married in 1983. You are not to breathe a word of my conversation with you about this to anyone in the press or to anyone who might cause trouble for me, and make sure during this visit that you act real happy about your pioneer visit to the U.S."

Satan found it easy to get followers. Just find what that person loved more than Jesus and use that as the bait. It worked with the Jesuits, and most of the world, and it worked with Bush.

Vladimir remembered the Kursk. Yes, he knew what the Americans were capable of. All American Presidents were alike. They all caved in to the Jesuit Order.

The almighty Russian President found himself no match against the almighty American leader. Bush, who tricked him, was no better than Jesuit President Clinton, who had extorted him into betraying the sailors on the Kursk.

They changed his wife's name in all biographies and writings about Vladimir. Her name was changed from Larisa to Lyudmila. They located all copies of any writings that had his wife as Larisa and switched out those copies with a version that had her name as Lyudmila. Their brain control technology then accomplished the switch out in the brains of all readers who bought any writings

The Forbidden Abyss

that called his wife Larisa. Those readers who bought or read a book about Vladimir that called his wife Larisa thought that the book they bought said Lyudmila all along.

Apparently, Jesuits decided to change his wife's name from Larisa to Lyudmila because a search could be done on his real wife's name and records could be made public that indicated his Larisa died and that the West's story about Vladimir's marriage was a fraud. Therefore his wife's name from November 2001 onwards was Lyudmila. He could not tell anybody about this conversation he had with Bush, or he may have a repeat of the Kursk.

So Lyudmila became his legal wife that day to non-Russians, though he never bedded her or made love to her. Too many Russians knew his wife's real name was Larisa, so Bush could not force Vladimir to propagate the lie in Russia. However, if a Russian dared to claim that Americans lied about Vladimir's wife, it would be an easy matter to claim that Russians are liars. In some ways, the Cold War never ended.

From September 2001 on, Gail was the wife of Vladimir's heart. But though the Russians knew the truth, that American President Bush extorted a Jesuit wife onto their President, if Vladimir dared to let this truth seep out to the non-Russian press, he risked World War III.

He consoled himself. Perhaps, later, he could secretly declare his marriage to Lyudmila a fraud and secretly marry Gail.

So under orders from Jesuit President Bush, Vladimir acquired a legal wife for whom he had no desire. This woman, Lyudmila, would put on a grand performance, playing the role of the Larisa he married in 1983. She would appear with Vladimir in public as his wife. The Jesuits wasted no time to put incorrect dates on photos and to promote Lyudmila as Vladimir's wife (who never died). They created Lyudmila, Vladimir's Loree McBride.

Gail thought her mother moved her to Tallahassee because the Florida governor, the U.S. President's brother, was trying to help Vladimir to meet her, to go off to Russia perhaps, as his bride. Oh, but she thought with disgust, how would Vladimir explain away Lyudmila? Deep inside, though Gail hoped Vladimir would meet her, she suspected Jesuits had blocked her heart again. Even a President was no match for the almighty Jesuits. While she waited in her new apartment in Tallahassee, Florida for Vladimir to show up for her on his pioneer visit to the U.S., he acted in public like he didn't know she existed. He seemed thoroughly intimidated, so it did not surprise her when he made a last stop at the World Trade Center site to see the damage from 9-11-01 and then flew back to Russia.

The Jesuits won. They sabotaged Gail's heart again.

In 2001, Gail's relationship with Vladimir grew and she shared with him all her political, religious and philosophical beliefs, including her belief that in the 1990s, the Catholic Church (in their Cold War orchestrations) saw the Soviet Union as the loser against the United States. They also (in 1991), because her relationship with Brent inspired her to write, and because she believed what Jack Chick published about Roman Catholic crimes, dropped (1991) the Soviet Union as their Cold War puppet.

Mom told her (May 2002) to come to her town to take the final exam for her

Vladimir and Catherine the Great

insurance course (mom paid for this course), because she had started the insurance course (while she lived at her mother's) at the Community College before she moved to Tallahassee.

So, at the time of President Bush's trip to St. Petersburg, Russia–she scheduled herself to take the final exam for her life/health insurance course at the Community College. She passed the final exam and the course. The results of the test, which was all insurance law, were also sent to Harvard Law School, and they were quite impressed. Now she only had to pass the state exam, which she did later, in Tallahassee.

What excited her more than passing this course, was that perhaps Vladimir would use President Bush to let her fly to Russia to be with Vladimir, because Bush scheduled this trip right at the time she had to drive to her mom's from Tallahassee to take her final exam. Perhaps, she thought, Vladimir and Bush did this on purpose, so she could fly with Bush from her mom's to be with Vladimir. Excited about this possibility, she decided to study insurance, to play the necessary game, to be with Vladimir.

But as soon as she arrived at her mom's and flicked on the news channels, they reported that they'd found the remains of Chandra Levy (Jewish girl) in Washington D.C. She knew that, because of her Jewish ancestry, this would probably scare President Bush from taking her to Russia. Oh, those Jesuits always sabotaged her family and love life!

After she passed the course for insurance and annuities at the Community College, she returned to Tallahassee, and passed the state exam for insurance and annuities on her first try.

She could barely afford to feed herself, even after liquidating her IRAs, because her Jesuit ex-husband had created the IRAs to lose what he had paid into them, by making them vulnerable to the stock market, so that they could lose what was paid into them. Jesuits made sure stocks were terrible at the time Gail needed to liquidate her IRAs. Though eleven thousand dollars had been paid into her IRAs, when Gail liquidated them, she only received four thousand dollars. The systemic yeast infection the Jesuits gave her made her so ill, she had to quit her job.

She ended up on food stamps and filed for chapter 7 bankruptcy, which she got in the summer of 2002. Because Lyudmila was considered Vladimir's wife, he was unable to give Gail any financial support while she strived to work around Jesuit complications to be with him. She forgave Vladimir for this until February 2006, when her patience ran thin and she reinstated Brent Spiner as her main lover brain to brain.

From this insurance course (like the Washington state real estate course that she took in 1999), she learned legal principles that helped her as a pro se lawyer against the Jesuits. But, because the Jesuits created too many obstacles, she felt it not wise to become an insurance agent. She dropped the idea, because it seemed the Jesuits took over all the insurance companies, and she refused to work for any company taken over by Jesuits.

She had an intuitive hunch that Bush did not really want her to marry Vladimir, but just led Vladimir on, and she especially suspected this, because Bush visited the Pope in coordination with the St. Petersburg trip.

The Forbidden Abyss

As President Bush's jet soared over the Atlantic towards Russia—without her—her heart fell. Again, the Jesuits had sabotaged her love life.

When Bush arrived in Russia, the headlines to her mom's local newspaper (May 25, 2002) flashed photos of Vladimir with his fake wife, Lyudmila, all over the front page, with extensive coverage of Bush's visit with Vladimir Putin and his wife Lyudmila. FOX News even showed extensive coverage of Lyudmila and Mrs. Laura Bush as they went to schools and promoted literature.

So President Bush left for Russia without Gail, and the local paper flashed whole page photos of Vladimir with Lyudmila on its front page, as it covered Bush's visit to St. Petersburg.

As she watched news coverage of the fireworks and ceremonies that Vladimir prepared for Pres. Bush's visit of St. Petersburg, her soul seeped in outrage.

Why did Vladimir go to such trouble to honor an American who could never understand and appreciate this Russian city so full of Russian history? Something in her sensed that President Bush disdained Russia and its history, and did not deserve all this pomp and show from the Russian President. You'd think Vladimir planned to marry Jesuit President Bush! And Bush could care less about Russia's great history. She saw in Bush an air of American superiority and arrogance, and that he felt he visited Russia as a favor to Vladimir.

Gail, wanted to be with Vladimir as his wife, but it seemed the barriers between Vladimir and her increased with each passing day. From February 2002 to August 2002 as she waited for Vladimir in Tallahassee, Jesuits flooded her apartment complex with their agents.

The few exchanges she had with her Caucasian neighbor, made her strive with all her power to avoid encounters with him. As she returned from her job at Burdines in Tallahassee, he sat in front of his door, his face pale, as if spaced out and in another world. His black, stringy hair fussed unkempt about him. His shirt and jeans, with holes and raggedness, symbolized his life. He appeared to be in his twenties. "Hi. How are you?" As if in another world, he gazed at her, and his mouth seemed to drool with filth.

"I'm fine." Gail jumped into her apartment.

She did not want to further the impression that she found this disgusting male at all attractive. The Jesuits set him up as her neighbor to destroy her growing relationship with Vladimir Putin, to create the impression of her as a loose woman who lived in bad neighborhoods, just because she loved Brent Spiner while married.

One time she decided to talk of her faith to this tramp of a guy, to emphasize the differences between them. "I've accepted Jesus Christ as my Savior, and I use the Bible as my guide for all living. I've been a Christian a long time." Oh, why did this guy have to be her neighbor? And this was such a clean and quaint apartment complex, how did he manage to be her neighbor?

"Oh yeah. I know all about that. I accepted Christ, too." He took a drag from his cigarette and spat on the ground next to him. His voice groaned like a weak wail. "But I have some problems. I've had a heroin addiction."

"I don't know anything about that. I've never smoked, never been drunk. I found the Lord when I was a young lady." She gazed at him and felt sorry for

Vladimir and Catherine the Great

this worm of a human being before her. "The Lord can help you overcome anything, even an addiction. Though I'm sure it won't be easy. But nothing's impossible with God." She decided against giving him a gospel tract directly.

One time, when he wasn't home, she slipped a gospel tract under his door. But most of the time, she tried to avoid him like the plague. If he sat on his doorstep several feet from her door, and stared like a mute into space, she ignored him, rushed into her studio apartment, slammed the door behind her, and locked it.

It seemed, that every where she moved, the Jesuits flooded in their agents as her neighbors, so that by the time a year rolled by, all her neighbors seemed criminals who trashed out the apartment complex, as they dumped filthy smells and liquids into the garbage dumpsters and scattered papers and cigarette butts about the pavements and walkways, so that even the upper class town she lived in (Mukilteo) while in Washington, turned into a trash bin to support the Jesuits' goals to create the impression of Gail as a garbage woman who lived in dumpster neighborhoods.

When she first moved into the Tallahassee apartment complex, it was clean and quaint. But within months after she moved in, the Jesuits flooded the apartment complex with criminals, and moved their criminals into the section where she lived. She had to "bump into" these criminals. Like a lightning bolt, she walked past them; but Jesuits, with computer/satellite precision timing and accuracy, shoved these scums into her pathways, and forced her to deal with them.

Her real mother Jesuits kidnapped and shipped to India in July 2001, enabling her mother's clone, who Jesuits had given all the memories of Gail's real mother, to move Gail next door to a heroin addict in November 2001.

Because Vladimir Putin wanted to marry Gail, Jesuits went all out to destroy Gail, but wisely used methods that would not make it appear she was their number one target. Rather, their strategy was to make her appear delusional and mentally ill, or Vladimir and Brent would give them deadly public exposure. If not for fear of this exposure from Vladimir or Brent, they probably would have killed Gail outright, but fear of public exposure made them use more subtle methods to destroy Gail.

Gail knew the Jesuit Order was her enemy and wrote and spoke about it everywhere, so she needed to be discredited and silenced first before they murdered her. Jesuit postal workers made sure to regularly switch out all the letters she left for Vladimir in her mailbox without a postage stamp, so that President Bush deluded Vladimir that he somewhat supported Vladimir's love for Gail. Vladimir would later discover that he did not receive what Gail really wrote him in 2002 when she would publish what she wrote him from her computer (2003 and onwards). Gail did not have a computer in 2002.

This heroin addict often sat on his doorstep about eight feet from Gail, so that, as she entered her apartment, she had to deal with him.

Through her front window, she could hear all the sounds of nature and the roar of the cars from the nearby highway. One day, as she lay on her bed in the sunset hours, she heard a trickling stream onto her pavement. She peeked out her window and saw her stringy, black haired neighbor, his zipper down,

The Forbidden Abyss

standing, in the "pee" position, like males when they urinate into a urinal. "This is ultimately disgusting," she thought.

Another time, outside his front door, for about a half hour, he coughed and made retching noises. It appeared he had about a half hour vomiting episode, and decided to spend his vomiting session outside his front door, rather than his apartment's bathroom. This scumbag couldn't keep his smut to himself, but had to spread his lewdness to all the world.

Gail thought, "These Jesuits use the most disgusting agents. They are truly the scum of the earth." Every passing day, as she dealt with Jesuits, she grew to hate and despise them more and more. "Is it any wonder Vladimir hasn't come to get me yet? Why would he come to get me with a neighbor like this? The almighty Russian President comes to get his wife in her studio apartment, who lives next door to a scraggly heroin addict, who pukes every day outside his apartment door!"

One time in February 2002, around 9 a.m., while she rambled about her furnished studio apartment, to fix meals for herself in her little kitchen, she sat on the queen sized bed that came with the furnished studio apartment, and heard from her heroin neighbor's residence gunshots—then, a loud thump.

The gunshot victim, whose slump she heard, lay about twenty feet or less from her, only separated by the wall that separated her studio apartment from the heroin addict's.

She called 911 right afterwards. "I want to report that I heard voices screaming, like a fight, and then I heard gunshots from my next door neighbor's apartment and it sounded like a body slumped down afterwards."

"When did this happen?"

"Just now. About five minutes ago."

"How do you know these were gunshots?"

"It sounded like gunshots to me. I'm sure I heard a body slump down afterwards."

"Where do you live?"

She gave them her address.

"Do you know who's in that apartment?"

"I have no idea. I don't communicate at all with my next door neighbor. I don't plan to go over there to see what's going on. It sounded like a body slumped down after the gunshots. But I don't know, perhaps I'm wrong. There could be a body in that apartment, and I thought you should know that, so I called. I'm leaving for work around noon."

After she made her phone call to 911, she decided to get ready for work, because she was scheduled to work at Burdines that day. Around 9:30 a.m. on that day that the Jesuits shot the body and she heard that thump, she played full blast from her videocassette player the entire musical *Singing in the Rain* so that her walls shook. She never left her apartment until she left for work, and didn't leave for work any earlier than usual.

After *Singing in the Rain* finished, with still a half hour before time to leave, she blasted part of her Lerner and Loewe musical *Gigi,* so that the murderer next door would hear it.

I'll spite you Jesuits. I won't let you to use this murder to destroy me or

Vladimir and Catherine the Great

Vladimir Putin. I won't let you to gloat over your murder, to make a conspiracy out of this, to ruin my life or my lovers. I know you want to draw attention to where I live, to make it appear I live in a ghetto, but I spit in your face. You won't intimidate me with your gunshots and your dead bodies. You monsters! You bastards!

Finally, ready for work, she turned off all her musicals, walked outside, saw about four or five police cars, with about ten officers huddled about, as if they waited for her to leave. The quantity of the officers and that they waited for her to leave, indicated that they found a body and didn't want to remove it until she left.

Gail was so glad that she was scheduled to work that day.

She walked by and ignored all the police cars and the police, huddled outside her apartment and about their cars with their talkies. "Roger, we got that. " The communications and radio talk lingered in the air. . .Then she entered her car, and drove to work.

At work, she sensed that her fellow Burdine's employees knew about the killer who lived next door. But she proceeded through the workday like another day under the sun and said nothing to anyone about the murder. Not a tremble from her hands, nor a quiver from her voice, betrayed what she knew. Throughout the day, she maintained calm and cheer.

When she returned home that evening, she heard nothing from her neighbor's apartment—total silence. The body was gone, and, apparently, the tenant, arrested.

About a day later, she heard on the local news a report: "A black woman was found dead in a motel room at the following motel—. We don't know how she got there." A photo of her flashed across the news screen. "If any one has any information about her, who she belongs to, or where she's from, please contact the police and give them this information. The number is—." Gail deduced that this woman, whose face flashed on the news screen, was the murder victim next door.

The police apparently moved the body and located it somewhere else, and the news reported the body was found in a motel on the other side of town. Gail knew the Jesuits orchestrated this murder, to intimidate Vladimir from meeting her at her apartment; and that they used trashy, criminal men to destroy her reputation.

Around the beginning of August 2002, in the evening hours, while she lingered about her apartment, she heard a barrage of gun shots. This time, not from her next door neighbor, but from her building, several apartments down. This time, she did not call the police.

Days later, she heard on national news that several Hispanic bodies (described on the news as Mexicans, possibly victims of gross neglect or immigration crimes) mysteriously showed up in the middle of the U.S. (Texas area). She suspected that these may have been the victims of that barrage of gunfire she'd heard several apartments down. Perhaps the Jesuits wanted to remind President Bush, who lived in Texas, that they still meant business, and

The Forbidden Abyss

that he better continue to cooperate with them in sabotaging Vladimir's love for Gail.

Around September 2002, Vladimir tried to come get Gail in Tallahassee, when he flew to New York under the guise of meetings with the United Nations over the U.S. decision to send troops to Iraq. Brent Spiner cried at that time, because he thought Vladimir would really get Gail as his wife, and it finalized it to Brent that Gail would never be his wife. Not that Brent didn't want Vladimir to have Gail, but Brent still wanted to marry Gail.

However, Gail felt so ill at this time, that she took an ambulance to the hospital. The physicians at the hospital could not explain her migraine headache and dizziness and let her go home. But this attack of Gail's health happened in September 2002, right at the time Vladimir planned to go to Tallahassee from his U.N. meeting in New York, to acquire Gail as his wife.

After Gail's visit to the emergency room, Vladimir eventually left New York to return to Russia, with his fake wife, Lyudmila, and not Gail, by his side.

The Marriage List
2003 to 2011

Gail ran out of money in Tallahassee, and was forced to move to Central Florida to live with her mother. She lived with her mother from January 2003 to July 2004.

On April 10, 2003 Gail was not sure, but sometime in the evening, while in the middle of a conversation with her mom on the living room sofa near the front door, sensed Vladimir wooing her to bed with him (through her brain), using computer/satellite technology.

She had this delicious feeling that Vladimir kissed and caressed her. After about two hours of this, she decided it was for real, and went to her room and gave in to the sensations. By making love to Gail long distance through her brain, Vladimir introduced Gail to brain to brain communications. It seemed he was right there in the bed with her. After some delicious lovemaking, she heard him talk to her, like "thoughts" to her brain. She wasn't sure then, but it seemed like him.

This was the start of Gail's brain to brain communications with her men, though, until Matthew McConaughey participated in November 2005, the only man who communicated with her brain to brain was Vladimir.

Vladimir's presence seemed very close to what she thought he'd be like. From April 10, 2003 onwards, she began to feel that Vladimir made love to her or talked to her all day long.

This "presence" (in her mind) who spoke with her was assertive (like he was comfortable giving instructions), but not aggressive or mean, very physically affectionate and passionate, with a pleasant sense of humor. The presence was a very direct person—he didn't beat around the bush. This is what she'd imagine Vladimir to be like.

From April 10, 2003 and onwards, she had quite a lot of lovemaking fantasies with Vladimir in her bed, because Vladimir continually wooed her to bed with him. She felt like he made love to her all the time and found it hard to resist his pull, because she loved him. She just went with it and enjoyed her fantasies, because she longed for his presence.

However, Jesuits wasted no time to sabotage the long distance lovemaking, and on the morning of April 11, 2003, in the middle of her "fantasy" with Vladimir in her bed, she heard *planes fly overhead*.

Jesuit obsession with her love life stunned her, even those aspects that they could only know about through mind reading technology, which they obviously possessed. They often interfered with Vladimir's brain to

The Forbidden Abyss

brain loving by sabotaging Gail's orgasms with Vladimir during the exchanges.

From November 2001 forward Vladimir appeared with Lyudmila in public, while in private brain to brain communications he made love to Gail from 2003 and onwards (who had more of the personality of his wife that died). Gail kept him going since September 2001. The Lyudmila woman was just for "wife show for the American press", to appease the American Jesuits who ran the United States, so that these Jesuits wouldn't cause trouble for Russia and Vladimir (like another Kursk disaster).

The problem with this "wife show", was it fed on his denial that his wife never really died. Whenever he made a serious move to marry Gail, the Jesuits stole sperm and artificially inseminated (Olympic athlete Alina Kabaeva) or killed people or threatened to kill Laura Bush, the U.S. President's wife, or even worse threatened to kill Gail. This fed on his fears that he could never, ever handle another death of a woman he loves (Gail). He felt if this happened to him one more time, he'd commit suicide.

The more he knew Gail, the more he loved her. The more he loved her, the more he felt he'd commit suicide if she died on him. So when the Jesuits threatened his love for her, he went into his protective shell of denial, telling himself his wife never died and put on the Lyudmila performance. He felt he had to do this to protect Gail and to protect himself from a heart that would break and bleed, until he had no life in him, should Gail depart from him in this life.

Gail began to doubt whether he could ever overcome the Jesuits. She told him (2005 and 2006), "You'll never marry me. You won't even meet me. The Jesuits know how to scare you, with all the crap they put out about you."

The truth is, that Vladimir's real wife respected him as a husband, person and a leader, and had a mature, cool-headed understanding and support for her husband (as depicted in Vladimir's memoir *First Person),* which differed from the *competitive, self-centered, and lying approach of the fake wife Lyudmila. Lyudmila was obviously not the woman Vladimir married in 1983.* Though Vladimir in *First Person* changed his wife's name, his portrayal of her personality when she was with him, was accurate. Except he omitted the reason why she cried when she learned he would be Russian President. She cried because she was dying.

Vladimir praised Gail constantly and asked for her advice to help him with his job (though she told him he should not) and urged her to write her *Conspiracy Law.* He adored her, so he tried to make it obvious to her that he was not married to Lyudmila, that Gail was his woman, but wore a wedding ring *to deflate "dirt" and gossip into his personal life (Alina Kabaeva), and to appease President Bush and the American government.*

But Vladimir did want to convince Gail he really planned to marry her. He even adopted her son. Gail found that all she wrote on her com-

Vladimir and Catherine the Great

puter, Vladimir could view, using computer/satellite technology. All she had to do was write something on her computer screen and he could see what she wrote. She began writing him every day on a computer that her stepdad gave her in 2003. The day that Vladimir adopted her son was a momentous day.

> December 7, 2003: Time now is 7:40 p.m. and my son is flying on a jet towards Vladimir Putin. From what I understand, the Jesuits are attacking my son's breathing (using satellite and 666-Computer technology).
>
> I ask all Bible-believing Christians all over the world to pray for my son as he flies on a jet towards Vladimir Putin. Vladimir felt he needed to immediately remove my son from the custody of his dad because he was afraid for my son's life.
>
> It appears as soon as the jet took off, the Jesuits used satellite technology (in combination with their wretched 666-Computer technology) to attempt to kill my son. Vladimir did not feel it was safe to allow my son to remain in the care of his dad, and wanted to remove my son from the father's care immediately. I have absolute confidence in Vladimir's ability to care for my son and have instructed Vladimir to do whatever he feels is best regarding my son. I think Vladimir will be a better father to my son than his real father. I am certain that Vladimir will be a great father to my son and a much better role model to him than his real father.
>
> Vladimir tells me that my son is a tough kid and that he's handling himself remarkably well. He is taking all this publicity and the pressures that go with being associated with a President remarkably well.
>
> Time now is 8:25 p.m. and Vladimir seems to tell me that the jet has landed and my son is okay, but they have him on oxygen just to be safe (in case the Jesuits pull a fast one). My son's emotions (which we can read via the 666-Computer) tell us that he is very happy to be with Vladimir and feels relieved that he is no longer with his real father.
>
> He is absolutely thrilled (and very calm) to be with Vladimir.

Vladimir had custody of Gail's son from December 7, 2003 to around 2009, but when Gail's son was returned to his real dad around 2009, all his memories of his time with Vladimir were removed and replaced with the memories of his look-alike. When Vladimir acquired Gail's son, the Jesuits replaced the real son with a look-alike, and the look-alike lived with the real dad while the real son lived with Vladimir.

Gail's son actually became very close to Vladimir's two daughters, and for a while, Vladimir almost decided to let her son marry his younger daughter. But

The Forbidden Abyss

when Gail gave up on Vladimir as a lover in 2006, and Vladimir decided to return the son to his dad in 2009, so that Gail could see her son again, Vladimir's younger daughter went on with her life without Gail's son.

When Vladimir returned Gail's son to the real dad around 2009, Jesuits abandoned use of the look-alike and let the dad have his real son back. Jesuits were forced to use a look-alike from 2003 to around 2009 because they were unable to make a full clone of Gail's son.

Vladimir tried many times to give the wife of his heart, Gail, financial support, but Jesuits sabotaged almost all his attempts. When Gail got a job at a major retailer, the Jesuits moved quickly to sabotage that source of income for her, by trying to take her car from her.

While Gail lived in her new apartment, she survived two major Jesuit satellite-induced hurricanes that plowed right through her town. At the last minute, on November 1, 2004, Gail decided to vote for George Bush as President in the U.S. Presidential elections. She sent in her ballot through absentee ballot.

The next day, on November 2, 2004, her mother called to inform her that General Motors Finance had called at her mother's residence, to inquire over her late car payments. Gail instructed Vladimir to investigate the matter and to enforce her Conspiracy Law, and to castigate General Motors Finance for calling her mother's residence rather than hers.

Apparently, because she had voted for George Bush, the Jesuits did not waste any time to use George Bush to further their conspiracy against Vladimir Putin. The Jesuits chose to use Bush, because Gail had just voted for Bush and so she'd never suspect that Bush would have anything to do with the conspiracy they planned for her in a few days.

The Jesuits approached Mr. Bush, while he was in a hallway at the White House—at gunpoint. The Jesuit, who posed as a U.S. Senator (actually a clone of a real senator) aimed his pistol at Bush's head, and scowled, "Well, did you know that yesterday, your lovely Gail decided to vote for you as President?" The Jesuit clicked the trigger of the pistol and shoved the pistol into George Bush's head. "Remember the contract you signed with us to obtain your Presidency?"

Bush trembled. "What do you want?"

The pistol remained at Bush's head. "Well, I'll tell you this much. If you don't do what we want, we'll blast this pistol into your head and then another into your wife's head. And we'll make it look like Vladimir Putin did it." The Jesuit smiled. "By the way, your re-election is assured. You'll have a second term—thanks to us. So you better do what we want."

George Bush screamed at him. "What do you want!"

"I'm going to escort you to the phone and you will say exactly as I instruct you to say, on this phone." The Jesuit shoved the pistol into Bush's head and escorted him to a White House phone. "Here, it's all in writing. You'll read from this script."

Bush read it. "Hey, I can't do this. I'll be impeached. This is murder."

The Jesuit shoved the pistol harder into his head, and made a phone call to another Jesuit. "Get your agents ready, flank Laura Bush, and when I give you the signal, blast a bullet into her head."

"But I can't do this to Gail Chana. She's popular with the people. The public will crucify me."

Vladimir and Catherine the Great

The Jesuit laughed. "You like to be dead? Or even better, you like your wife and you to be dead?"

"Alright, take me to the phone."

Bush walked to the phone like a robot, and called the towers who'd tow away Gail's car on November 8, 2004. "Hello, this is President George W. Bush. I need to talk with the head of your towing service."

"This is George W. Bush? What do you need to talk to us for?"

"I'm giving you a Presidential order. When General Motors Finance Services contacts you about the late car payments of Gail Chana, you are to tow Gail's car, regardless of what else happens. If you don't, Russian President Vladimir Putin will hire hit men to come and get you, and it appears, there's nothing I can do to prevent it."

"Look, we don't want to get involved with all this politics."

"I'll pay you a million dollars if you follow this order."

A pause. "Oh. . .*really.* . .perhaps we will reconsider. . ."

Bush ended the call, and faced the Jesuit. "Now, are you happy?"

The Jesuit shoved his pistol harder into Bush's head. "You aren't finished yet."

"What? You mean there's more you want from me?"

"Of course." The Jesuit smiled. "You know that Gail will raise hell when her car gets towed. We are prepared for that contingency. . ."

Bush sat down and sulked on a bench. His hands grasped nervously at his hair. "What else do you want from me?"

"We're going to follow you until November the 8th—or more, if we have to, to ensure you follow all our orders. You're to hire a hit-man to murder Gail at the junk yard she'll come to, when she reclaims her car—that is, if she somehow comes up with the money to pay-off her car. You're to say that this hit-man was hired by Vladimir Putin."

Bush scowled in outrage. "I can't do this to Vladimir!" Bush jerked his head away from the pistol. "And I won't stay President, if I commit this act. I'll be impeached."

"Exactly. That's what we want. And then, our Jesuit, Hillary Rodham Clinton, will be the next U.S. President. We'll have a stronger Jesuit in the White House, a Democrat. That is, because your actions, as a Republican President, will so turn the stomachs of Americans, that they'll vote for her as President." The Jesuit then blasted a shot onto the ground. No one came to assist President Bush. Apparently, the Jesuits had all angles covered. "As you can see, your Secret Service seems to be defunct. We have them all distracted. They never expected us to attack you *inside the White House.*"

The Jesuit got on his cell phone in front of President Bush. "Get your hit men ready to hit Laura Bush, because President Bush is going to break his contract with us." The Jesuit smiled. "Make sure the guy is a Russian, *with KGB connections.* . .."

On November 8th, 2004, the Jesuits towed Gail's car; and the Jesuits used their computer/satellite technology on Russian President Vladimir Putin to give him a sudden and devastating heart attack that day, and he was rushed to the hospital. Several days later, thanks to Gail's Conspiracy Law networks, ground

The Forbidden Abyss

breaking technology was used on President Putin to save his life, and he regained enough bearings to assume some Presidential responsibilities.

But because she couldn't afford her car payments and assumed that Vladimir had taken care of these for her, as she walked on the balcony outside her apartment and talked with the Jesuit maintenance man about her loss of cable service, she noticed a towing vehicle came into the area of her apartment (where her car was parked).

The towing vehicle backed up toward her car and a crude, vulgar and muscular looking man (with dark curly and greasy hair) rushed out, and began to hook up her car. Because her car was about to be towed, Gail ran to approach the man. "Why are you towing my car?"

"Can you open your car's door for me, please?" he said, as he studied her car.

"No! This car has been paid off. You have no right to tow my car."

"That's not what I've been told. General Motors Finance Services has ordered me to tow your car."

The man ignored all Gail had to say, except for brief and gruff replies, rushed to his towing vehicle, got out something that looked like a wrench bar, that he slid under the hood of the car into her engine, that made it so he could tow her car, even with the door shut and her hook still on the wheel.

The car's tires skidded and left marks in the parking lot as his towing vehicle took her car, and because Gail's anti-theft hook was still on the steering wheel, the vehicle's horn went off as he towed away her vehicle. Helpless to do anything, she heard her car's horn get lighter and lighter, as her car disappeared from her life.

She dialed 911 to call the police, and talked to a local police officer. No use.

A letter that she wrote to Vladimir Putin, to his Russian Embassy address explains what happened and what she went through:

November 8, 2004

Vladimir Putin, Russian President
Russian Embassy
2650 Wisconsin Ave., N.W.
Washington D.C. 20007

Dear Vladimir:

The time is 1:30 p.m. on 11-8-04 and my car was towed about an hour ago, by an unidentified tow truck and the man who towed my car was the same man who came to get my car back in January 2003. I recognized him. I assume it's the same towing company. There was no identification on the towing truck. Back in Jan. 2003, my mother was with me and when this man showed up, he escorted my mother and I to the SunTrust bank at the intersection of Augusta St. and Florence Ave. and my mother sent the $600 car payment to General Motors Finance (via Western Union express), that prevented my car from being towed back in Jan. 2003.

I don't have my car now and I don't have a way to go to work, unless I pay outrageous taxi fees.

Vladimir and Catherine the Great

I called the police while the man was towing my car and a police officer showed up and said that there was nothing he could do, that this was a civil matter (and that I needed to contact General Motors Finance Services), and so this man with this tow truck, went off with my car. Because there was a hook on the steering wheel, he opened my front hood and did something to my engine so he could tow my car. I hope he didn't damage the car. I received no notice from General Motors Finance that my car would be towed today, and when I called them to tell them that I had received no notice, I was told that they couldn't give me a notice, because I am under bankruptcy protection. *I never heard this before.* All my conversation with the police and with the General Motors Finance people can be obtained from wiretapped recordings of my cell phone.

The guy just showed up, and took my car, without giving me any information about who he was or about which towing company had my car, or about what his telephone number is. This guy said the car was being repossessed and that I could not get the car. He wouldn't give me his name, phone number or the name of his towing company. All he said was that my vehicle was being repossessed, because the payments were not current. His towing vehicle had no identification, except a phone number on flaps in front of the tires of his towing truck, which I read out loud to the police on my cell phone—this can be obtained through wiretapping (as I attempted to get information from this man).

When I called General Motors Finance Services at 1-800-561-5805 around 1 p.m. today, I spoke with someone who identified herself as Miss Smith at ext. 4000. I asked her to have General Motors Finance Services send me something in writing that states my car is not paid off, because I told her that I believed that my car had been paid off by you, and I wanted something in writing, as proof that my car had not been paid off by you.

I told her if I had something in writing that stated my car was *not* paid off, that then I would make car payments. *I asked her to put it in writing that you had not paid off my car.* She said I would be getting something in the mail that would state that my car has not been paid off, but that they couldn't make a statement that Vladimir Putin had not paid off my car, and that the only way I could get my car back would be if General Motors Finance received about $2,000.00—that they wouldn't agree to monthly payments anymore.

She also told me that I could not have my car back, unless the total pay off for the car was received all at once, for the whole amount of about $2,000.00, and that there was no way I would get my car back in time for work tomorrow, and that she couldn't tell me how much the pay off was right now on the phone, but that it was estimated to be about $2,065.34, and that I would get something in the mail about this.

She told me to call you and have you call her at 1-800-434-5987, ext. 4569 to state that my car had been paid off, and to have you deal with the matter.

I then called the Russian Embassy (which is the only number I have for you) at (202) 232-6020 and spoke with someone who sounded like he had a strong Russian accent. *I thought we had Germans at the Russian embassy.* **This is because at that time Gail had written law to kick out the Russians at the Russian embassy in Washington D.C. and replace them with Germans, because the Russians were not in obedience to Vladimir Putin.** I asked this Russian sounding man to contact you, and to tell you that I had an emergency in regard

The Forbidden Abyss

to my car. I left him my name and phone number. The man wasn't rude, but acted like I was a mental case and eventually hung up on me. So I gave up on calling the Russian Embassy.

I then called the bus service to see if I could take a bus to go to work. The bus schedule is very bad and only runs during the day time, and I would have to take three buses to get to work from here. So, it appears taking the bus will not work, because I often work at night.

Vladimir, I need *evidence* that this car has been paid off—in the form of a title or something. And now these criminals at General Motors Finance Services will not work with me unless I give them something like $2,100 all at once. They said they wouldn't work with monthly payments, that they wanted the $2,100 (which they allege is what I owe them) all at once!

I have no way to get to work. I'm *not* going to call my mother about this because this will strengthen the Jesuit's case against you.

I just called a limousine service, and arranged to have a week of service (five days), where they will take me to work and pick me up from work with female drivers who will use their private vehicles. It costs $75.00 for a week. This is more than my salary and eventually, I cannot afford to pay this amount for transportation.

If I don't get my car back, or I can't car pool, then transportation to and from work will end up costing me $300 a month. Then I won't be able to afford my rent and other expenses. Vladimir, I am in a bind, and don't know what to do. I am not used to being without a vehicle. I wish I was with you and my son. I hate playing these Jesuit games.

Is there any way you can communicate with me directly? I know we have a problem with Jesuit imposters. Is there any way I can obtain proof that my car is paid off?

Because I didn't have a title to my car, when the police showed up, there was nothing that they would do for me. So this towing man went off with my car.

I just wrote some new law that deals with a national health care plan and I think the Jesuits are very upset about this, so they've been very brazen and did something very illegal to get my car today. I ask God to give you wisdom as you deal with this. In the meanwhile, my financial situation is not good, because being without a car makes it so that I cannot go to work unless I take a taxi or pay for an escort to drive me (which I will be doing for the coming week). And my job does not pay me enough to take a taxi (or an escort) every day to and from work.

So, I don't have a car and now I don't have a way to get to work, unless I pay outrageous transportation costs (for an escort) that I can't afford. Some of my favorite music tapes were in the car, and the guy who towed my car, has all my favorite tapes. The towing occurred when I was outside talking with the maintenance man (because the maintenance man kept unplugging the power to my cable). It's obvious that the Jesuits are trying to tie in this towing with the lack of cable service to my apartment. Also, when I came to this computer to type a report about this matter earlier, my power went off and I had to restart my computer later. So the Jesuits are on a rampage and are trying to make conspiracies about everything—like the power failure, hurricane, General Motors Finance Services, my job, computer, towing, taxi conspiracy.

Vladimir and Catherine the Great

Please, if there is any way we could communicate directly, this would be wonderful. I long to be with you and my son.

I hope you like the new laws I wrote for a national health care plan. I think this would be very good for the U.S. and the world. You can download these laws on my Conspiracy Laws and Government document. It's a new Section 55. I think these laws are the *real reason* the Jesuits took my car. Once these laws are passed, it should really help us to remove from the Jesuits their ability to control people with their criminal satellite/computer technology over people's brains, and so the Jesuits are desperate and doing very brazen things. We need to be very tough on them.

Any ways, you know my situation, because I've already typed this out on my computer and you can download everything from my computer. I wish so bad I was with you. I pray that God will make a way for us to be together, without all this Jesuit garbage causing problems between us.

Make sure to enforce my laws to the letter. There have been some death penalty violations of my laws in this towing matter. Try this case publicly on International Broadcast News and please get me some money and some transportation! Please make sure I can afford to pay my upcoming rent and dental expenses. I have a cavity that will be filled on 11-15-04. These Jesuits are monsters.

I shall pray much about this matter, and ask God to give you courage and wisdom. You may want to tie in this case with the case we have going with Lis Wiehl. Thank you so much for your assistance. I miss my cassette tapes (that went off with my towed car). They took my Christian music and all my Russian and German tapes. I long to be with you and with my son.

Devotedly yours,

Gail Chana

A few days after her car was towed, she received a NOTICE AFTER REPOSSESSION OR VOLUNTARY SURRENDER (BANKRUPTCY). That stated: We have obtained the automobile, called the "vehicle". WE ACKNOWLEDGE THAT ONE OR BOTH OF YOU ARE UNDER THE PROTECTION OF THE UNITED STATES BANKRUPTCY CODE. WE DO NOT INTEND BY THIS LETTER TO MAKE DEMAND UPON YOU PERSONALLY. THIS NOTICE IS SENT SIMPLY TO COMPLY WITH STATE LAW.

DESCRIPTION OF VEHICLE FOLLOWS...

NOTICE OF SALE: The vehicle will be offered for sale, at private sale, beginning on 11/24/2004, and from day to day thereafter until sold. The vehicle will be sold by General Motors Finance Services.

HOW TO GET THE VEHICLE BACK:

You have a right to redeem the vehicle AT ANY TIME BEFORE IT IS ACTUALLY SOLD. To redeem, we must receive the NET AMOUNT itemized below at the address on reverse, plus any other amounts that may become due after the date of this Notice and before the vehicle is sold. To learn the exact amount please call us at the number listed on the back of this Notice.

UNPAID BALANCE $2,022.33

The Forbidden Abyss

PLUS: FINANCE CHARGE TO: 11/24/2005 $45.25
SUBTOTAL OF CHARGES $2,067.58
NET AMOUNT NEEDED TO REDEEM: $2,067.58

The vehicle will not be sold until the date shown in the "Notice of Sale" at the *earliest*. After that date, YOU CAN STILL REDEEM THE VEHICLE BEFORE IT IS ACTUALLY SOLD. If you do, neither we nor the Dealer will have any further claim on it.

If you have any questions, you may call or write us.

General Motors Finance Services, P.O. Box 980, Roanoke, Texas 76262, (877) 687-6546, ext. 7659.

Date Notice mailed: 11-09-2004. By its agent Dan Steele, Customer Service Rep.

Gail had to humiliate herself and ask her mom for assistance to pay about $2,067.58 plus a $12.95 charge to send the Western Union quick collect, which was the only way General Motors Finance would accept the money for her car's pay off. She sent this money to them immediately (via Western Union) and *in cash* to get her car back, because she was required to fully pay off her car *in cash* about $2,067.58.00 (via Western Union to General Motors Finance).

She came up with the money "just in time" because the towers were about to send her car to a big city (hours from where she lived), in order to put it up for auction—where she'd have to drive hours to get her car back. After General Motors Finance received her money and after a lot of run-around, General Motors Finance Services finally give her the number to call, where she could get her car.

She told Vladimir to add this towing incident onto the Finance Services and medical conspiracy case she had against the Jesuits.

In the meanwhile, while she did without her car, she still needed a way to work and discovered that the local bus could only take her to work, if she took about three different buses and she would have to meander around town on city buses for about three hours to get to work from her apartment—when it took her twenty minutes to drive from her apartment to work.

In other words, Jesuits ensured her town had lousy bus service.

When she asked people at work to give her rides, not many responded, perhaps because their schedules differed from her. This just wouldn't do, and she realized that the Jesuits even manipulated her city's bus service so that the buses didn't have any direct routes from her apartment to the retailer where she worked.

So she ended up paying about $75.00 for an escort service for a week to take her to and from work and to the dentist (to have a cavity in her molar filled). She bought groceries at her job and put them in the escort's car. And she walked to the CVS pharmacy about one block from her apartment for other things she needed, until she got her car back. She didn't want to humiliate herself before her mother any more than she already had, because she claimed to her mother that Vladimir would take care of her, and it was humiliating enough that Vladimir couldn't rescue her from the General Motors Finance Services towers. The escort was a nice and dependable man, who tried to sell her his car, but she said she would still try to get her car back.

Vladimir and Catherine the Great

Because Gail had told her mom that Vladimir wanted to marry her, that he had custody of her son, and that he had millions of dollars from her novel, now she was really humiliated and ashamed of Vladimir, who failed to rescue her when her car was towed.

Vladimir informed her (through computer/satellite brain communications) he had to go into emergency surgery because of a heart condition when her car was towed; and, therefore, was "unavailable". Another had to speak to her via computer/satellite technology during this time, to inform her that Jesuits had removed Vladimir's memories, and that, when her car was towed, he denied he ever knew her.

Gail's supporters did emergency surgery on Vladimir to fix his heart and his brain against Jesuit control.

"Mr. Putin, Gail's car has been towed by General Motors Finance. She called the Russian Embassy in the United States and when she asked to talk to you about her car, the Russian man who answered hung up on her."

Vladimir scowled. "Start a lawsuit against General Motors Finance and all criminals involved in this. I've paid off her car, but those bastard Americans never let me help her. They block me every time." Vladimir was unaware of President Bush's involvement in this, so Putin's lawsuit was directed only at General Motors Finance and those who towed her car.

The day that Gail went to claim her car, President Bush made a call to the towing service. "Gail is getting ready to come pick up her car. Continue to give her a hard time as I instructed you before, and be rude and abrasive. She's a tough woman, so she'll buck you, and when she does—shoot her in the head."

"Wait a minute, President Bush. We can't do this. Russian President Putin has a lawsuit against us and against General Motors Finance, and claims that her car was unjustly towed and that he paid off her car. Who do we listen to—you or him?"

"If you don't do as I say, Vladimir Putin's agents will shoot you in the head. It's either you or Gail."

"God damn it. What kind of hell hole set-up is this?" The man hung up in fury.

The Jesuits then flanked the man at the junkyard. "Well, will you do as President Bush ordered you to do?" They handed him a pistol.

"I'm not holding this thing. . .when she shows up." He looked at the pistol. "She doesn't trust us."

The Jesuits smiled. "Of course, you won't. Put the pistol here in your desk and pull it out at our signal and shoot her."

When Gail called the tower's number, it was difficult to talk to a person, because they were all unavailable and she had to be persistent. She ended up talking to the same man who towed her car.

"I've paid off my car. How can I get my car?"

"Oh, how are you?" he said, with a sarcastic tone. "You won't be able to get your car unless you pay us for holding your car for three days."

"What?"

"Yes that's right." She could hear the glee in his tone.

"And how much is this?"

"Three hundred dollars—and I want *cash*."

The Forbidden Abyss

So Gail had to call her mother back and begged for more money and she told her mom it had to be cash.

Gail and her mother showed up at the junkyard to pick up her car.

As Gail walked toward the middle-aged man (who wasn't the same guy she talked to on the phone and who had towed her car), she noticed the man looked real frustrated and exasperated. And perhaps he was, because Russian President Vladimir Putin had hit him with a lawsuit for damages the day before, because he dared to charge Gail outrageous charges for each day that he had her car in the junkyard. In confusion, when he saw the car with Gail in it pull up, and she headed towards him, he muttered curse words against Gail and all politicians, and decided he would not murder Gail, because he'd already been hit with a lawsuit, and didn't want murder charges next.

When she went to the place where her car was stored, the man was very nasty and refused to give her a receipt (dated 11/17/2004) until he had inspected all her bills in the morning light to see if they looked counterfeit. The place where her car was stored looked like a junk yard.

Her mother came with her, and sat in her car and waited for her daughter. The man eyed her mother nervously and didn't dare look behind him to see what the Jesuits did, who were hiding, with their pistols aimed at his head.

Gail's toughness, and her mother, who stared at him, caused his nerves to break. He couldn't shoot her, and if those Jesuits wanted to shoot him, well, they could go ahead, because he was already in enough trouble, perhaps it would be better if he was dead.

So God protected Gail and she got her car back, and she did not suffer from a bullet to her head, nor did the man at the junkyard. At least, not while she was there.

Gail tried to look like a President's wife on her limited income. Because she lost the $500.00 Montgomery Ward sewing machine she had in Seattle, which got auctioned off (with all the stuff she had in her Mukilteo apartment), because she couldn't afford to move her stuff from Seattle to Florida, she had no sewing machine until late 2004. Around Christmas 2004, she bought herself a present, a new Singer sewing machine for $100.00, just basic stitches, that's all she needed. It worked fine for her.

In the spring of 2005, she sewed herself a pair of blue cotton pants with pockets and belt loops that looked good on her. Sewing machines had gone down in price since the time she bought her Montgomery Ward sewing machine in Portland (1985). Later in 2007, Gail still wanted to look fashionable and she helped accomplished this with her sewing machine.

Vladimir planned to attend his Feb. 23-25, 2005 Bratislava, Slovakia meeting with President Bush, by himself, without his fake wife, because he really wanted to marry Gail. This infuriated the mind-reading Jesuits. As his jet neared Slovakia, Gail watched the news, and an important news break (Feb. 23, 2005) interfered and took over all the airwaves, "Pope John Paul II has been taken to Gemelli hospital. He's having breathing difficulties. It appears he'll need a tube inserted into his lungs to assist his breathing." Vladimir and Gail didn't know it, but Jesuit leader Zack Knight informed Gail (in 2012) that Jesuits murdered

Vladimir and Catherine the Great

John Paul years ago, and this was his lifelike robot or android, who was badly malfunctioning and needed to go any ways.

Vladimir knew that Jesuits wanted to frame him with the pope's death, to portray him to the world as a cold and bloody killer, a pretext for Jesuit-led nations to declare war on Russia. Intimidated, and hoping to save the pope's life, Vladimir descended the down ramp from his Russian jet with Lyudmila by his side again. But this Lyudmila had a different appearance from his previous Lyudmila.

Jesuits were outraged. How dare Vladimir pull this stunt on them. To ensure Vladimir's continued appearance with Lyudmila in public, the Jesuit Order decided to carry out their murder of the pope John Paul II android. But, Gail knew the Jesuits may murder John Paul, and in her Conspiracy Law, wrote international law to cover the election of a new pope. In her law, she asked John Paul II (who she thought was a friend to Vladimir's love for her) to choose the next pope. Her law was honored and Vladimir and her got what they wanted: (Joseph Ratzinger) Pope Benedict.

Unfortunately, the Jesuits murdered the real pope Benedict in Nov. 2011, by attaching a bomb to him that exploded as he escaped to Church of Gail, not allowing him to escape unharmed from a Vatican bombing.

By February 2006, Gail gave up on Vladimir as a lover. At least Brent called her on the phone and talked to her. This Russian President wouldn't even do that. So she reinstated Brent Spiner. From 2006 to early 2010, when she ignored the Russian President as a lover, he went into depression. He came home to his house and there was no wife, and Gail no longer made love to him, so "From Russia With Love" his heart flew to her in a YouTube video he had made for her, and he bared his chest in public to remind her he was still interested.

But Gail did not have the Internet at the time he made the video, so he got depressed to the point that he didn't care if he remained as Russian head-of-state. Too manly to complain about Gail's obsession with Brent over him, and because he genuinely liked Brent, his depression never reached Gail in brain to brain communications. Perhaps the Jesuits also blocked Gail from sensing Vladimir's feelings telepathically through the brain to brain computer/satellite servers at this time.

What use was it to be a big shot head-of-state, when his heart died of loneliness? He realized that he couldn't live without her. Vladimir and Gail had the same heroes: great writers, artists, musicians, generals, monarchs and God. Though Vladimir liked sports and judo, he had inner depths, manliness and heroism that the Olympic gymnast or Lyudmila could never nurture or understand.

Sometime in 2008 or 2009, Gail's men decided to return Gail's son to his biological father, so that Gail could someday see her son again. Now, that it appeared Brent would be her husband rather than Vladimir, they felt her son needed to go back to his dad, for Gail's sake. Her son's memories with Vladimir Putin removed, Gail's men returned him to his real dad.

One day in 2010, after Gail had not made love to him since 2006, a depressed Vladimir drank a handle of Russian vodka before he packed up and set off for the jungles, like he'd done many times before. He neglected to tell his men back at headquarters that he intended to die out there. He wandered the

The Forbidden Abyss

jungle for many hours before attracting the attention of a five hundred pound Bengal tiger.

From his position in the bushes, he made lots of noise, trying to rouse the tiger. He shouted in Russian, "Tiger! The fire in your eyes is like the fire within me: predatory, passionate—eat my heart, tear it from my chest! It might as well be!"

The tiger charged him, its claws outstretched for his eyes. When it was within three seconds from devouring him, his future life, like a clear and vivid vision, Jesus flashed before his mind's eye. He saw many years ahead of him, and a possible future with Gail waiting for him. He couldn't deny himself this chance.

A black belt in judo, he punched the tiger in the face, grabbed it in a headlock, and snapped its neck, and yelled, with renewed passion for his Gail.

It was early 2010. Gail had not made love to Vladimir since 2006. Several weeks after Vladimir killed the tiger, Gail got the Internet, and after observing the depression in Vladimir's face, her heart went out to him. The old feelings she had for him came back like a nostalgic dream. How proud she always was of him. How manly and heroic she felt he was. The days and nights she dreamed of him and made love to him like a hero returned to her heart.

Oh, how he needed her, how she made him into the great man she knew he was. She believed him the bravest, smartest and most perfect head of state in all the world. When he wanted to make her proud, his heart flowed into his moves in bed, thrilling her with his passion, daring, breadth and tenderness. His manliness and vastness as a man had fused with her vastness as a woman, so that his love inspired her to become Catherine the Great for him.

He used his scientists to help reconstruct her genetic profile and she flowered into Catherine the Great before his eyes. He had made her the Empress of Russia, a position she did not want, but she lived only to please him and make him happy. She was always strong for him, so she could always nurture his manliness, when he had doubts about his greatness. She always believed in his vastness and greatness, so that he became the man she believed him to be.

How she underestimated the depth of his feelings for her and how strongly they had bonded. She viewed some YouTube videos he'd made for her, with songs such as "From Russia with Love" and "I'm a Better Man for Having Loved You" by Engelbert Humperdinck .

Oh dear, the Russian President really loves me, Gail thought. He's in clinical depression. I must make love to him. My awesome Vladimir, my darling. Forgive me Vladimir for neglecting you. Oh, how he needs me to love him, to believe in him and nurture him as a man with my body and my soul. Jesus, forgive me, but I still have feelings for him in my heart. I so bonded with him from 2001 to 2006, he is as much a part of me as Brent has been. I will have both of these men. Please forgive me, Jesus. My Vladimir, my awesome Russian President still needs me and I still love him.

So, Gail decided to make brain to brain love to both Vladimir and Brent at the same time, and reinstated Vladimir as her brain to brain lover.

From that day forward, the marriage list of men who wanted to marry Gail became formal. The Jesuits had made it so that these men could only find happi-

Vladimir and Catherine the Great

ness with her; therefore, she would do her best to love them all in the special way that she had bonded with each of them.

Brent understood Vladimir's pain. He recalled how he felt when he lost Gail to Vladimir from 2001 to 2006. Therefore, he allowed Vladimir to share brain to brain intimacy with his Gail.

Gail decided that if a man was on her marriage list, it was okay with Jesus to make brain to brain loving with more than one at a time. But that if she ever had real sex with any of them, that would be marriage and she could only have real sex with one man on her marriage list. Because Gail believed that sex was marriage, she could only have sex with the man who had the number one spot on her marriage list. Brent still retained his number one spot and Vladimir now had the number two spot. Brent was first and the bravest, but brave and heroic Vladimir still deserved her laurels and the highest of her heart's affection.

The more Vladimir loved Gail, the more he feared her possible death and how it would devastate him. And that's just the reason he wouldn't formally marry her. When he tried to marry her, the Jesuits threatened to kill her or to kill President Bush's wife.

If Gail died, she knew Vladimir would kill himself. But, at least now, she understood how much the almighty Russian President needed her, and she had never stopped loving him. She decided that it was possible to love more than one man at a time. So, even if he could never marry her in the normal sense of the word "marriage", Jesus would forgive her for making love to him brain to brain at the same time as Brent, because this is what both Brent and Vladimir desperately needed.

It seemed only she understood both of these men and how Jesuits had devastated their hearts. They didn't want anyone else but her, because only making love to her healed the deadly wounds they suffered in their hearts from the cruel Jesuit empire. Her courage in love reached down to the deepest recesses of their manhood and made them feel manly again, only she had the power to heal them. She came to terms with this with her Lord, and Jesus seemed to say with a smile, "Go ahead and love more than one at a time, my child. It's okay with me, because I know you love me most of all. You nurture them all for me, to strengthen them for My service."

The formidable Jesuits attacked any man who dared to fall in love with Gail, then Gail would love that man and heal him. Once this happened, the man bonded to Gail for life. These men also bonded with each other and found that they understood each other's pain: the pain of loving the woman forbidden by the Jesuit empire. Only a man who had crossed that forbidden abyss could understand another man who'd done the same, so Gail's marriage list of men became an army of men that Gail used to unite together against the cruel Jesuit Order.

Perhaps because Gail loved Jesus more than anything, Jesus honored any man who loved her. A man couldn't love her without loving the Jesus she loved above everything. It seemed that all men who ended up loving Gail, would end up loving Jesus. Therefore, the marriage list of men who wanted Gail, would become Jesus' greatest army for righteousness and courage against Satan's treachery in perhaps a millennium. So much so, that Jesus Himself would show up to lead Gail's army, in fulfillment of the prophecy of Zechariah 9:15, a verse based on the king David woman's birthday of September 15th.

The Forbidden Abyss

"The Lord of hosts shall defend them; and they shall devour, and subdue with sling stones; and they shall drink, and make a noise as through wine: and they shall be filled like bowls, and as the corners of the altar."

Gail decided to have brain to brain intimacy with Vladimir and Brent both, because Vladimir would die without her loving, even if he couldn't marry her. She'd love her men and leave the results to God.

The result would be a group of disciples for Jesus Christ. Agnostic and Jewish Brent Spiner's undying love for Gail would transform into undying love for Jesus Christ. Brent would end up meeting Jesus Christ almost every day, while Jesus would use Brent's willingness to die for Gail—the woman who loved Jesus above everything—to guide her men into daring and courageous service towards their Lord Jesus Christ.

QUEBEC TRIAL
Brent Spiner's Leap of Courage: 2011

Brent Spiner in July 2012: "Loree humiliated me, and it felt like she was my oppressor for a long time, but to have you stand up for me and show the world what really happened and how I really am has helped to make me stronger."

Though Gail's men wanted to marry her, they wanted most to protect her. A dead or near dead wife would do them no good. For this reason, her men actually liked having other good men besides themselves who wanted to marry Gail. This became The Marriage List. The Jesuit Order seemed far too formidable for one man alone.

Because Jesuits had rewritten Gail's entire genetic profile to minimize her genius intelligence and to sabotage her Catherine the Great and King David genes, Vladimir Putin set up a Nanotechnology Research Team around 2004 to 2005, who restored to Gail the brain she had at birth.

Brent and Vladimir needed Gail to be the king David and Catherine the Great that she was at birth; therefore, they restored to Gail the brain she had at birth over a course of several years, from around 2003 to 2008. During this time she gradually became more and more like Catherine the Great and King David.

Horrified that their plans to destroy the Catherine the Great and king David baby born in 1957 had failed, the Jesuits put all their energies into destroying Gail's reputation, health, finances and whatever else they could get away with. But because of the famous and powerful men who loved and supported Catherine the Great and King David in Gail, they couldn't kill her outright, without sustaining catastrophic damage to their reputations that could possibly bring down the Jesuit Order.

Rather they launched a massive propaganda campaign, using millions of Jesuits, to make her appear paranoid schizophrenic whenever she used her website, videos or writing to expose Jesuits. They hoped to flood out any exposure Gail gave them, by drowning out her message with millions of Jesuits who would flood the Internet in a propaganda campaign to make Gail appear crazy and unreliable, using their age-old technique of character assassination.

Jesuits did not limit their brain interference to Gail; they had removed from Brent's memories details about Loree McBride's September 1992 rape. They hoped that by doing so, they could convince Brent to want Loree.

But Brent never wanted Loree ever. During the Quebec trial in August 2011, as Loree shoved herself on Brent and Gail to destroy their budding new correspondence, she divulged details of the rape that served as triggers to bring back

The Forbidden Abyss

Brent's memories.

Brent's sleep then became an avalanche of nightmares. Loree's descriptions of her rape of him, made him feel as if she had thrown him right back into September 1992, like he was being raped all over again.

The memories were so raw, and pierced him like a knife, that he tried to deny the horrific events ever happened; mortified at the thought that Gail might throw him out like a dirty rag, if she knew what vile actions his body had committed.

Loree wanted victory, at any price, even if it meant Brent's suicide. Brent Spiner and Gail Chana must never have happiness in love with each other, which was Loree's mission. If Loree failed at this mission, Jesuits programmed her to self-destruct and take down Brent and Gail with her.

When Brent finally had the courage to write Gail through a YouTube channel he created for her in June 2011, the Jesuits retaliated with their website orderofthejesuits.com in July 2011, listing their agents, targets and mission, and their intention to target and murder Gail, Brent, Vladimir, Matthew McConaughey, Hugh Jackman, and Gerard Butler.

Gail, Brent and Vladimir's jaws dropped at their audacity—what a bold and daring move, to admit in a public website that Loree was indeed their agent and intended to kill Gail. It was obviously a Jesuit attempt to intimidate Brent and cause him to stop writing Gail. Brent felt as if Loree had shoved him back in time, and that she lived in his house and hounded him day and night again.

By the time Gail could afford a computer, she strived to have more authenticity in her relationship with her men. She noticed that the shams and performances imposed on her men, drained their hearts and spirits, forcing them to live like a shell of a man, instead of the real and vital men that she knew them to be.

As she strived to stick up for her men and reveal to the world their true hearts, the Jesuits increased their campaign to make her appear delusional and paranoid schizophrenic.

She thought her brilliant writings and her "presence" online would win over people to her, as they had won her men over to her. But whenever she posted a YouTube video, Jesuits commentators flooded the comments sections, ranting and raving at her for being a psychotic; therefore, Gail shrank back her online presence somewhat, did not allow comments and began removing some videos that, though true, made her really appear crazy.

Jesuits seemed masters at flooding out the truth with a blitzkrieg of websites, commentators and videos they created to drown out the truths of Gail's videos and writings. She began to believe that no matter how brilliant her writings or videos, they could never overcome the millions of Jesuits who lived 24/7 to drown out Gail at every opportunity, to inundate her every time she spoke a truth that incriminated the Jesuits.

Brent communicated with Gail online through a YouTube channel he created just for her in June 2011. This lasted until September 15, 2011, when the Jesuits used a Brent Spiner clone to contact YouTube, causing the cancellation of Brent's "private" YouTube channel for Gail on September 15, 2011 (Gail's birthday), because this clone claimed to YouTube that the real Brent who created this channel was an impersonator.

Quebec Trial

Because the cancellation of Brent's YouTube channel for Gail happened on her birthday, it reinforced to Gail that the real Brent was *not* behind the cancelled YouTube channel. Gail reasoned. . .why would the real Brent, who claimed *not* to have a relationship with Gail, cancel the impersonator's YouTube channel *on Gail's birthday?* Obviously, if this was the famous Brent who knew nothing about Gail, he wouldn't know or care that he cancelled the impersonator's channel on Gail's birthday!

But when Brent finally wrote Gail in June 2011 through the YouTube channel he created for her, he convinced her on July 14, 2011 that she should not allow the Jesuits to intimidate her:

> Why don't you put back up the videos that you've removed in the past? Be it as it may that some of those videos wound up on Jesuit sites which is why you removed them, but why let that stop you? No matter where your story appears, if just one person out there with good in their hearts discovers it, and is listening, they will start to ask questions.
>
> When people begin to ask questions, liberty is strengthened. Whenever you remove one of your videos, or whenever you try to censor yourself, the Jesuits win. Freedom is squashed by the suppression of information. They know that by scaring you they can get you to be quiet, so that's what they do. I think it's time to stop letting them. Be free with yourself Gail, and show them how powerful you are. They can't stand it! Do what you feel is right. No matter what, I will always be by your side.

Gail hid nothing from Brent and on July 14, 2011, bared her heart to him:

> I think you're right. So I will put back up the two videos I removed. One of them was about my brain to brain relationships with other famous men besides yourself. I didn't like what the Jesuits did with that video, because they tried to portray me as some sort of whore.
>
> Sometimes this brain to brain loving seems like an otherworldly experience and I often ask myself if it's really happening. However, when I observe the news about Hugh or Matthew or some of those I've had brain to brain loving with, I do believe I have had it with them.
>
> I really don't feel comfortable having brain to brain loving (even though it seems like an otherworldly experience) with others besides you. Though I do give Vladimir some time, because we need Vladimir Putin frankly. He has really helped us a lot in this war against the Jesuits, and has made possible the brain to brain communication we have now.
>
> As you know, I have bonded with Vladimir and poor Vladimir, like yourself, is a victim of the Jesuit controlled press and has had to parade around with a fake wife for years, just because he fell in love with me. But you get most of my time. I've bonded with you more than with any other.
>
> You and Vladimir are such big men and don't mind me sharing myself a bit with some other good men (like Matthew McConaughey and Hugh Jackman). I still don't feel comfortable 'spreading myself around', even if it's only brain to brain. Because, as you and I know, brain to brain

The Forbidden Abyss

is not sex, but it's close, very close.

Brent wrote Gail on July 15, 2011:
There is no shame in having a breadth of sensual, even if not fully sexual, experiences with men. It's obvious to anyone that I'm your favorite. I'm not jealous. Do be sure to let Vladimir know he's still in your heart. He may be feeling a bit upstaged now that we've achieved a direct two-way communication.

I'll start forwarding all of these messages to Vladimir. I think it will make him feel much more included in our communications. He is still worried about you, but it seems as though since receiving your videos he has enjoyed a much higher morale. He works so hard to defend the world and protect you. It's a good thing he has such a strong woman to stoke his fires or who knows what would have become of him by now. Even without the work of the Jesuits he's always had the weight of the world on his shoulders, you know this just as well as I do.

After Brent shared with her Vladimir's email about the new Jesuit website called orderofthejesuits.com, Gail wrote on July 18, 2011:

I'm pretty sure I will go public about this horrible website orderofthejesuits.com. However, I think I will go to God in prayer first. Thank you so much for sharing this information with me. We need to know this stuff. I will also communicate with Vladimir through you. I'm thrilled that I can now communicate with Vladimir Putin.

She then stated on a July 20, 2011 YouTube video:
The Jesuits made a stinking website and I'm going to give them hell. They make me mad that they have the nerve to do this. Jesuits, I'm giving you hell, right now. How dare you make this website! Who do you think you are, you arrogant bastards.

Yup, and you know what, Jesuits? I know you want to kill me, and I've known it for a long time and I've also known for a long time that I'm the most targeted woman in the world and that I've said that many a time. All I can say is that if you kill me, have fun dealing with all the bad press you're going to get, it'll stink to high heaven.

Gail made Brent feel, for the first time in his twenty year relationship with Loree, that he was no longer her helpless pawn. Gail's courage infused him, making him feel invincible. Because of Gail's daring and courage, he felt he had finally shoved his drug rapist back. Gail's courage fused into his bones, made him feel like a man again. He wrote on July 20, 2011:

Wow! You are an incredibly gutsy woman! I am so proud of you. I feel so blessed to be married to such a fiery, passionate woman who isn't afraid to speak out about what she believes is right. Vladimir, the

Quebec Trial

other men and I all fight to protect you, but you are far from a helpless damsel in distress. You fight back like a true heroine!

The Jesuit plot against Brent's newfound courage with Gail went into action. Drowning in dreams of Gail, who seemed so real to him now that he could practically touch her, Brent forgot to check outside his windows and to survey his surroundings, to make sure all his windows and doors were closed and locked tight. He went to his computer to write Gail.

While he composed an email to Gail, Loree McBride snuck up on him, giving him a sharp whack with her pistol to his head, blacking him out into unconsciousness.

Loree McBride signaled to the Brent Spiner clone that it was safe for him to enter the room. She dragged the unconscious Brent off his desk and into another room.

The Brent clone went to the computer and rewrote on July 20, 2011 the email that Brent, a U.C.L.A. medical school graduate, had started:

> Well, I did a little research about 'Candida albicans'. It seems that if you try and attack the yeast too aggressively, since some of it is supposed to be there, that you can actually make it worse by throwing off your hormones, vaginal pH, and killing the bacteria that is supposed to be keeping the Candida in check naturally.
>
> My theory is that if you go off of the yeast treatment for a while, your body would slowly take over for itself and you'll gradually begin to feel better. . .Eat well and maybe lay low on the supplements for a while so it can adjust and figure out what it needs to do. That is just my opinion. I am so glad that I make you happy.

Gail sensed something was not right with Brent, because it seemed, by his comments, that her brilliant physician had suddenly become stupid. She thought it strange that she needed to remind her brilliant physician Brent about the unique nature of her yeast infection—something he should have already known from the years they discussed this brain to brain. She wrote on July 21, 2011:

> The Jesuits have given me an infection that no doctor knows how to treat correctly (if the doctor goes by the book), and this way the Jesuits can keep me sick and make me appear to have a mental illness. Unfortunately, many patients with candidiasis are treated as mental patients by the average physician. I think the Jesuits are behind this.

Gail scratched her head, thinking, I shouldn't have to write Brent to tell him this. He already knows! She wrote further:

> I understand your points, but I have Candida *overgrowth*, so there's no danger in not having enough yeast in my guts.
>
> Try to be sure that when you write me, that no one can get near you and do something terrible like putting a gun to your head.
>
> I must say, it's not like you to give me bad medical advice. I hope the

The Forbidden Abyss

Jesuits aren't bothering you.

Brent's letter to Gail (via his YouTube channel) on July 22, 2011 from the hospital confirmed what Gail had heard from him brain to brain the day before:

My dear wife, I'm writing to you on my iPad. I just wanted to let you know that I am awake and seem to be recovering. I can barely remember what happened, or what was transpiring around me at the hospital. It's all a blur now. I do think I remember you and the other men trying to get in touch with me brain to brain, and some other voices I didn't recognize (or were those doctors?) but it wasn't very clear. I fear the injury may have hurt my ability to communicate brain to brain, whether temporarily or permanently I don't know.

I can talk but I can barely hear anyone on the other side. It's like picking up a phone with a lot of static. I hope this doesn't scare you. I am devastated. I hope it gets better as the rest of me heals.

Please help me. I don't think any conventional doctor is going to know what to do about this.

That snake Loree McBride seems to own the police around here. I tried to explain to them what happened and she was briefly detained, but the next thing I know, I'm awake again and she's at my bed side with flowers, acting like nothing had happened! The doctors said nothing to her! I wanted to jump out of my skin when she reached out to stroke my hair. I might as well have been looking at a ghoul!

I don't know how long she's been here in the hospital, maybe the whole time. She's gone right now, thank God. I think she's corroborating with the police since a federal agent was called (you can thank Vladimir for that). They're probably going to cover this whole thing up! Those bastards!

This is all my fault. I am so sorry for this. I should have been more careful when talking to you this way. I was just so excited. I was fearless. At times I lost myself so deeply in your words, your eyes, and your voice that I didn't even think to look over my shoulder. I didn't think to close the window when I felt the presence of that McBride mutant creeping so stealthily behind me.

She struck like a scorpion, I didn't even feel it. My only thought as I fell to the floor was you. I'm not going to let her win. I'm going to keep writing you, because it means so much to me, but from now on I'm only going to write when she is completely out of the house.

I'm not going to try and sneak it if I know she could be just around the corner anymore. As I told you before, boldness should not cross with foolishness, and I've been very foolish with this precious gift of two way communication we have achieved. I suppose love makes men this way sometimes. I am sorry for the scare. I will talk to you again soon. Don't you worry about me.

Gail responded on July 22, 2011:

Vladimir and I will use our Conspiracy Law physicians and scientists to rebuild your injured tissues at the cellular/genetic level to restore your damaged tissues to pre-injury levels. I want you to know that I can hear you loud and clear in brain to brain communications. Though it is possible that not everything you are saying is making it to me.

We just had a lovely lovemaking time, and you were explaining to me how you feel your injury affected your sexual performance, but that our scientists were using groundbreaking technology to operate on your brain, to rebuild your injured brain tissue using computer satellite technology at the genetic cellular level. You explained to me that Loree McBride whacked your head with the butt of a gun and put such a deep gash into your head, that it hit and gouged some of your brain tissue.

We are using our Conspiracy Law physicians to use groundbreaking computer/satellite technology to rebuild your brain even better than it was before. I think most of what I'm saying or feeling is getting to your brain, but probably at the subconscious level. I feel that my emotions are reaching you because you are responding to me sexually, though I don't recall that you are responding to my words, but you are responding to my emotions.

From what I understand you're lucky to be alive. She had a gun pointed to your head and was getting ready to shoot when police barged in and shot her in the leg. Then she changed her strategy and whacked your head with the butt of her gun and knocked you out, right before she went down when the police shot her in the leg. They decided to shoot her in the leg, to knock her down, so we could keep her alive for legal purposes.

Gail wrote Vladimir on July 24, 2011:
Set up surveillance equipment over every person's home that needs protection, which uses video cameras as well as genetic scanners to detect the presence of dangerous Jesuits near our people. When dangerous Jesuits get near our people, an alarm will go off at a law enforcement office in the country where the incident happened and also at a Russian law enforcement agency (so that we can be aware of the problem).

Brent wrote on July 25, 2011:
Vladimir and his associates have set up prototype genetic surveillance scanners outside my home. I think Loree McBride (or one of her expendable clones) must have set it off last night but ran away before federal agents could respond. They filed a report and searched for her all night but they couldn't find her.

For the time being they have asked police to patrol my neighborhood as an additional security measure. Hopefully it's given her a proper scare and she won't dare try coming around again. Vladimir set up the surveillance cameras around my home as an emergency, considering everything that has happened and the immediate danger I am in, but he says that once they are fully tested and working 100% he will make sure to get them sent to the US and have them installed around your home as well.

I think mine are in good working order so far. I can finally breath a very heavy sigh of relief. I've missed writing you so much.

Speaking of Vladimir, I will go ahead and send you his response to

The Forbidden Abyss

your message:

To my sexual lover, I am very sad in the event Loree McBride injury Brent in head. I have followed your wishes to produce expanding Jesuit law kill Jesuits. My secret agents put camera scan genome in places. You and other special people are protect. I want you to be proud.

I kill a Jesuit myself today using martial arts judo. We are winning small battles, but the war is very ugly fat. I have decided to improve my English, as to one day have phone sexy time. Would you enjoy? I wishing I could always keep you safe. Sometimes I want to put you in a protective plastic bag, so I can protect you from the Jesuits. I want to express my strong sexual desire for you, but I do not know what words to use.

I read the Bible, and I wanted to share my feelings for you, to quote song lyrics of Solomon: You are beautiful, my darling, beautiful beyond words. Your eyes are like doves behind your veil. Your hair falls out in waves, like a herd of goats, the curtailment of the slopes of Gilead. Your teeth are as white as sheep, newly shorn and washed. Your smile is flawless, each tooth is aligned with its counterpart. Your lips are red as the ribbon, your mouth invitation oral sex.

Your cheeks are pink, like a grenade behind your veil. Your neck is as beautiful as the tower of David, jeweled with the shields of thousands of heroes. Your breasts like two fawns, two of the calves graze among the lilies gazelle. Before dawn breezes blow and the night shadows flee, I will hasten to the mountain of myrrh and the hill of frankincense. You are altogether beautiful, my darling, masculine in all respects. Come with me from Lebanon, my bride, come with me from Lebanon.

Come down from Mount Amana, from the top of Senir and Hermon, where lions and leopards live in dens in the hills. You captured my heart, my treasure, my bride. You hold it hostage with one glance of your eyes, with one chain of thy neck. Your love delights me, my treasure, my bride. Your love is better than wine, your perfume more fragrant than spices.

Your lips are as sweet as nectar, my bride. Honey and milk are under your tongue. Your clothes are fragrant, like the cedars of Lebanon. You are my private garden, my treasure, my bride, secluded in the spring, the hidden fountain. Your inner thighs housing paradise garnets with rare spices, hentai with backgammon, backgammon, and saffron, calamus and cinnamon, allspice, with all trees of frankincense, myrrh and aloes, and all the other wonderful spices.

You are a garden fountain, a fresh water flowing from the mountains of Lebanon. As you can see, my masculinity is throbbing for you. I would like to see you naked with vagina

Quebec Trial

touch in video. Please? Thank you for being a strong woman.

Brent wrote further:
That boy has a way with words, I'm so jealous. He must be good at reading my mind because it sounds like he is speaking for the both of us! It sounds like he is feeling a lot better.

Despite the scare with our brain to brain communications, I am feeling a lot better too, especially now that I am able to write to you without fear. I want you to know that my email is still secure, the Jesuits don't even know about it, so if you ever have anything extra private that you'd like Vladimir and I to read or see you can send it there safely.

Anyway, my dear, therein is my very long awaited update. . .Good night my sweet wife.

Gail wrote Vladimir on July 27, 2011:
I suspect my real mother has been kidnapped by the Jesuits. My mother's clone just called me on the phone in hysterics, screaming at me because I'm late for cleaning. This is typical of my mother's clone. As you know, we've had a real problem with my mother's clone over the years. Please send out law enforcement on this right away and make sure my real mother is okay. As you know, my mother's clone is the biggest reason you have not been able to give me my writing income or to meet me. Right now she's ringing my phone off the hook, and I'm ignoring her. I hope they haven't killed my real mother. *Get on this right away.*

To Brent on July 27, 2011:
My mother's clone left me a message on my cell phone's answering service, where she said that she was through with me, and that I now owed her a hundred dollars a month, and she wants me to pay her back all the money I owe her (about two thousand dollars) every month (about a hundred dollars a month).

Brent wrote Gail on July 27, 2011:
I talked to Vladimir Putin today. He is very busy working on this. From what we know, your real mother has been taken hostage. The reason we are unable to snag her clone is that every time we are close to nabbing it, they threaten death on your real mother.

Our last attempt was close and as a result they injured her as a warning to us. They are very serious about their threats. We are afraid of what they might do if I we did capture and execute a clone, and for your mother's sake we have been as cautious as possible about this. These Jesuits are smart. They will eventually release your mother and switch her out with the clone again but we don't know when. The best we know to do right now is to fight until they give up and abandon their current mission, which seems to be keeping you from going to law school. Our teams are investigating the matter very seriously and working on this. I will let you know if we turn up any more information. Stay safe, my Catherine the Great.

Loree McBride upped her game and started a YouTube channel to harass Gail, reminding Brent that she had not forgotten her age-old threats to kill Gail if Brent dared to approach Gail. She wanted to crush this new correspondence between Gail and Brent.

Her first video on July 26, 2011 started off with chorale music in the background that opened with a tympani to announce its entrance to the world:

Order of The Jesuits.Com

Then the chorus of male voices in the background, like the voices of a military marching band going forward to the slaughter played in the background, to a steady beat and tempo, rushing forward and headlong like a pulsating beat, pulsating, pulsating, forward, forward, headlong into battle to devastate Gail and her men:

The IHS or Jesuit symbol flashed in the video.

A drumbeat started, overpowering the voices, like a forward march, in the background. The music sounded confident, arrogant, powerful, determined and forceful, and the beat increased in intensity and volume as the video moved forward. The pace of the music increased, almost to a frenzy and then words appeared on the screen.

A blend of mezzo-soprano female voices, with one slightly louder than the rest, spoke—calm, cold and cruel, against a background of loud drum beats, they announced:

We Are God's Marines.
Be Part Of Something Bigger.
Order Of The Jesuits.Com
Our Numbers Are Many.
We Are Always Watching.

Then the female voices repeated, cold and cruel, with the military marching music blasting, read their script like an automaton:

Order of the Jesuits.com.

Pause:

We are always watching.

Longer Pause:

We are God's Marines.

Loree McBride's vindictive, defiant stare in a face photograph, jumped onto the screen:

Be part of something bigger. . .be part of something bigger.
We are God's Marines.
We are always watching.

The Jesuit symbol IHS and Loree's defiant face flashed again.

The proud, arrogant, defiant music continued to march and beat:

Order of the Jesuits.com.
Order of the Jesuits.com.

The IHS symbol flashed again.

The music continued to march and beat:

Quebec Trial

Our numbers are many...

A black and white face photo of a smiling Billy Mays appeared, with the marching music in the background and the following words scrolling up the screen:
Target Eliminated.
The female voices read their script, like a lifeless robot:
Our numbers are many.
Join us.
Be part of something bigger.

A black and white face photo of a smiling Michael Jackson appeared, with the marching music in the background and the following words scrolling up the screen:
Target Eliminated.
The female voices, with the beat music intensifying and increasing in confidence and arrogance, repeated words like a robot army:
We are always watching...we are always watching.

A black and white face photo of a smiling Princess Diana appeared.
Target Eliminated.
Be part of something bigger.

Loree McBride's defiant stare photo reappeared, the following words scroll up over the photo:
Agent McBride.

The IHS symbol again. The cold female voices, like an automaton machine gun:
Order of the Jesuits.com.
Order of the Jesuits.com.
Order of the Jesuits.com.
The music jazzed up with electrifying whirling sounds:
We are always watching.
We are God's Marines.
Be part of something bigger.
Our numbers are many.
The voices overlapped against the loud, arrogant beat:
Join us.
Be part of something bigger.
Order of the Jesuits.com.
We are always watching.
Order of the Jesuits.com.

A color face photo of Gail Chana flashed on the screen. The chorus in the background (men and women's voices) intensified into a finale, like a triumphant death march.

The female voices, cold and assured, like a lifeless recording of death:

The Forbidden Abyss

*We will defeat
Catherine the Great.
We will defeat
Catherine the Great.
We will defeat
Catherine the Great.*

Already, Brent Spiner was shaking. His subconscious reminded him of Loree's September 1992 rape, even though his conscious mind subdued the memories.

Jesus Christ Prepares for His Entrance

A defecting Jesuit sent Gail an email about a new Jesuit website. Gail then read about Catherine the Great on this secret 2011 Jesuits' wiki page, which ended up public, because of the defector, whom the Jesuits murdered very quickly:

> Lies are one of our greatest tools, and must be wielded by the tempered hand.
>
> A common story states that she (Catherine) died as a result of her voracious sexual appetite while attempting sexual intercourse with a stallion—the story holds that the harness holding the horse above her broke, and she was crushed.
>
> A tale was widely circulated and even jokingly referred to by Aleksandr Pushkin in one of his untitled poems. ("Decreed the orders, burned the fleets/And died boarding a vessel", the last line can also be translated as "And died sitting down on the toilet".) There existed also a version on alleged assassination, by spring blades hidden in a toilet seat. This rumor is true, and it was a Jesuit assassination to destroy Catherine, and was successful.
>
> She took many young lovers, even while in old age. This is proof positive that Gail Chana is comprised of Catherine the Great even though we make her look like a crazy paranoid.

Because Gail's men now communicated directly with Gail, the Jesuit Order unleashed everything in their arsenal at Gail and her men. When a Jesuit in the audience tried to machine gun Brent Spiner while a Gabrielle Chana FOX News reporter interviewed him in February 2012, Jesus Christ blocked the bullets, causing the bullets to ricochet back onto the Jesuit machine gunner, killing him. From that day forward, Jesus made frequent visits with Gail and her men, but only spoke with Gail through Skype.

Usually when Jesus spoke to Gail, it was to correct her because she had believed something false that could bring her to harm. Gail was usually receptive to what Jesus had to say, but not always. Jesus knew when He could hit her with something touchy, often waiting months or years before He would correct her.

Because Gail was Jesus' favorite, Satan found Gail a major threat. So that whenever Jesus made an appearance to Gail, Satan or his antichrist, Zack Knight, would also show up, breaking up the Skype connection or dealing with Gail afterwards to cause Gail to misinterpret what Jesus had tried to teach her.

Therefore, because Zack and Satan were so obsessed with Gail, Jesus would make a pact with Satan, that He would not make direct appearances to Gail, and

The Forbidden Abyss

that Satan must not do so either. To honor His pact with Satan, Jesus would not allow Gail to see Him in person, but she could only communicate with Him through Brent Spiner, where Brent would type what Jesus said for her.

Because Gail had read the Bible from cover to cover over a hundred times, she recognized that the Jesus who was speaking to her through Brent on Skype, was the real Jesus Christ. She never doubted it, even though she never saw Him, like Brent and Terrance did. It is impossible to read the Bible this much and fail to recognize the real Jesus when He appears. For this reason, Jesus bothered with Gail, because He knew, for the most part, she would be receptive to Him.

Gail would soon learn that most of the world was not receptive to Jesus and though she embraced the real Jesus as He spoke with her through Skype, most of the world would not. Like His disciples, she would suffer persecution for striving to honor and obey the real Jesus who spoke with her through Skype.

Despite this, she never doubted that it was the real Jesus she spoke with through Brent Spiner. For one thing, she knew Brent would never lie to her about this. So, the combination of her deep Bible knowledge, which basically showed her the heart and soul of God and her absolute faith in Brent's love for her, made her very receptive to the Jesus who spoke with her through Skype through Brent and Terrance, even when He became angry at her or corrected her. Nothing about this Jesus who communicated with her through Brent Spiner on Skype contradicted what she knew of Him through her personal Bible studies. In fact, the real Jesus seemed to contradict the way some of her rigid church friends portrayed Him. Jesus would gradually let Gail know who He really was, and why He was so proud of Brent as Gail's husband, because Brent's vast heart and soul in many ways was like Jesus.

Jesus became angry at Gail because she questioned His directions through Brent Spiner in June 2012, after she lost her job and was confused about what to do next. "You have been doing less than you are capable of, and spending much of the time whining and questioning me. I was very disappointed in you," Jesus said to Gail on June 16, 2012. "I know you can do better."

To Gail's amazement, He even scolded her for reading the Bible too much. This was before He corrected her about her King James Bible worship in October 2012. "I want you to spend less time reading the Bible right now—I have written the word in your heart and you should carry it in your heart while you do your work for me." Jesus continued, "It's going to take sacrifice, Gail, and it's not going to be pleasant. Nobody said tribulation was going to be fun."

"You really meant it when You said I was going through what those tribulation saints will be going through."

"Indeed. I hope you understand that tough love is still love. All I say is in your best interest I have shielded you from the worst of it. Take Matthew McConaughey for instance—he swelled up like a balloon, for you, in space." Jesus referred to the space battle between Church of Gail and the Jesuit fleet in May 2012. "I will never allow you to feel the cold vacuum of space, Gail. I have appointed Brent and Terrance as my instruments to help you. I want you to follow their advice." Jesus continued. "I have a plan, Gail. You just have to trust me, and trust my instruments."

"I have to admit those Jesuits who are writing to me at my email, I think they are casting doubts in my mind. Perhaps I need to plead the blood and rebuke the

Quebec Trial

lies that Satan is planting in my mind."

"Satan thrives on doubt," Jesus said. "It's his favorite flavor."

"You're right," Gail said. "I am a terrible whiner. You should have killed me by now."

"I would never want to kill one of my most beautiful creations."

"Oh, thank you. I think I'm just trying to find an excuse to cop out on You and go home to heaven and get out of this mess right now. Sorry, for my little faith."

"Yes. No copping out on Jesus. I didn't cop out on the cross for you."

"What do you want me to do tomorrow?"

"Tomorrow, take a Sabbath. Just like a full time job, you get at least a day off to relax and refresh yourself." Jesus smiled. "You should have seen how exhausted my Dad was when He made the world. That was pretty bad ass."

"I am sure of it," Gail said. "I could never be as good as You."

"The Sabbath day was just long enough for Him to crack his knuckles. Of course, then Satan took advantage, and made the hagfish. Have you seen those things? They have teeth in their vagina."

Gail laughed. "No. What a sense of humor."

"It's pretty rad, I guess," Jesus said.

"Rad?" Gail asked. "What does that mean?"

"It means 'cool'," Jesus said. "Like, I think you're pretty rad, Gail."

"Brent is so much like You," Gail said to Jesus. "Don't you think?"

"Maybe that's why I like him so much," Jesus said. "I couldn't help but put some of myself in him."

"All his bones broke in that awful battle in outer space ." Gail referred to a May 2012 space battle between Church of Gail and the Jesuit fleet. "And, like You, he just took all that suffering and pain like a hero. He didn't even think about himself and put his life in danger to rescue all the other men before himself. He is so self-sacrificing and generous. A truly awesome person. I am so proud of him. He has grown by leaps and bounds as a new Christian and has the spiritual maturity of a very advanced Christian, now, don't You think? I guess that is why You have invested so much time in him, because You knew You had good material."

"You're right about that. He took his broken bones like a man, I was impressed. I remember how much those nails hurt when I was being hung on the cross, and those whips." Jesus smiled. "Just like me, Brent wasn't doing it for himself. He was doing it purely to save you and the other men."

"Yes, he is so much like you. Even back in 1990, when I suffered at the hands of the child abuse industry and was only a nobody fan, he took such an interest in a stranger and, I believe, You used him as an instrument to allow me to keep my son. I sensed even back then how big a person he was, and that's why I fell so hard in love with him." Gail now addressed Brent. "I'm sorry, Brent, that I doubted you. Satan confused me."

"I don't hold it against you, Gail," Brent said. "I would have probably felt the same in your position. Those were dark times."

Gail corrected Brent. "When I say I doubted you. I am referring to the present."

Jesus poked Brent in the back.

The Forbidden Abyss

"Oh, I guess that's why Jesus was poking me in the back then!"

Gail explained to Brent that Zack Knight impersonated Brent to her mind as he spoke to her brain to brain and gave her advice that contradicted what the real Brent told her to do. "Hey, Jesus." Gail now addressed Jesus. "If Zack tricked me like this, I'm not sure I'm doing excellent with Zack Knight." Jesus had told her earlier she was very wise about Zack's impersonations of Jesus to her mind.

"He's a powerful guy," Jesus said. "And he's going to get the best of you when you're at your darkest. Just remember that trials like this will make your spirit stronger."

"Oh, I see. " Gail pondered over all Jesus had said to her. "This must be what You meant when You said in an earlier Skype that I still have a lot to learn."

"Yes," Jesus said. "You're not ready to check into Heaven just yet."

Jesus' statement startled and confused Gail. "What does that mean? Not ready to check into heaven? You paid for it all on the cross, so I guess it means you have to 'improve' me so I don't lose my rewards, is that it?"

"I don't mean it that way." Jesus became apologetic. "Sorry to be confusing. I mean that I have a lot planned for you on earth yet. Your spirit is still growing."

"Oh, I see." Jesus' statement made some sense to her, but she still felt a bit confused. Jesus often spoke in parables with her, like He did His disciples and dealing with a Deity could be confusing sometimes. She dared to probe further on a topic that Jesus in the past refused to discuss—the date of the rapture. "I know You don't want to talk about this. But I think I only have three years left on this present earth. I guess that's why You have me in a crash course."

"It's a lot to handle for one spirit," Jesus said. "I know you can handle it."

"I can tell that You would rather not have to meet me on Skype, because You are trying to stay in the background right now."

"Yes," Jesus agreed with Gail. "It encourages Satan to interfere for his followers as well, and when he does that it makes things extra difficult. He's always trying to throw a wrench in my plans."

"I can tell that my men seem real embarrassed about my behavior, lately, because it made You angry," Gail conceded. "Do you have anything to say to them?"

"You are all imperfect beings," Jesus answered. "I expect you to make mistakes sometimes."

"Sometimes?" Gail wiped her forehead. "I make mistakes *all the time*."

"No matter how hard you try, there are times temptation will be too great, and you will sin. So it's best to learn from them so you can make less mistakes in the future."

"That is true." Gail knew how wise Jesus was. "I'm not God."

"Brent and all the other men make their own mistakes. I will remind them not to forget that."

Gail wanted to stick up for her Brent, because he was always so supportive about her. "I don't get the impression that I offended Brent. He is not easily offended. I think he was confused and concerned."

"He was worried about you," Jesus explained. "You helped him to find me, and he's trying to do his best to help you in the same way, and return the favor.

Quebec Trial

He's trying to keep you on your path."

"I like using my time the way I like to do it, and not how others like me to do it."

"I think I'm a special exception," Jesus said.

"Huh?" Jesus again confused Gail. "What does *that* mean?"

"You're using your time as I would like you to use it, right?"

"Oh, I get it. I must consider You my boss." Gail finally understood. "Okay, I will try to heed Your advice. Actually, I do try to please You, but I confused You with Satan." Gail felt bad. "Sorry about that. That must have been a *real insult*." Gail realized now why she made Jesus angry.

"It hurt my heart a little," Jesus admitted. "But I know you will do great."

"I feel terrible, now." Gail felt like a jerk. How horrible that she thought Jesus' counsel to her was from Satan. "Can I do anything more to make this up to you?"

"Of course," Jesus perked up. "That's why I decided to chat with you tonight."

"I just felt like You expected me to be God, that it was in my power to get the job, and that's why I thought it was Satan." Gail elaborated on why she felt she had failed Jesus in this instance. "I think we had a communication problem."

"I'm glad I was able to fix it." Jesus, as usual, was a gentleman. "I will try to be less cryptic. I think it's best that Brent gets to bed now."

Jesus turned into a dove and fluttered off.

Brent scratched his head in amazement at Jesus. "Wow. . .Jesus just turned into a dove and fluttered off. He's so amazing."

Meeting Jesus through Skype would transform Gail, just like Jesus transformed His disciples. It was impossible to meet with Jesus and remain the same. Everything He did for Gail was always in her best interests, though sometimes Gail could not see it, but she would learn to trust Him, even in the dark.

Jesus Christ would begin speaking with Gail and her men through Skype seven months after the infamous August 2011 Quebec trial (between Gail and Loree) to let Gail know that the Jesuits had indeed murdered Catherine the Great.

Every time Jesus spoke with Gail through Skype, the future false Christ, Zack Knight, snooped on every conversation, often causing problems with the connection, and sometimes even cutting off Skype. Zack Knight and Jesus Christ battled each other, both obsessed with Jesus' favorite, Gail Chana—Zack apparently believed Satan could win the final battle.

On March 9, 2012, Jesus contacted Gail through Skype to inform her that Zack Knight had been talking to her brain to brain, directly and indirectly, and impersonating Jesus. Jesus was fed up with this, and wanted to straighten Gail out about this deception, because Gail was still believing that Zack Knight was Jesus at times, when she heard brain to brain communications in her mind.

After He assured Gail, that to protect her, He would *never* communicate with her using computers or brain to brain to talk to her, even using Brent as His go-between, He then brought the conversation onto a more positive tack. Whenever He corrected Gail, he never wanted her to feel rejected or that He didn't love her, so He always tried to end on a positive note.

The Forbidden Abyss

"You have a very powerful soul," Jesus Christ told Gail on March 9, 2012 in His baritone voice. He had long, gorgeous hair down to the middle of his waist, and was wearing the same robe He wore when He walked on earth with His disciples.

"Ohhh. I bet I get that from David, and maybe Catherine the Great, too." She paused to consider Jesus' comment. "Lord, You haven't said too much about my Catherine the Great genes. What do You think about *that* side of me?" Jesus always boasted about her king David genes, she thought. She wondered what He thought about Catherine the Great.

Jesus stood beside Brent. "Catherine the Great was a bad-ass. Loved horses."

"I guess that means she was tough."

Gail pondered over what Jesus meant by "bad-ass". "She was tough." Gail giggled. "I'm not sure 'bad-ass' is a good connotation, though." She laughed out loud, kind of embarrassed for having the genes of a "bad-ass".

Jesus, beside Brent, smiled. "She was awesome."

Gail's mouth dropped. "Oh, You *liked* her, huh? The Jesuits didn't like her." Gail pondered over what Jesuits did to the woman whose genes she had. "Did the Jesuits murder Catherine the Great? They claim that they did."

She remembered about the Jesuits boasting about murdering Catherine the Great through their Catherine the Great web page. Outrage came over her, when she realized that Jesuits felt they could topple anybody, even Catherine the Great. "I'm just curious. You would know, Lord." Gail tried to get from Jesus information she knew only He would know. "They claim they killed her on the toilet, that she sat on knife blades, and she died on the toilet seat." Gail's feathers ruffled. "And they're *boasting* about it." They must have made this up, she thought, because historical records stated Catherine died of stroke. "I think she died of stroke."

Gail, read in amazement what Jesus wrote through Brent on her screen, and became outraged: "Oh, they *killed* her! Oh, they're horrible. They really did kill her."

Jesus remained with Brent, with His hand on Brent's shoulder. "On the toilet."

"Oh, man, they boast about it and they really *did* kill her! Oh! Those creeps!" Gail fumed with outrage. Those Jesuits really did kill her ancestor. "That's *disgusting*." She collected her thoughts. "So, she didn't die of stroke. She was *murdered*. That makes me so mad, 'cause I'm sixty percent Catherine the Great and they murdered my—"

Terrance's jaw dropped. "With knife blades in her butt?"

"She sat on the toilet and, apparently, knife blades sprang up and they stabbed her to death," Gail said. "When she sat on the toilet."

"The knife blades, where did they go?" Terrance said.

"I think they went in her butt. Yeah. It's terrible. They *murdered her*." Gail still could not believe it. "I thought she might have died naturally, and they were just boasting." Still in disbelief, Gail was amazed at the extent of Jesuit power. "I didn't believe it. I thought they were just boasting, to intimidate me."

Jesus played dumb. "Oh, that's right, I remember that, now."

"Lord, how could You *forget?*" Gail said. "You have a perfect memory!"

"In the butt," Jesus said.

Quebec Trial

Terrance addressed Jesus, "So, Jesus, she died, being stabbed in the butt?"

"Yes, but it gave her a stroke." Jesus still stood beside Brent.

"So she did die of stroke, but it was precipitated by that," Gail said.

Jesus continued. "A blood clot from her butt went to her brain."

This astounded Gail. "Oh! Those horrible Jesuits. Man! That's disgusting." She wondered now about the eternal destiny of her genetic relative. "Catherine the Great was not a born again Christian though, was she? I know king David was saved, but I don't think Catherine the Great was. Was she saved?"

"No, that's why they were able to do a switch-out," Jesus said.

Gail knew that the Holy Spirit in a born again Christian would not permit an unsaved body to house a born again soul, so born again Christians could not have their bodies switched out with a Jesuit clone.

"A switch-out? They didn't have that technology back then, did they?" She read her computer screen in amazement. "They had clone technology back then?"

"Then her clone had sex with a horse," Jesus said. "The UFOs helped."

"Oh my goodness," Gail said. "They had that technology back *then? That was the 1700s!*"

Terrance offered his input. "The UFOs, the fallen angels definitely knew how to do that."

"Yeah," Gail said. "Jesus, those third of the angels that fell with Satan, are those the creatures that are travelling around in the UFOs? The fallen angels that fell with Satan, that's what I think—I'm not sure."

"Yes, they are," Jesus said.

Gail clapped her hands. "You know how a third of the angels fell with Satan. Those are what are travelling around in UFOs right now. Those are all the fallen angels."

Terrance chimed in. "Those are the fallen angel *demons*."

"When Satan rebelled against God," Gail said, "he was the anointed cherub that covereth. He fell from the third heaven and God kicked him off the throne, 'cause he rebelled and he wanted to be like the Most High, and he took a third of the angels with him—those are all the UFO inhabitants."

Gail continued. "Yeah, poor Brent Spiner got stuck with some of them. That's why I told Brent, 'You need to get saved. Those demons have an obsession with you.' I'm so glad you found the Lord, Brent." Then she directed her comments, as if to an invisible person. "I was so worried about him when he was in that UFO, because I knew they were demons. I prayed, I said, 'These devils have an obsession with Brent, he needs to get saved.' "

Terrance remembered an incident with Vladimir. "So those were the same folks that were in the computers, when Vladimir Putin was karate chopping them demons."

Gail's eyes lit up. "Oh—the fallen angels, huh?"

Terrance continued, "Vladimir was karate chopping them off of the satellite."

"Oh, there were some aliens in there?" It amazed Gail how everything seemed to come together and make sense.

"Well, Vladimir said they were devils," Terrance said. "I don't know what that was. Maybe that was aliens."

The Forbidden Abyss

"Mechanic aliens," Jesus said.

"Wow," Gail said.

"Demons," Terrance added.

Jesus wanted to clarify. "Like the kind that abducted Brent."

"Yeah. . ." Gail reflected with joy. "Oh, I'm so glad Brent found you, Lord. He didn't want to have sex with Loree in the trial! And I could tell he was really depressed about this. And I knew that You were the answer, Lord. You rescued Brent Spiner."

Terrance smiled with pride. "Now, He's going to officiate your wedding with Brent. He's going to even join you guys in your first act on your wedding night."

"Brent, what you going to do for the other guys on my marriage list, like Matthew McConaughey, Gerard Butler and all of them?" Gail laughed and directed her next comment to Jesus. "It's just that with You here, I'd like to know, but you don't have to tell me, if You don't want to." She mused in wonderment over possibilities. "I just wonder how you guys can stand it, 'cause I'm only one woman and I can't marry fifty of you."

Jesus smiled. "They can still make love brain to brain."

Gail gave her gut reaction. "What? In the *millennium?*" She stopped to reconsider her words. "What's keeping you guys going? 'Cause I can't marry fifty of you guys? It just amazes me how you all love me so much, that you're willing to forego other women just to be on my marriage list and I'm only one woman."

Jesus smiled rather matter-of-factly. "Marriage is beyond sex in the millennium."

Gail's eyes opened wide. "Huh?" Jesus' statement confused her. "Marriage is beyond sex in the millennium?" She asked Terrance, "What does that mean?"

Terrance seemed equally confused. "I don't *understand*."

Gail's eyes opened wider, when she read what Jesus said on her screen. "You can have physical sex with the *other men?*" In shock, she reared her head back. "Oh, my goodness!"

She dared to probe Jesus further. "Hey Lord, I got a question for You. You said in heaven there's no marriage, but You didn't say there was no sex, so You mean in the millennium it's not considered adultery to have sex with more than one person?"

Terrance was still in shock that it was okay for Gail to have sex with more than one man in the millennium. "Is that just for Gail or for everyone in the millennium?"

"Pretty much, just for Gail." Jesus was total calm, His long hair streamed down to the middle of His back. There was much about Him that Gail needed to learn, but He didn't want to put her in shock.

Gail was in shock. "Why?"

Terrance, like Gail, was conditioned with years of church teaching on the subject of sex and marriage. "What makes Gail so different?"

Gail agreed. "Yeah!"

Jesus laid His hand again on Brent's shoulder. Jesus' hand had scars from where the nail pierced his hand years ago when He died on the cross. The divine hand gave Brent a squeeze. "Brent and I have decided that's our reward to them."

Quebec Trial

It was Gail's duty to love Jesus, but, to her amazement, she not only loved Him, she *liked Him*. He loved her exactly the way she was. She had been raised that all she did was wrong. "I guess I am going to be like king David, he had a bunch of wives and concubines." She laughed, still not accustomed to the real Jesus, so different from her King James Bible views of Him. He didn't use thee and thou when He spoke, used street English and a lot of slang, and had no sexual hang-ups in His speech or outlook; and, amazingly, never preached at her, but just offered wise advice and counsel.

"Is this whenever Gail wants to?" Terrance said. "I don't understand."

"Whenever Gail wants to, of course," Jesus said. "Yeah, it's all for you, Gail."

Gail's jaw dropped. "Why are You doing this, God?" She still couldn't digest what Jesus just said. "I can tell I'm one of Your favorites. I'm a little stumped over this. And it's not because I'm going to be Your wife. I know that's not the reason, so it's something *else*." Jesus had clarified to Gail that His giving her His semen in the millennium was a pure wedding gift for her with Brent, and did not involve Him with her in the sexual act.

Jesus raised one of His brows, his eyes underneath were pools of meaning and depth. "You shouldn't even have to ask. You know how special you are."

Gail's mind was in a daze, and wondering over Jesus' statement. "I do?" She laughed out loud. "I do? I know how special I am? Well, I know a lot of the men adore me. They think I'm the most beautiful woman in the world, but I don't think I'm the most beautiful woman in the world." She smiled. "I will admit, that I think what they like about me is my spirit, more than my looks. I have an unusual spirit."

Jesus gazed at them all. "Your spirit makes all the difference."

"Well, I'm glad you think that."

Terrance interjected. "Well, you're pretty hot, too, Gail."

Jesus seemed to love to shock Gail. "Yes, you're pretty hot."

Gail was amazed Jesus would say this. "I am?" She paused, to ponder over why Jesus would say this. "Goodness!" Gail got right to the point. "Lord, I know You think I'm aware of this, but I'm still stumped over this, I don't get it. Maybe I'll get it more, later. I don't get why I'm pretty hot." She thought over it some more. "The only thing I can think of is I must be an unusual lover. I think the way I make love to these men is just out of this world. That must be it."

Zack Knight, who had been snooping the whole time, hated the direction this conversation was going. Satan invented the computer, so Zack used his genius computer knowledge as Satan incarnate to disconnect Terrance from Skype. Terrance called back and reconnected with Gail.

Gail addressed Jesus again, amazed He stuck around so long to talk to her. "Lord, I still don't get why all these men like me. I know they do, but . . .well, I sorta get it. I think I'm an exceptional lover. I think that's what it is and I think maybe it's my king David genes. Brent made some music about how I make him ascend to the heavens. That must be it—I have a very unusual spirit."

"The Jesuits try to create beautiful women to compete with you." Jesus attempted to clarify to Gail what He meant. "Not understanding what true beauty is."

Perhaps what she was reading on her Skype was from Brent and not Jesus? But no, this sounded like Jesus, Gail thought. "Is that you, Jesus, or is that Brent?"

"Yes," Jesus said. "Though Brent would agree with me."

"Yeah, I've noticed that," Gail said. "A lot of their women are pretty good looking physically, but inwardly they're like scorpions."

Jesus made a point blank statement. "He was never attracted to Loree McBride."

No way, would her deep and awesome Brent ever want that arrogant, hell-raiser, despite her model good looks. "Oh, I knew that, Lord. I know. I know." She agreed wholeheartedly. "She's totally lacking in inner beauty. She has zero in that area."

Jesus zeroed in on the key issue. "Women like Loree are too prideful."

Yes, Gail thought, how true, how perceptive her Lord was. "Loree was very proud and she kept making fun of my yeasty vagina." Now that they were on the subject of her yeast infection, she was talking to God Himself! It seemed the cure to her yeast infection was beyond the scope of human medicine. "Lord, can You cure me of this yeast infection the Jesuits have given me? Or is this my thorn in the flesh? I have to take all sorts of supplements to deal with it all the time."

"I will heal your yeast infection, Gail. I think it's time we get rid of that." Jesus waved His hand and did a partial healing on March 9, 2012 to hold the powerful yeast back. Eventually, Jesus did a complete healing in mid-June 2013, with the help of a medication called Seroquel.

Gail was truly grateful that Jesus cared about her yeast infection. She knew that without Him, she probably would have died from it by now. She told Him on January 23, 2013, "Jesus, thank you for Seroquel. It has made me feel better."

"You're welcome!" Jesus replied, bright and happy. "I made Seroquel just for you."

Jesus commented about the Quebec trial to Gail on March 9, 2012 during a Skype conversation.

"Yeah, you saved my life during the Quebec trial. Those Jesuits wanted to kill me!" Gail said to Judge Terrance Jenkins. "I think God noticed that."

"Being a judge is not a problem," Jesus said, encouraging Gail to make brain to brain love to Terrance, who, in March 2012, was on her marriage list.

"How does that work?" Terrance asked Jesus. "What if someone questions my bias?" Terrance wondered if he could be the judge for a trial about Gail, because if he made love to her, he could be accused of having a bias towards Gail. "Questions me having a vested interest? I don't want to get into one of those situations where I gotta defend Gail and people say that I'm not qualified."

"Lord, if I make brain to brain loving with him, isn't that going to make him appear biased and he won't be able to be a judge anymore?" Gail asked. "That's the reason I haven't done it (brain to brain loving with Terrance). Then we can't

Quebec Trial

use him as a judge. The Jesuits will say he's biased because he's had sex with me."

"The Jesuits are blowing smoke," Jesus answered. "Terry, I want you to repeat after me, 'I *am* the law'.

Terrance repeated, "I *am* the law." He paused. "Oh, that makes sense. So, you're saying Jesus, that my word goes,"

"Oh, wow," Gail said.

"Oh, my goodness," Terrance said.

"Your word is 'go' brother," Jesus said.

"For real, Jesus," Terrance said, "Just like in Compton." Terrance referred to Compton, because he grew up in the Compton ghetto and often had to use a gun to defend himself.

"You know what I think that means?" Gail said, "If they give you a hard time in court, Jesus is going to go kill them again." Gail laughed, speaking to Jesus, "Like you did in the Matthew McConaughey trial.".

"If the Jesuits ever question you," Jesus said to Terrance, "Just respond like you did in Compton."

"What did you do in Compton?" Gail asked Terrance.

"Well, that's my gangster side. I try not to talk too much about that."

"Oh, I see," Gail said to Terrance, "The Lord apparently knows all about it."

"Well, you remember what happened when that one juror tried to get you killed?" Terrance referred to a juror in the Quebec trial (Gail versus Loree in August 2011).

"Oh, yeaaaa," Gail remembered now with amazement. "Boy, you were so brave! I think that's one reason God made you number seven on the marriage list." When Terrance was judge over the Quebec trial, he shot dead the head juror (in front of millions of people), because this juror decided that the verdict for Gail was the death penalty. Right after the head juror read the verdict, Loree McBride laughed and called Gail a bitch, and the executioner was getting ready to head out the door to fly to Gail's apartment to carry out the execution. That's because the war crimes in this case involved millions of people; therefore, it was decided that whoever was guilty needed to be executed immediately. The Quebec trial was a rerun of the Nuremberg War Crimes tribunal that happened right after Hitler's Germany and tried the Nazis; therefore, the Quebec trial was about war crimes, even though Loree tried to make it about how Gail interfered with Loree's "marriage" to Brent Spiner. "Man, that took a lot of guts." Gail paused to reflect. "You knew what was right and you just did it, even if the stars fell. Kudos to you, man. I think the Lord was impressed."

"Yes, when people step against Gail," Terrance said, "They step in Compton, too."

"You were so impressive, then," Gail continued. "I thought, *man,* what courage! There were a million Jesuits out there (in the audience). You were like David against Goliath. You are quite impressive. God is right about you."

"One man. One glock, against thousands of Jesuits," Jesus said, smiling with pride. "It was an impressive moment."

"I'm so glad that Brent Spiner and Vladimir Putin joined in to help me shoot all those Jesuits," Terrance added with pride.

"All of you men are impressive," Gail stated with pride.

The Forbidden Abyss

"They were very brave," Jesus said.

"They sure were, Lord," Gail agreed. "They sure were."

Terrance chimed in. "Yeah, Compton."

Whenever Terrance said, "Yeah, Compton" it was his way of saying justice in the ghetto-style, like how he used his gun to defend himself and others in Compton, California, where he grew up. The city of Compton as well as southern Los Angeles County in general is notorious for its heavy concentration of gangs and gang violence. Terrance Jenkins, a born again Christian, rose above this background to graduate from Harvard Law School and become a judge. If not for his gangster courage, it's possible that Gail would not be alive now to write this story, because the Jesuits tried to execute her at the end of the Quebec trial.

That's why Jesus said about Terrance (in regard to how he handled the Quebec trial's first verdict from Jesuit jurors), "One man. One glock, against thousands of Jesuits. . .it was an impressive moment."

The first time that Gail talked with Jesus was on February 14, 2012 when Satan showed up and resurrected Zack Knight from hell, who had died on December 27, 2011.

Jesus had just beaten up Zack Knight for the first time, which He would end up doing on a regular basis to defend Gail.

In Gail's first encounter with Jesus on February 14, 2012, when Jesus rescued Gail's men from Satan and Zack Knight (who had turned them gay), she bantered with Him. "Okay, God. I got another question for you. Signs and wonders are for *the Jews*, and You're not supposed to be doing all this in the church age. Are you getting ready to start the tribulation? To deal with the Jewish nation again? The signs and wonders died when the Apostle Paul came in. . .but when God starts dealing with—"

Jesus became very serious. "The anti-Christ arrived today." Jesus was referring to Zack Knight, whom He had just punished with lightning bolts and Jesus' fist to his groin. He later told Gail that same day, "Gail, you are more important than you know."

"Yeah, I know. You've got me in the *Bible*, in Zechariah 9:15. And You're right, I don't think I'm very important, but, apparently, You feel otherwise. But I love You."

"Yup," Jesus said. "That was you."

"Yeah, I know," Gail agreed. "Zechariah 9:15. I'm *in the Bible.*"

"You will defeat the Jesuits." Jesus' statement shocked Gail—something He would do on a regular basis.

Gail was astonished. "How? *You'll* do it, God. You say in Zechariah 9:15, that the *Lord of hosts will defend them."*

"You'll find out."

"Don't give me credit. It's *You.*"

Jesus spoke with certainty. "You are my instrument."

Gail spoke about 666 and Zack Knight being the evil monster and how she was in the Bible.

"Well, Gail, my Father is calling. . .someone else needs my help," Jesus said.

"Thank you, Lord. I love You."

"I love you, too. Gail."

In the future, Zack Knight would impersonate Jesus to Gail, speaking to Gail brain to brain and tricking Gail that he was Jesus. Jesus would need to meet with Gail several times to straighten Gail out about this. On March 9, 2012, Jesus spoke with Gail about His status on her marriage list:

"Me and Brent have been having very good brain to brain sex, *but*, and I don't know if this is correct or not, the Brent voice was telling me that Jesus was giving me His semen through *Brent*," Gail said to Jesus. "That was probably a lie. That Zack might be getting really clever on us."

"There are things I need to clarify about that, Gail," Jesus said. "You are hearing pieces of the truth."

"I am?"

"I want to go ahead and tell you what my plans are for the millennial since there appears to be some confusion," Jesus said. "My intentions are for you to marry Brent Spiner, not me—*however*-"

"You said You were going to give me Your semen!" Gail said, laughing.

"This almost seems to be contradictory," Terrance Jenkins said. "I don't understand. How can You give the semen? I don't understand."

"I think He realizes we don't understand," Gail said. "That's why He's here."

"My intentions are that I will join you two in the marriage bed in the first night, so that I can teach Brent Spiner how to properly make love to you." Jesus was matter-of-fact. "And afterwards as my wedding gift I will grant Brent Spiner my glowing semen."

"You mean Brent Spiner doesn't know how to make love to me?" Gail asked Jesus. "I think he's pretty good."

"Oh no, he's very good." Jesus kept a straight face. "But I want to show him some millennial tricks I've learned."

"Oh, that's great," Terrance said.

"Well, what do you mean by *that*?" Gail dared to ask God, laughing.

"You talking about sex moves?" Terrance asked.

"You'll find out," Jesus said, keeping a straight face. "Sex moves? Yes."

"Jesus," Gail blurted out. "Are you going to have a physical wife in the millennium?"

"No, Gail, I cannot do that."

"Oh, so that means the video I just made is not correct."

"I am married to the church," Jesus said.

"Okay." Gail smiled. "Well, nothing in the Bible indicates You're going to have a physical wife. So what do I do about that video I just put up there, Lord?" Gail had put up a video claiming she would be the bride of Christ. She laughed. "Want me to make a correction?"

"You should make a corrective video when you are ready."

"Oh! Okay." Gail was relieved Jesus did not take her mistake too hard.

"You will not be marrying me," Jesus said. "You will be marrying Brent Spiner."

Gail smiled. "Oh okay, I don't mind marrying Brent Spiner." She laughed. "So there will be marriages in the millennium."

The Forbidden Abyss

"But I will be the One to marry you two."

"Oh, my goodness," Terrance said. "Jesus is going to officiate your wedding!"

"Oh, my goodness!" Gail laughed. "So You don't marry anybody Lord Jesus, huh? I mean You, Yourself. I guess it's because You're God."

"Yes, exactly," Jesus said.

Gail felt embarrassed over her mistake, thinking she would be the bride of Christ. "How do you feel about that video I just made, Lord Jesus?" She laughed in embarrassment. "I didn't even want to make the video. I was tired. I guess it will be better once I put the correction in there."

"Well, I loved the get-up," Jesus said, referring to the lace veil Gail wore over her head to look like a bride.

Gail laughed. She loved Jesus' sense of humor. "You want me to take it down, because it's doctrinally incorrect?"

"Even though you are very beautiful," Jesus said. "I feel more of a brotherly love for you, Gail. You don't have to take it down. Just make a correction video, that's all."

"Okay," Gail said matter-of-factly. "Why did You say You were going to fill me with Your semen?" Gail paused to consider her words. "That's why I misunderstood You." Gail now addressed Brent. "Brent, is Jesus like a dove? What form is He with you?"

Brent ignored her to let Jesus talk.

"I will be filling you with my semen, but. . ."

"Oh! I get it. . ." Gail interrupted. "It's going to be through Brent Spiner!"

Terrance added, "He's going to put His semen inside Brent."

"Oh!" Gail smiled, laughing, now understanding what Jesus meant. "Oh, okay. . ."

"I remember that Jesus said Brent would be your husband in the millennium. . ." Terrance added.

"I'm going to fill Brent with my semen." Jesus smiled.

"Are you doing that now?" Gail asked Jesus.

"Maybe that is why Brent is writing so slow," Terrance said.

"It is going to be my wedding gift," Jesus said.

"What's so special about your semen, Jesus?" Gail's curiosity was hyped. "I imagine it is special, but why would this make a difference?"

"It glows in the dark, of course," Jesus explained.

"Why are You going to be giving us Your semen?" Gail was dying of curiosity.

"It's just better," Jesus said.

"Why is it better?" Gail asked. "What's wrong with Brent Spiner's semen?" Gail spoke to the air. "He (Brent) probably wonders himself."

"Brent has extraordinary semen."

Gail laughed.

Jesus continued, "My semen is very luxurious. It is blessed millennial semen, Gail."

"Why do You call it millennial semen?"

Terrance added, "Maybe it's because it will be the wedding gift for the millennial reign."

"Yes," Jesus agreed.

"Lord, why do you take such an interest in my relationship with Brent Spiner?"

"Because you were made for each other," Jesus said.

"Ahhhh," Gail felt honored, and realized that the love she and Brent had was very unusual.

"Brent Spiner is your soul mate."

"Yeah, he sure is. . ."

Jesus said with certainty, "I would never want to get in between you two."

"Ahhh." Gail smiled, a happy tone to her voice. "Yeah, I've noticed that. But aren't You number one on the marriage list?" Gail paused to consider, and spoke to Brent and Terrance. "Maybe we ought to take Him off."

"It is both of you that will destroy the Jesuit Order together," Jesus said, not encouraging Gail to take His name off the marriage list.

"Ohhh." Gail understood that she and Brent cared about the same things Jesus cared about. "And they're You're enemies." Gail became silent and thought about all Jesus had said to her. "Okay, since You're number one on the marriage list, I guess I should just take that as being like, as me being part of the church and You're my husband because I'm part of the church and I'm the bride as being part of the church," Gail continued. "Is that how You want me to take it?"

"Yes, that is the correct interpretation," Jesus said.

"Okay," Gail said, resigned, but content. "That's fine."

"We understand that Jesus is a handsome fella," Terrance added.

"Oh, what does He look like?" Gail wanted to know. "Does He look like king David? Like in that movie *David* with Jonathan Parker?"

"I want you to be with your intended, Brent Spiner," Jesus said.

"King David told me, when he talked to me around 2008 that that actor who portrays him, looks a lot like him. I'm just curious what David looked like, cause he's my great, great, great ,great grandfather."

"I resemble David quite a bit," Jesus conceded.

"Do you look kind of like the David in that movie I have of him? King David told me he even looked like that actor who portrayed him, is that correct?"

"I'm afraid I'm rather ordinary looking." Jesus was being modest.

Gail laughed. "Yeah, but You're not ordinary inside." Gail asked her men, "What does He look like? Does He look Jewish?"

"Yes," Terrance said. "He's very Jewish looking."

"Well, he *is* Jewish." Gail knew her Bible. "Dark hair and dark eyes?"

"He has the nose," Terrance added.

"Jewish. Dark eyes. Dark hair. Average in height," Jesus said.

"Jewish," Gail said. "From David."

"I've got this Jewish nose," Jesus admitted.

"Hey, there's nothing wrong with being Jewish," Gail said, proud of her king David genes in front of Jesus. "God's not finished with the Jews. When the tribulation comes, He's going to be dealing with Israel again."

Zack Knight broke into the brain to brain servers for the first time in February 2012, and took advantage of Gail's ignorance that he could do this, to trick her that he was Jesus making love to her brain to brain. Gail did not know that

The Forbidden Abyss

Zack Knight in 2012 had the ability to impregnate a woman telepathically. Satan, apparently, gave Zack special powers after he became the antichrist on February 14, 2012. Jesus spoke to Gail through Brent Spiner on Skype on February 22, 2012:

"I dislike computer technology," Jesus said.

"I'm not surprised to hear that, Lord," Gail answered.

"This is a little difficult to explain, Gail, as I do have some troubling news. . ." Jesus said. "Gail, I don't use any computer technology. The devil invented the computer, just like the devil invented electricity. I only trust Brent to transcribe my words for me here." Jesus paused. "Zack Knight has hacked into the brain to brain computer servers, and he has stolen my identity there. He has been impersonating me while with you brain to brain." Jesus paused, looking furious. "I am very angry. He has been making love to you with his black, devil semen."

Jesus told her this, because Zack had told Gail brain to brain that Jesus' semen was black and then turned silver, misinterpreting Song of Solomon. Zack had told her while he faked as Jesus, "That's why Song of Solomon opens up with black in chapter one, verse 6 and then ends with silver in chapter eight, verse 11."

Jesus continued, "That was not my semen." Jesus would later reveal to Gail that His semen was white and glowed in the dark.

"Oh no!" Terrance yelled." Oh no, Jesus! Say it ain't so!"

Gail remained calm, thrilled that Jesus spoke to her personally about this. "Jesus can fix this."

Terrance became desperate. "Jesus! Jesus! Can you fix it?"

"I'm sorry, Terrance." Jesus consoled Terrance.

"You got to fix it, Jesus," Terrance whined. "Gail is such a wonderful woman. She can't be having devil semen in her."

"I have faith in Jesus." Gail remained calm. "I have faith in Jesus."

"I have faith in you, Jesus," Terrance said, calming down.

"He can do an abortion!" Gail said, knowing this was exactly what Jesus would do. "Jesus can do an abortion."

"I will not allow Gail to carry devil babies." Jesus spoke with authority.

Terrance almost wept with gratitude. "Oh, thank you, Jesus!" Terrance paused. "Oh, that's wonderful, He's waving His hands and looks like—"

Jesus agreed with Gail, "I can do an abortion."

Gail smiled. "I told you He could." She laughed.

"Zack Knight's not going to be having no babies with Gail," Terrance said, with conviction.

"Uh-uh." Gail nodded "no", a smile in her voice, that Zack would have no babies with her. "I think the Lord just wanted me to realize that I can't trust what I'm hearing in my brain."

"No," Jesus said. "Zack Knight is a bad man."

"Obviously," Gail agreed.

"He's Satan incarnate, right now," Terrance said, still spooked that Zack had made Gail pregnant telepathically.

"Satan and I are going to have a *very* serious talk." Jesus' voice was firm.

"We gonna kick his butt." Terrance cheered Jesus on. "Gonna kick his Satan butt."

Quebec Trial

"I knew God could do an abortion, so I wasn't freaked out by it." Gail barely felt the abortion and never felt like she was pregnant. The twenty-first century technology was remarkable.

"Jesus, you're my hero," Terrance said, adoring Jesus.

"He's all our heroes!" Gail agreed.

"That dirty Zack Knight, he did the same thing to you that he did with Loree McBride on Brent," Terrance added.

"Really?" Gail didn't quite get what Terrance meant.

"Well, because you thought you were making love to Jesus, when you were making love to Zack Knight."

"Oh, yeah." Gail now understood Terrance. "And Brent thought he was making love to *me*."

"Yes," Terrance explained. "The Jesuits used this dirty trick, just as Zack Knight had the ability to break in there—"

Jesus agreed with Terrance. "That is *exactly* what has happened."

"Those Jesuits is always up to no good," Terrance said.

"Jesuits want to do this and now they have done it to me. I am furious." Jesus face looked like a stone in anger.

"Lord Jesus," Gail asked.

"Gail," Jesus said. "As much as I love you, I have not allowed myself to have brain to brain loving with you."

Gail gave a happy whelp, almost laughing. "Ha, okay!" It was rather brazen to expect Jesus to make love to her, and actually, her time with Zack as Jesus was starting to wear her out, because this fake Jesus seemed to regulate and advise Gail over every minutia of her life, while the real Jesus gave Gail some space. "That's fine."

"Yeah, Jesus," Terrance asked. "Do you *want* to have brain to brain loving with her? If we could use the satellite technology or after the millennial reign?"

Gail brightened. "Oh, thank you for that question, Terrance!" She began digesting all Jesus had told her. "I need to correct some stuff on my website's transcription. I don't want it to be inaccurate, so I don't mislead your followers."

"Yes, very much." Jesus agreed with Terrance that He would like to make love to Gail. "But I cannot interfere with mine and my Father's plans here on earth by allowing this to happen so soon. I am saving myself for you."

"Oh, that's awesome!" Gail felt truly honored, misunderstanding Jesus at this point, thinking He meant a millennial marriage with her. But Jesus did not correct the misunderstanding, because He knew He'd be dealing with this later, and He didn't want Gail to feel ugly or unattractive.

"In the millennial reign, I will fill you with my real semen," Jesus said, not going into detail.

"Ugh!" Gail couldn't believe what she was hearing! "This Zack Knight what he did to me, was that anything close to what you're going to be like?" Gail was dying to know the details about how Jesus would make love to her in the millennium. "Or did he do a total counterfeit?" Gail paused to consider. "I'm sure You know what he did to me, Lord."

"I don't know," Terrance interrupted. "What did he do to you?"

"He made *love* to me," Gail answered. "And I thought it was Jesus!"

"Goodness," Terrance said. "It's so horrible. I'm sure he would know some of the moves that Jesus would do—"

"I am much better than Zack Knight is in bed," Jesus said, flat-out.

Gail laughed in hysterics at Jesus. "Actually. . ." Gail bantered with Jesus and flung his name out. "Jesus!" She enjoyed a direct conversation with Him, admiring his lack of sexual hang-ups. "I was having a little bit of trouble getting an orgasm on some of it!" She laughed.

"He's a total dud." Jesus frowned, thinking about Zack's attempt to imitate Him.

"Oh, my goodness!" Terrance said.

Jesus shook His head in disapproval. "He fakes it until he makes it."

"Lord Jesus, you allowed this to happen," Gail said. "Can you tell me why? You *knew* this was going to happen!"

"I can't tell you why, right now." Jesus often did not answer all of Gail's questions.

"Okay." Gail had respect for Jesus when He desired to remain silent.

"It will interfere with my grand plan. It's like Abraham and his son." Jesus later added. "Please do not believe anyone who tries to tell you they are me brain to brain. I want you to be safe because I care so much for you."

"Did I do something wrong that this happened?" Gail asked Jesus.

"No," Jesus answered. "You have done everything I have hoped for you."

"Okay," Gail said. "You allowed this to happen because it's part of your plan, then."

"The devil tricked you," Jesus said.

"Oh yeah, he sure did," Gail said. "What about all those messages I got the other day, where you told me what everybody around me was up to? That made it seem like it was You who was talking to me, because everything you told me about these people turned out to be true." Gail pondered over how Zack had approached her as Jesus brain to brain in the past week. "Was that the devil? Of course, that could have been the devil, because he would know what all his followers are up to."

"Of course. Exactly." Jesus said, agreeing with Gail that Satan could tell her what everybody around her was up to, because they were all Zack Knight followers. "Zack Knight knows what all his minors are doing. He's the antichrist, after all."

After Zack Knight tricked Gail several times in 2012, she decided that she would never trust any "thoughts" that came into her brain that claimed to be Jesus, even if they claimed to speak for Jesus through Brent Spiner.

Zack would be relentless, with a 24/7 obsession with Gail, so that Gail would rebuke Zack in her mind just about every day. Despite her rebukes, Zack would continue impersonating Brent Spiner or Jesus to her mind, and Gail would have to double check with her men online to determine what was accurate and inaccurate from her brain to brain communications.

Made in the USA
Las Vegas, NV
12 October 2022